AMERICA'S *Choice* ☑

The Election of 1996

Editors

William Crotty
Northeastern University

and

Jerome M. Mileur
University of Massachusetts

Dushkin/McGraw·Hill

A Division of The McGraw·Hill Companies

Dushkin/McGraw·Hill

A Division of The McGraw-Hill Companies

Library of Congress Catalog Card Number: 97-65305

ISBN 0-697-36982-X

Printed in the United States of America

10   9   8   7   6   5   4   3   2   1

This book is printed
on recycled paper

Preface

The election of 1996 could prove to be historic, leading to a presidency of distinction and legislative results of consequence, but there was little in the campaign to suggest such an outcome. The divided government resulting from the 1994 midterm election—a Democratic president and a Republican Congress—will continue. The tone of government, however, may be more accommodationist and less confrontational than that of the term that preceded it. As a result, better working relations between president and Congress may emerge as the election's most significant contribution. On the other hand, charges and countercharges of the unauthorized raising and use of campaign funds and other abuses could continue the hostility between the two branches of government that marked the years leading up to the election.

The presidential race was, for all practical purposes, decided early. Incumbent Bill Clinton began with a number of advantages. He faced no primary opposition. He enjoyed the perks and attention his office gave him and used them artfully. He campaigned as a centrist, presenting the Republicans with a difficult target against which to campaign. Overall, he ran a close to letter-perfect campaign. His challenger Bob Dole's situation was quite different. Dole emerged scarred from a strongly contested prenomination race, and his campaign was poorly organized and presented few consistent themes to the American public. The case for replacing the president was not made, and Clinton won handily on election day.

Ross Perot was not the third-party factor he had been in 1992. He was virtually ignored by the press and the public until late in the campaign season, when the Dole campaign attempted to list his support.

The campaign was the most expensive in history. Campaign finance laws were bent and may have been broken, a concern that has surfaced in a number of recent campaigns. An extensive congressional review of alleged funding abuses is likely, and major campaign reform is possible. However, while endorsed by the leadership of both political parties, support for it on Capitol Hill is likely to be lukewarm at best.

The Democrats had hoped for big legislative gains. Although they made inroads on the Republican majority in the House, cutting it by 10 seats, the party actually lost 2 seats to the Republicans in the Senate. The upshot is that the Republican Party remains in control of both houses of the Congress.

What is the significance of the election? What were its dynamics and what explains its outcome?

To address these questions, a distinguished group of political and social scientists have brought their academic expertise to bear in the essays that follow. We think you will find their views both informative and provocative. Their work should provide a context for informed classroom discussions and exchanges.

We would particularly like to thank Marie Arnberg of Northeastern University, Scott Spoolman of Brown and Benchmark, and John Holland of Dushkin Publishing/McGraw-Hill for their significant contributions to this volume.

William Crotty

Table of Contents

Chapter One

A Bridge to the Twenty-First Century?

William Crotty

The midterm congressional success of the Republicans in 1994 was a key point of reference for the 1996 election. With it came Republican control of both houses of Congress and a new class of freshmen pledged to a conservative political agenda—downsizing government, cutting or even eliminating social programs, balancing the budget, doing away with cabinet departments, returning power and responsibility to the states, and generally enacting the provisions of the "Contract with America." The determined push to follow this agenda eventually led to the shutdown of government on three occasions. Ultimately, President Clinton chose not to accept the Republican program. He emphasized his commitment to a balanced budget (his administration had already reduced the deficit by 60 percent) and a more streamlined and efficient government. But at the same time, he presented himself as the champion of moderation, the guardian of federal aid to education and efforts to clean up the environment, and the protector of working-class Americans, whose interests he said he would defend.

Clinton's strategy worked, and the shutdowns boomeranged on the Republicans. They and their leader, Newt Gingrich, were characterized as extremists who would go to any lengths to impose their will on the nation. It was a characterization the Democrats were quick to exploit and one that hurt the Republicans in the campaign. Clinton returned to this confrontation repeatedly in his campaign and used it to frame his reelection. His position caught the essence of his presidency.

THE CANDIDATES

Bill Clinton liked to refer to himself as "the man from Hope." A young governor of a small southern state, articulate, charming, and a self-confessed "policy wonk," Clinton won the Democratic Party's presidential nomination in 1992 in a weak field and went on to defeat the incumbent, George Bush. Underlying economic anxieties that the Bush administration had failed to address in the public euphoria that followed victory in the Persian Gulf War, as well as the formidable political skills of an underrated challenger, contributed to Bush's defeat.

However, despite a campaign with a heavy policy emphasis, the Clinton administration came into office with no policy commitments ready for legislative enactment. The Clinton White House was described in the national press as disorganized, unfocused, and politically naive. Journalist and author Bob Woodward used such terms as "sloppiness and chaos" to describe it. The president's staff was described as young, inexperienced, and too eager to please the chief executive. The man in charge was seen as having little sense of direction, ineffective in delegating authority or in establishing discipline. Candidates nominated by the administration for key appointments were repeatedly withdrawn. It was, in Woodward's terms, "a presidency in real trouble."[1] Bill Clinton was unprepared to deal with the Congress or to manage in an intensely partisan political environment or to perform in front of a hypercritical national press. He gave his one major policy initiative—national health insurance—to his wife, Hillary Rodham Clinton, to implement, and its failure almost sank his presidency. The program proved to be excruciatingly slow in taking shape, ambiguous in design and benefit, complex and poorly conceived, and amateurishly marketed to the American public. This and other unsuccessful efforts served to place congressional Democrats in uncomfortable positions. They paid the price in the midterm elections of 1994. In fact, the results were nothing short of a political revolution.

> ## The midterm elections of 1994 were nothing short of a political revolution.

The Republicans came out of the 1994 election with a 26-seat majority in the House and a six-seat majority in the Senate (gains of 54 and 10 seats, respectively), as well as a coherent policy agenda and an ideologically committed majority that would provide a new dimension to contemporary American politics.

In the two years leading up to the presidential election of 1996, the strain between Clinton and his party, especially the Democrats in the House, was clear and never satisfactorily addressed by the White House. The House Democrats put forth their own policy agenda, often in direct competition with the president's. The party's House leadership, spearheaded by Minority Leader Dick Gephardt, made it clear that they felt Clinton was an unreliable ally, one prone to compromise too quickly with Republicans.

Clinton's first term was marked by a constant barrage of ethics charges—improper use of government influence both as governor of Arkansas and in the White House; profiteering, along with Hillary Clinton, from various land and stock deals; engaging in sexual misconduct as governor of Arkansas; improper firing of White House personnel, especially the staff in the travel office; obstructing justice over the handling of FBI files by lower-level White House officials; in the White House allowing documentary files demanded by the Special

Counsel and congressional committees to disappear and reappear; peddling influence and raising funds illegally; and so on. The list seemed endless, and congressional Republicans did their best to keep the controversies alive with a constant barrage of charges and countercharges, Senate and House investigations, and personal attacks on the president.

Bob Dole provided a stark contrast with Bill Clinton. A generation older, he is a scarred and decorated veteran of the Italian campaign in World War II, with a permanently disabled arm. His war record and commitment to country were often compared to Clinton's alleged "draft-dodging" and his opposition to the Vietnam War.

Dole was the product of a small Kansas town, raised in the Calvinist traditions of hard work, perseverance, and self-reliance. Where Clinton is outgoing, voluble, and friendly, Dole is undemonstrative, introspective, and self-effacing. On the campaign trail, he often seemed angry and at times even bitter. His speeches, again in contrast to Clinton's, were generally poorly delivered, lacked coherence and a clear message, and depended on the repetition of key words or short phrases for effect.

Dole differed from Clinton in another fundamental respect. He was the ultimate Washington insider, an experienced politician who had served in Congress since his election to the House of Representatives in 1960. He had been elected to the Senate in 1968, serving as minority leader and later majority leader when the Republicans won control in 1994. He was known as a skilled legislative tactician, more moderate in many respects than members of the most conservative wing of his party. He was typically interested in getting a deal done and moving legislation rather than in fighting ideological battles. His crisp, punchy, darkly humorous style, effective in the Senate, was poorly suited to the campaign trail.

THE PRIMARIES

For the first time in memory, there was no competition for the Democratic Party's presidential nominee. One reason was that the Clinton campaign amassed large sums of money early—large enough to scare off any would-be challenger. Secondly, Republican success in

1994, the ideological positions pushed by the new majority, and the shutdowns of government operations in the budget wars convinced Democrats that there was too much at stake to risk weakening the president's reelection efforts. Consequently, both liberal and moderate Democrats rallied behind the President, allowing the Clinton campaign to conserve funds for the major general election drive and to enunciate its campaign themes early.

The situation for Republicans was quite different. Bob Dole was the acknowledged front-runner from the beginning, but his campaign stumbled often. In addition to the primary loss in New Hampshire, the campaign's message was unclear, Dole was an indifferent campaigner, and funding ran out before the primaries ended.

Dole's competitors in the prenomination phase were all well funded, with expenses estimated at between $20 and $25 million *prior* to the start of the campaign in January of 1996.

A surprise candidate, Steve Forbes, publisher of *Forbes* magazine and son of the late Malcolm Forbes, spent an estimated $35 million or more of his own money to run. His single issue was a flat tax, a plan that would have benefited him enormously. Forbes was a political novice who campaigned primarily through expensive, well-made television commercials that proved effective with voters. Before his campaign faltered, he did unexpectedly well—further testimony to the power of money in politics.

Another contender was Lamar Alexander, former governor of Tennessee and a cabinet secretary in the Bush administration. Pat Buchanan reprised his 1992 role as point man for the party's cultural conservatives. Although he proved to be an effective speaker, he was the weakest-funded among the major contenders. Texas Senator Phil Gramm, an acerbic right-wing conservative, was expected by many to be Dole's principal rival, but his appeal even among Republicans proved limited. Others with even less vote power were Congressman Bob ("B-1 Bob") Dornan of California, who lost his bid for congressional reelection in his home Orange County; Alan Keys, a black candidate and former State Department official in the Reagan administration; Senator Richard G. Lugar, a moderate and former governor of Indiana who emphasized foreign policy issues; and the un-

known millionaire, Maurice "Morry" Taylor. It was a long, heated, and costly fight with consequences for the Republican Party and its candidate in the general election.

THE GENERAL ELECTION CAMPAIGN

Political consultant Dick Morris, who had helped Bill Clinton to regain the governorship of Arkansas after his 1978 defeat, worked with the president (before Morris's withdrawal as an adviser in the wake of a sex scandal) to fashion a strategy for reelection that proved highly successful.

The Democrats prepared to respond instantaneously with the spin they wanted reported.

The campaign plan they devised involved seven major tactics:

- Oppose the Gingrich-led Republicans in the House and, in particular, the proposed budget cuts. Protect spending for education, the environment, Medicare, and the interests of working Americans.
- Avoid bold initiatives in the campaign. Stick to middle-range proposals that call for little or no government action.
- Remind the voters of foreign policy successes and improved economic conditions during the first four years of the administration.
- Raise money early and aggressively, to frighten challengers out of the nomination race and allow the president to get his message out to the media promptly. Ultimately, the Democrats raised and spent less than the Republicans, but the level of funding and the tactics used in fundraising became liabilities in the later days of the campaign.
- Develop a quick-strike capability to answer Republican charges immediately. Whatever the issue, from the quality of jobs available to peace efforts in Haiti to attacks on White House ethics or the

3

president's character, the campaign was prepared to respond instantaneously with the spin they wanted reported.

- Secure the Democratic strongholds—the industrial states of the Northeast and the Midwest and the Pacific states, particularly California—and then take the campaign to Republican strongholds. Force the opposition to spend time and resources defending their base. The Clinton-Gore team executed this tactic well.
- Finally, position the president above the battle, as a nonpartisan, reasonable, and moderating influence representing all Americans. The more intense and partisan aspects of the campaign could be carried out by the vice president, members of the cabinet, the Democratic National Committee, supportive outside groups (such as organized labor), and through media advertising.

The Clinton effort was cohesive, well-oiled, and carefully managed. From the earliest-ever media advertising (begun in June of 1995, 18 months before election day) to the experienced campaign team led by a consummate professional, the campaign could serve as a model for future incumbents.

An additional advantage was that the Republican issue agenda in Congress set the political tone and context; Clinton simply ran against it. Here are the assessments of two campaign insiders. From a Clinton strategist early in the campaign: "The Republicans have given us great gifts. . . . Whether it's shutting down the Government or the revolutionary rhetoric of Newt Gingrich above Dole's inability to articulate a message, they all compound to create a much more favorable climate for Bill Clinton."[2]

A Dole strategist commented on the sound economy, the lack of international threats to the nation, and the brutal primary battle the Republicans had undergone: "Combine [these] with the fact that Clinton has the best candidate skills of any Democrat in at least a generation. . . . I don't think any Republican would have won this year."[3]

The Dole campaign was easily among the worst-run in the modern era of presidential elections. The candidate contributed his own weaknesses—his age; his poor speaking, debating, and media skills; and his inability to clarify staff responsibilities or settle on long-term strategies. Dole was clearly uncomfortable in the electoral arena, unable to delegate authority effectively, or to settle on a single message—a 15 percent tax reduction; Clinton's character and trustworthiness; and Dole's own integrity, legislative skills, and war record were all used, virtually interchangeably. The campaign staff was weak and inexperienced, and the candidate was ultimately unable to wrest the political center from Clinton.

The one tactic used that was universally lauded was Dole's choice of former congressman and Bush cabinet secretary Jack Kemp as his vice presidential candidate. Dole and Kemp were neither personally nor politically close. In fact, Kemp's advocacy of supply-side economics during the Reagan years had been repeatedly rejected by Dole. Nonetheless, Kemp brought a freshness and independence to the campaign that briefly revitalized it and proved attractive to both the media and the party faithful.

The Issues

Bill Clinton strove to make it tough for a Republican to run against him. Just prior to the general election campaign, he signed a Republican-sponsored welfare bill that many in his party opposed (liberal Democratic critics charged that a million children would be forced into poverty). To take another issue away from his opponents, he signed a $256.6 billion military appropriations bill, $11.2 billion over what he had requested from Congress. "The bill makes good on our pledge to keep our armed forces the best trained, the best equipped fighting force on earth," the president said.[4] He endorsed several initiatives to restore family values—an antistalking measure, school uniforms for children, extended hospital stays for mothers after delivering babies, and other issues that had significant political support and required little government implementation.

The economy was good and the nation was at peace. The economic anxieties that had contributed directly to George Bush's defeat in 1992 no longer appeared so pervasive. And, despite his lack of experience, Clinton had proven surprisingly successful in managing the nation's international relations.

Clinton preempted major Republican issues, from support for deficit reduction and a smaller government to anticrime and pro-police measures. And the president stood up to the

Gingrich-Dole Congress, as the Democrats liked to call it, on the budget and the government closings showdown.

The Clinton-Gore themes were consistent and repetitive: the Dole tax reduction was "risky"; "it could blow a hole in the deficit . . . and raise taxes on 9 million of the hardest-working Americans." Clinton proposed a tax break for middle-class parents to pay for their children's college education. The "Republicans want to cut Medicare deeply—$270 billion. . . . We'll protect Medicare, Medicaid, education, and the environment." "We passed welfare reform . . . , created 10½ million new jobs, and moved a million people from welfare to work." For a centralizing theme, the Clinton administration was "building a bridge to the twenty-first century."[5]

The Dole campaign, by contrast, appeared to back different messages at different points in time. There was the 15 percent tax cut: "It's about youth, it's about jobs, it's about opportunity, it's about the private sector," Dole contended in his speeches. His economic plan in addition was to balance the budget and halve the capital gains tax.

The economic emphasis was alternated with a more complex message about ethics, personal integrity, and trustworthiness. The implication was that Dole had these qualities and Clinton did not. Dole emphasized his record in World War II, his serious injury in the Italian campaign, and his professional success in the face of his disability. The contrast with Clinton's opposition to the war in Vietnam and alleged "draft-dodging" was brought into play.

The campaign wavered on whether Dole should attack Clinton's character directly regarding his ethics. When given the opportunity in the vice presidential debate, Kemp said he would not do it, but within days, Dole was on the attack. While the issue had sometimes been sidelined in favor of the economic message or the "tax and spend" labeling of Clinton, it was to take center stage in the last days of the campaign.

There was much grist for an ethical attack on Bill Clinton, including past land deals and investments, charges of sexual harassment and misconduct, cronyism in and out of the White House, improper use of FBI files, concealment of files in the suicide of White House aide and Clinton confidant Vince Foster, and the alleged firing of the White House travel office staff to make way for political appointees.

When he did attack, Dole said:

> No administration has shown more arrogance. But few have displayed more ethical failures. . . . Among members of this administration there is a growing gap of integrity between the low standards they have adopted and the high honor they hold, a gap between their swagger and their public scandals. . . . What bothers us most is not just the wrongdoing but the excuse making. . . . The goal is always to conceal ethical failure, not confront it."[6]

This was the most fully articulated packaging of the character issue that the Dole campaign offered. It came principally in the later of the televised presidential debates two weeks before election day. Dole had not laid any consistent groundwork for an evaluation or an understanding of the charges. At best, the stratagem was not effective; at worst, it backfired.

With the failure of this last-minute attack, the outcome of the election was inevitable.

After a week of such attacks, a *Newsweek* poll of registered voters found Dole "more negative and nasty" than Clinton (59 percent to 11 percent), and Clinton was seen as having the better personal character to be president than Dole (48 percent to 36 percent). Ten percent of the registered voters felt that character made no difference.[7] With the failure of this last-minute attack on Clinton's character, the outcome of the election was inevitable.

Whither Candidate Perot?

Ross Perot was a factor of consequence in the 1992 election, the most successful third-party candidate since Teddy Roosevelt in 1912. Perot's success was due to his folksy, common-sense discussion of issues; the half-hour "infomercials" that proved to be popular, breaking all the rules of slick television programming and 30-second commercials; and, not least, his personal fortune—he was said to have put up

5

to $60 million of his own money into his campaign. Perot's Reform Party received 19.5 percent of the vote in 1992, qualifying it for federal election financing of $29.2 million in 1996.

The 1996 election year proved to be quite different from the earlier campaign. Perot was no longer a novelty and, in fact, was seen as something of an eccentric; media interest waned and focused primarily on his quirkiness—his seeming indecisiveness over running, a controversial nominating process within his party when a formidable challenger, former Democratic governor Richard Lamb of Colorado appeared—and Perot's reluctance to campaign personally.[8] He was also excluded from the presidential debates by the commission charged with developing guidelines. For the candidate and his party, this was a death blow.

What had changed between 1992 and 1996? The issues Perot emphasized in the weeks preceding the election were vague and confusing: "If you're among the 50 percent who don't vote, vote for Perot; if you are between the ages of 18 and 35, vote for Perot; if you don't want to see our government for sale, vote for Perot; if you're in the military or own a small business or want millions of good-paying jobs, vote for Perot." The message was muddied still further by the campaign's slogan: "Don't waste your vote, vote Perot."[9] The wasted-vote argument is one that the major parties use successfully to undercut third-party candidacies.

Nevertheless, Perot received 8.5 percent of the vote, and his party again qualifies for federal funding in the election year of 2000.

THE ELECTION RESULTS

President Clinton won 390 electoral votes, carrying 31 states and the District of Columbia. Bob Dole won 159 electoral votes and 18 states. Ross Perot won no electoral votes and no states. Clinton won 49.8 percent of the popular vote, Dole 41.7 percent.

For Clinton it was an improvement over his performance in 1992, when he won 370 electoral votes and 43.0 percent of the popular vote (to George Bush's 168 electoral votes and 37.4 percent of the popular vote).

Clinton's strength was in the Northeast, Midwest, and West Coast. In addition, he carried seven southern or border states, including Florida, normally a Republican stronghold. Clinton's electoral vote was the highest for a Democrat since Lyndon Johnson's 1964 landslide, and his proportion of the popular vote the largest since Jimmy Carter's victory in 1976.

Two basic questions emerged from the results. The more pressing was whether the victory was decisive enough to give Clinton the political muscle he will need for a successful second term. The likelihood is that the operative words in Washington will be negotiation, teamwork, and bipartisan cooperation. Second, did the Clinton pattern of electoral college support herald a new era of Democratic Party supremacy? The likelihood is that the electoral map may well be more flexible than it has been in the recent past, an indication of the political and demographic changes taking place at the state level.

Turnout

The 48.8 percent turnout in the election was the lowest since 1924 and the second lowest since 1824. Turnout was down in every state. However, the fact that only about half the eligible electorate votes has been true for quite some time and is generally accepted as a fact of political life in the United States.

The low rate of participation occurred despite the introduction of "motor-voter" legislation since the last election. The National Voter Registration Act of 1993 allowed people to register in 34 states and the District of Columbia when receiving a motor vehicle license or in unemployment offices, libraries, military recruitment offices, or other federal or state offices.

As a result, between 8.8 and 11.5 million new voters were added to the rolls. Although registration is often considered the chief structural barrier to voter participation, the level of participation declined in 1996 despite the change.

A number of factors are suspected as causes. First, interest in the 1996 elections was down from that in 1992. As examples, 50 percent of voters in a *New York Times*/CBS News nationwide poll taken during the campaign described the election as dull (compared to 39 percent in 1992), and those paying "a lot of attention" to the campaign were down from 54 percent in 1992 to 42 percent in 1996.[10]

Others see socioeconomic class distinctions as a problem. The Gallup organization reported that turnout in 1996 for those earning $75,000 or more was 62 percent, against 39 percent for those with incomes under $20,000. In an analysis of elections from 1976 to 1992, it was reported that the states with the fairest tax laws and the smallest gap between the rich and the least well-off consistently had the highest turnouts. An official of Human Serve made the point: "When you have a class-skewed electorate, only the better-off people end up determining policy."[11]

Demographics of the Vote

President Clinton did well among women (54 percent of the vote), African Americans (an impressive 84 percent), and Hispanics (70 percent), the youngest (53 percent) and oldest (50 percent) age cohorts, low-income voters (60 percent of those making $15,000 per year or less against only 40 percent of those whose incomes exceeded $100,000), those with the least formal education (58 percent of the voters who did not finish high school) and those with the most (50 percent of those with postgraduate courses), along with Jews (80 percent) and Catholics (50 percent). He lost among Protestants (41 percent) and the religious right (only 26 percent of the vote). Although he ran as a centrist and a nonideologue, his voter profile is classically Democratic. See Table 1.1.

Those using the Internet regularly favored the Clinton-Gore ticket (59 percent to 39 percent), apparently responding to the talk of the electronic "superhighway," one of the administration's most fierce enthusiasms. A majority of gun owners voted for Bob Dole.

There are strong indications in the exit polls from the *Washington Post*/ABC News of a policy-driven, partisan, and ideological vote. Liberals, those who favored and supported Clinton's policies, consistently voted Democratic. Those who feared a Republican-controlled, conservative Congress or had an unfavorable opinion of Newt Gingrich, as well as those who voted for Clinton in 1992, also supported him, often with overwhelming majorities, in 1996.

Clinton voters felt that the president was in touch with the 1990s and cared about people like themselves. Those who felt that education, Medicare/Social Security, or the economy/jobs were the most important issues in the campaign, all Clinton campaign themes, voted for the president. The party differences on the various indices measuring these concerns are very clear and consistent.

There is another indicator of policy commitment and party cohesion that is equally impressive. In an era of declining party loyalties, those who voted for either Clinton or Dole were also likely to vote for their party and ideological preferences in other races. Eighty-four percent of the Clinton voters supported Democrats in House races, 82 percent in Senate contests, and 69 percent in gubernatorial elections; the equivalent Republican figures are 78 percent, 77 percent, and 80 percent. It was a divided electorate, but one whose issue positions, party support, and candidate preferences appeared to be both cohesive and in line with voters' own values and partisan identifications.

Congressional Races

The most interesting aspect of the election, and what may well be its most important, was the congressional races. Local concerns, personalities, efforts by the Democrats to regain their majorities and of Republicans to vindicate their legislative record, the fate of the 73 freshman congressmen chosen two years earlier, the future of Newt Gingrich as Speaker—all hung in the balance. More than in most presidencies, the administration would need to adjust to those in control of the new Congress.

Despite the campaign drama, the new Congress closely resembled the old.

Despite the campaign drama, the new Congress closely resembled the old. Republicans, despite losing 10 seats, remained in control of the House and added to their margin in the Senate, gaining two seats.

In the aftermath, winners and losers, president and Congress appeared subdued,

(Continued on p. 10)

7

Table 1.1

Results of the 1996 Presidential Election (in percentages)

Characteristics	Candidate			Characteristics	Candidate		
A. Social Characteristics	*Clinton*	*Dole*	*Perot*		*Clinton*	*Dole*	*Perot*
Gender				Whites—Religious Right			
Men	44	45	9	Yes	26	65	8
Women	54	38	7	No	55	35	8
Race				Do you have a union member in your household?			
White	44	46	8	Yes	59	30	9
Black	84	12	4	No	47	44	8
Hispanic/Latino	70	22	6				
Asian	41	49	9				
Other	60	23	11	*B. Economic Conditions*			
Age				Financial Situation Compared to 1992			
18–29	53	35	10	Better	68	26	5
30–44	49	41	8	Worse	27	58	13
45–59	47	43	8	The same	46	46	8
60+	50	43	6				
Income				Condition of the Nation's Economy			
<15K	60	26	11	Excellent	77	19	4
15–30K	54	36	8	Good	63	31	5
30–50K	49	40	9	Not so good	32	55	12
50–75K	46	46	6	Poor	19	55	22
75–100K	44	49	6	Country is on the . . .			
Over 100K	40	54	5	Right track	71	24	4
Education				Wrong track	21	62	14
No High School	58	29	11				
High School Grad	51	35	13				
Some College	48	41	10	*C. Personal Character*			
College Grad	43	48	7	Personal character and values	18	71	10
Post-Graduate	53	39	4	Did these candidates attack each other unfairly?			
College Education				Clinton did	16	82	2
Not Completed	51	37	11	Dole did	87	7	5
Completed	47	44	6	Both did	41	46	11
Religion				Neither did	33	57	8
Protestant	41	50	8				
Catholic	53	38	8	Do you think Clinton is honest and trustworthy?			
Other Christian	49	38	12	Yes	88	7	4
Jewish	80	16	3	No	17	68	12
Other	62	25	7	Is Clinton telling the truth regarding Whitewater?			
None	57	26	23	Yes	88	6	4
Religion—Whites				No	25	63	11
Protestant	37	52	9	What is more important in a president?			
Catholic	48	42	9	Highest personal character	14	77	7
Jewish	79	16	3	Understanding the problems of people like you	68	24	7
Other	53	30	10				
None	54	30	13				

Characteristics	Candidate		
	Clinton	*Dole*	*Perot*

D. Party and Political Factors

Which party did you vote for in the U.S. Senate race?

Dem	82	11	6
GOP	15	77	8
Other	33	18	22

Which party did you vote for in the U.S. House race in your district?

Dem	84	8	6
GOP	14	78	7
Other	22	22	43

Which party did you vote for in the state governor race?

Dem	69	21	8
GOP	13	80	7
Other	—	—	—

Party ID

Dem	84	10	5
GOP	13	81	5
Ind/Other	43	37	16

1992 Vote

Clinton	85	9	4
Bush	13	82	4
Perot	23	45	30
Other	30	34	8

Ideology

Liberal	78	11	7
Moderate	57	33	9
Conservative	20	72	7

Approval of GOP-led 104th Congress

Approve	15	78	6
Disapprove	78	9	11

If Clinton is reelected, would you rather have the U.S. Congress controlled by:

Democrats	85	7	6
Republicans	15	76	8

Are you concerned that a Democrat-led Congress will be liberal?

Yes	21	69	8
No	78	13	6

Are you concerned that a Republican-led Congress will be conservative?

Yes	81	10	7
No	25	67	7

In your vote for the U.S. House of Representatives, how important were Clinton and his policies?

Very important	65	30	5
Somewhat important	51	40	8

	Clinton	*Dole*	*Perot*
Not too important	27	59	11
Not at all important	15	69	12

In your vote for the U.S. House of Representatives, how important were Gingrich and his policies?

Very important	52	41	6
Somewhat important	41	52	6
Not too important	45	45	8
Not at all important	57	33	8

Do you think the government can cut the deficit and cut taxes at the same time?

Yes	39	52	8
No	64	25	9

Do you think Dole would be able to cut the deficit and reduce taxes by 15% at the same time?

Yes	11	84	4
No	67	22	8

If Clinton wins, what describes your feelings about his second term?

Excited	93	4	2
Optimistic	85	9	5
Concerned	27	57	13
Scared	2	84	12

What statement describes your opinion of what Clinton wants to do in the next 4 years?

Support almost all of it	93	5	2
Support some of it	65	21	10
Support only a little of it	8	75	15
Oppose almost all of it	4	87	8

Do you think Dole understands the problems of people like you?

Yes	18	76	6
No	79	7	12

Do you think Dole's age would interfere with his ability to serve effectively as president?

Yes	79	12	7
No	33	58	7

Who is more likely to reduce Medicare and Social Security benefits?

Clinton	52	43	5
Dole	64	29	6
Both equally	33	55	10
Neither	33	46	18

Which party is likely to reduce Medicare and Social Security benefits?

Characteristics	Candidate		
Democrats	42	51	6
Republicans	69	24	6
	Clinton	*Dole*	*Perot*
Both equally	33	55	10
Neither	28	62	8
What's your opinion of Hillary Clinton?			
Favorable	82	11	5
Unfavorable	14	72	12
What is your abortion position?			
Should always be legal	69	22	7
Mostly legal	55	34	9
Mostly illegal	33	57	9
Always illegal	25	67	7
Do you think the federal welfare law . . .			
cuts too much.	69	18	9
does not cut enough.	34	58	8
is about right.	55	37	7
Are you a gun owner?			
Yes	39	51	9
No	55	37	6
Do you regularly use the Internet?			
Yes	51	39	8
No	47	44	7
Are you gay/lesbian/bisexual?			
Yes	67	18	10
No	47	44	7
Which one should be the highest priority of the new administration?			
Family values	30	63	6
Funding Medicare/Social Security	69	31	6
Keeping the economy healthy	59	32	7

Characteristics	Candidate		
Cutting the size of government	17	67	9
	Clinton	*Dole*	*Perot*
Reforming the health care system	74	19	6
Cutting the middle class taxes	42	50	8
Improving the education system	65	26	8
Which one issue mattered the most in deciding how you voted for president?			
Taxes	18	75	6
Medicare/Social Security	69	24	6
Foreign Policy	30	60	9
Deficit	29	53	17
Economy/Jobs	60	28	10
Education	79	16	3
Crime/Drugs	42	48	8
Which quality mattered most in deciding your vote for president?			
He shared my view of government	43	46	8
He stands up for what he believes in.	42	42	14
He cares about people like me.	72	16	10
He is honest and trustworthy.	7	86	6
He is in touch with the 1990s.	90	6	4
He has a vision for the future.	77	12	9

Source: ABC News/*Washington Post*, exit polls, November 5, 1996.

even chastened. Clinton repeatedly indicated his intention to work with the congressional leadership to fashion a legislative agenda and announced a willingness to accept some form of balanced-budget amendment to the Constitution, a staple of Republican rhetoric and a part of the Contract with America. For his part, Speaker Gingrich said that he and his party had "an absolute moral obligation" to cooperate with the president to make the system work.[12]

"If the last Congress was a confrontation Congress, this Congress will be an implementation Congress," Gingrich promised his fellow House Republicans.[13]

Such postelection rhetoric from all sides is not uncommon in American politics. Still, it is a world away from the combativeness, ideological fervor, and lack of respect that marked the 104th Congress. In this sense, it may be closer to what Americans expect from their political leadership.

Referenda

Referenda have assumed increasing importance in recent decades in setting the nation's political agenda. The historic leader in this regard has been the state of California. From antismoking initiatives opposed by the tobacco industry to car safety measures and setting limits on local and state government spending, the battles have been fierce, costly, and, as often as not, trend-setting.

In 1996 several California initiatives had national ramifications. First, Proposition 209 bans sexual and racial preferences in government hiring, contracting, and education, effectively ending affirmative action programs. It passed 54 percent to 46 percent. Other states are likely to follow California's lead, and several court battles over the issue are already under way.

A second initiative in both California and Arizona proposed to legalize marijuana use for medical purposes. Opponents saw it as the first in a series of efforts to repeal or weaken drug laws. Both initiatives passed, although federal statutes outlawing marijuana conflict with the new statutes. These initiatives have also been taken to the courts.

A third California initiative, Proposition 211, would have facilitated stockholder suits against corporations for securities fraud. The measure was soundly defeated, 74 percent to 26 percent, the victim of the most expensive opposition campaign in California history.

In other issues of broad interest, Colorado defeated measures to give parents the right to control the education of their children and to allow governments to levy property taxes on churches and not-for-profit groups. In all, some 90 initiatives, most on matters of local concern, were decided in 20 states.

BUILDING THE BRIDGE?

Following the election, a number of top administration officials, some of their own volition, others at the will of the president, announced their resignations. They were led by the secretary of state, Warren Christopher, and White House chief of staff Leon Panetta. The resignations positioned Clinton to put into place a new team for his second term.

Many observers interpreted the election as a mandate for moderation and cooperation. To quote the president, "[The voters] are sending us a message: Work together."[14]

This view has been the dominant assessment, because enacting any legislation under a divided government is difficult, and Clinton campaigned as a moderate.

However, there are alternative interpretations. George F. Will, a nationally syndicated conservative columnist and television commentator whose wife was an official in the Dole campaign, sees the outcome as a continuation of the conservative hegemony:

On the 30th anniversary of the beginning of conservatism's ascendancy, voters produced another advance for conservatism. They gave Clinton what history says is a recipe for disappointment—a second term. And they allowed Republicans to retain control of the engine of government in this era of restored congressional supremacy.[15]

Lyn Nofziger, conservative political consultant and former adviser to Ronald Reagan, sees the outcome as reaffirming the agenda of the Contract with America, which, according to Nofziger, was "more widely approved at the grassroots level than the national news media and the Democratic leadership would have us believe."[16]

Labor, by contrast, saw the results as "a sweet victory" that forced its liberal agenda onto the Congress and the nation and one that unified working-class America. According to AFL-CIO president John J. Sweeney, it "demonstrated that labor was once again a powerful player on the national scene."[17]

Others yearn for the New Deal/Great Society of Franklin Roosevelt and Lyndon Johnson and, in the words of historian Irvin Unger, "faith in rational, benevolent, centralized planning in a world of graft, inefficiency, consumer vulnerability, predatory economic power and social inequality."[18] Their view is that such traditions gave much to America and that Clinton in a second term might consider something of similar stature. However, the president's postelection speech to the centrist Democratic Leadership Council outlining his programs for the second term and his cabinet appointments suggest a modest set of initiatives focused around a concern with deficit reduction and stable economic development.

Finally, there is the cynic's view, captured by cartoonist Szep, in a drawing that shows a beefy Clinton flashing the V-for-Victory sign and saying, "Re-election wasn't everything. . . . It was the only thing!!!"[19]

*Second terms have histori-
cally been less productive
than first terms.*

Bill Clinton is the first Democrat since Franklin Roosevelt to win a second term and one of only eight presidents in the history of the nation to do so. But second terms have historically been less productive than first terms. In effect, a second term is usually a lame-duck presidency, with attention shifting to new centers of power and new candidates and coalitions—in short, to the next election.

Clinton is the first president to be reelected with the Congress under control of the other party. His opposition has a strong ideological agenda and equally strong political ambitions. In the Senate, Republicans hope to increase their margin in the midterm election of 1998 to the 60 votes needed to override a presidential veto.

On the other hand, the Democrats in the House have the largest minority body representation in 40 years, since the Republican margin was reduced by 10 votes. Democratic majority leader Dick Gephardt promised a new and more aggressive Democratic Party presence in policy making.

President Clinton is also likely to face investigations by the Congress (promised by congressional leaders immediately after the election), a special counsel to investigate possible ethical and financial indiscretions, and scrutiny in other venues of charges of sexual misconduct.

David S. Broder of the *Washington Post,* one of the most respected of the nation's columnists, summarized the election this way:

With the end of the Cold War, both sides of the equation changed. The "big issues" are no longer the threat of Soviet expansionism and nuclear war, but job security, crime, drugs, welfare, education, the environment and . . . health and retirement benefits. Those are the issues on which President Clinton twice campaigned successfully and where the most prominent Republicans in Washington were found wanting. . . . The voters reelected the Republican Congress to keep the pressure on

Washington to balance the budget within the next few years. They put Clinton back in office in order to see that his priorities—which are also their priorities—remain at the top of the list, i.e., to protect what are now the most important things in their lives.[20]

The ultimate meaning of the election, of course, will be left for the future to decide. One thing can be said with certainty in all of this: The race for the presidential nomination in the year 2000 has already begun. The front-runners appear to be Al Gore for the Democrats and Jack Kemp for the Republicans. And within days of the election, Lamar Alexander, the moderate who did poorly in the 1996 Republican primaries, announced that he, too, would be a candidate again in four years.

Each of the chapters that follow focuses on a different aspect of the 1996 contest. We trust you will find this second look at *America's Choice* enlightening and enjoyable.

ENDNOTES

1. Bob Woodward, *The Agenda: Inside the Clinton White House* (New York: Simon & Schuster Pocket Books, 1995), p. 395.
2. Alison Mitchell, "Stung by Defeats in '94, Clinton Regrouped and Co-opted GOP Strageties," *New York Times,* November 7, 1996, p. B1.
3. Associated Press, "Dole's Campaign Staff Looks Back, with Hindsight," *Boston Globe,* November 9, 1996, p. A9.
4. Todd S. Purdum, "Clinton Signs Bill for $256.6 Billion for Armed Forces," *New York Times,* September 24, 1996, p. A1.
5. Michael Wines, "Campaign Travel: The Presidential Race," *New York Times,* October 12, 1996, p. A14.
6. Deborah Orin, "Dole Comes Out Swinging at Clinton Ethics," *New York Post,* October 16, 1996, p. 4; Brian McGrory, "Dole Aiming at Clinton's Character," *Boston Globe,* October 13, 1996, p. A1; Katherine Q. Seelye, "Changing Tactics, Dole Challenges Clinton's Ethics," *New York Times,* October 9, 1996, p. A1; Andrew Miga and Joe Battenfield, "Tough Talk: Dole Slams Clinton on Ethics, Broken Promises," *Boston Herald,* October 17, 1996, p. 1; and Jill Zuckerman and Brian McGrory, "Dole Targets White House 'Sleaze Factor,'" *Boston Globe,* October 18, 1996, p. A1.
7. Associated Press, "Clinton Seen Leading Dole on Character Issue," *Boston Globe,* October 20, 1996, p. A19.
8. Gerald Posner, "Perot, Alone," *New York Times Magazine,* November 22, 1996, pp. 82ff. See

also Gerald Posner, *Citizen Perot: His Life and Times,* (New York: Random House, 1996).

9. Advertisement for Perot Campaign, *Boston Herald,* November 4, 1996, p. 27.

10. Bob Minzesheimer and Martha T. Moore, "Why Voters Didn't Turn Out," *Chicago Sun-Times,* November 10, 1996, p. 39.

11. "The Electorate: 48.8%, Lowest Figure since 1924, Said to Have Gone to the Polls," *Boston Globe,* November 11, 1996, p. A39.

12. David Rogers, "Gingrich, Accepting Speaker's Post, Sees 'Moral Obligation' to Work with Clinton," *Wall Street Journal,* November 21, 1996, p. A24.

13. Chris Black, "Chastened Gingrich Reelected Speaker," *Boston Globe,* November 21, 1996, p. A3. See also Todd S. Purdum, "Clinton Suggests He May Not Resist Fiscal Amendment, *New York Times,* November 13, 1996, p. A1; Adam Clymer, "House Leader Tries to Replace Ethics Panelist," *New York Times,* November 21, 1996, p. A1; and R.W. Apple, Jr., "Despite Some Words of Bipartisanship, More Political Storms Are Likely," *New York Times,* November 7, 1996, p. B6.

14. Michael Kranish, "Campaign '96: Letter for the President," *Boston Globe,* November 10, 1996, p. D4.

15. George F. Will, "Conservative Voters Batted Three for Four," *Boston Globe,* November 8, 1996, p. A23.

16. Lyn Nofziger, " 'Contract' Is Alive and Kicking," *Boston Globe,* November 12, 1996, p. A17. Also on the Contract and the legislative goals of the Congress, see Jeffrey M. Berry, "The Real Powers on Capitol Hill," *Boston Sunday Globe,* December 5, 1996, p. C1.

17. Steven Greenhouse, "Despite Setbacks, Labor Chief Is Upbeat over Election Role," *New York Times,* November 15, 1996, p. A20; Bernard J. Wolfson, "Labor Declares Election Victory," *Boston Herald,* November 7, 1996, p. 40.

18. Quoted in Donald M. Shribman, "Public Policy: Will There Be a New New Deal?" *Boston Sunday Globe,* November 10, 1996, p. D1.

19. "Szep's View," *Boston Globe,* November 8, 1996, p. A22.

20. David S. Broder, "A Political Role Reversal," *Boston Globe,* November 13, 1996, p. A15.

Chapter Two

The Context: Policies and Politics, 1993–1996

John T. Tierney

However else one may interpret the outcome of the 1996 elections, it's difficult to see it other than as an endorsement by American voters of political moderation. The voters restamped Bill Clinton's ticket to the White House, but only after he backpedaled from the liberal postures he had struck earlier in his presidency and successfully repositioned himself squarely at the center of the political spectrum. Voters in 1996 also returned Republican majorities to both houses of Congress, but only after being satisfied that the fires of conservative zeal that had been burning bright on Capitol Hill since 1994 no longer threatened to rage out of control. In short, the most striking feature of the political climate prior to the national party conventions in 1996 was the simultaneous retreat on the part of both the Democratic president and the Republican Congress to a centrist or moderate posture on issues of national policy.

Important as it was in shaping the election's outcome, the wholesale retreat to moderation by the two political parties was obviously only part of the story. The voters' decisions in 1996 were reflections of other factors as well, such as the strong performance of the economy throughout Clinton's term in office and the persistence of a gender gap that has plagued Republicans for years, this time swallowing Bob Dole. Going into the election year, the Republicans also were in trouble with older American voters, many of whom were politically alienated by what seemed to be Republican plans to reduce spending on Medicare. Thus, one of the remarkable things about the 1996 elections was the extent to which many of the electoral foundation stones on which Clinton's reelection victory eventually was built were already firmly in place as the election year began.

This chapter will map out the broad context of policy and politics as the general election campaign geared up in mid-1996. Toward that goal, I focus on the Clinton administration's record in its first two years, the Republicans' victorious assault in the 1994 midterm elections, and the political events and circumstances that seemed to be shaping voters' attitudes as the presidential and congressional elections of 1996 drew near.

THE POLITICAL LEGACY OF THE 1992 ELECTIONS

The 1992 election did not send Bill Clinton to the White House with any clear mandate, but to the extent that the voters were sending any message that year, it was that Washington needed to change. And having aggressively presented himself to the voters in 1992 as an agent of change, Clinton could take from his victory a sense that the people had spoken in its favor. After all, the best means available to voters for bringing about changes in government policies and practices in a democratic society is to elect the candidate of the party that is not in power. And that's what they did, rejecting a Republican president who seemed to be ignoring their concerns.

Speaking to weary middle-class Americans when he accepted his party's nomination for president in July of 1992, Clinton indicated that he had heard their anger and frustration, and he held out to them a promise that, under his presidency, attention would be paid: "In the name of all those who do the work, pay the taxes, raise the kids and play by the rules—in the name of the hard-working Americans who make up our forgotten middle class, I accept your nomination for president of the United States. I am a product of that middle class. And when I am president you will be forgotten no more." Thus, Clinton presented himself as someone who would pay attention to ordinary Americans. Indeed, that promise on Clinton's part was a large part of what helped him recapture the support of such segments of his party as the Reagan Democrats who had been siphoned off by Republicans in preceding elections.

As he discussed his agenda during the 1992 campaign, Clinton styled himself as a "New Democrat," separating himself from traditional Democratic politicians by his support for welfare reform, vigorous anticrime measures, and deficit reduction. In addition, Clinton promised to "change the way Washington works," with pledges to reform campaign financing, lobbying, and the operation of Congress. Thus, like other modern presidents who preceded him, Bill Clinton had helped to generate the inflated public expectations of his performance that he carried with him to the Oval Office.

And for Clinton, fulfilling those expectations would be an especially complicated task. First, although the president's party controlled both houses of the 103rd Congress that was seated in 1993, its majorities were slender: the Democrats had 258 seats in the House (10 fewer than in the previous Congress) and 58 seats in the Senate (shy of the number they would need to close down Republican filibusters). And of those congressional Democrats, a smaller number were the president's political supporters. Moreover, having won only 43 percent of the popular vote, the new president lacked the sort of victory margin that might incline others in Washington to cut him much initial political slack. In particular, the Republicans on Capitol Hill saw little to gain by cooperating with Clinton and the Democrats.

CLINTON'S EARLY POLICY AGENDA: LOOKING LIKE A LIBERAL

Although Bill Clinton had campaigned for the presidency as a new brand of moderately conservative Democrat, by the time his administration was nine months old, its policy initiatives had given it a distinctly liberal veneer. None of these initiatives should have come as any particular surprise to anyone who listened carefully to candidate Clinton throughout 1992, but for less attentive voters who were expecting a Democrat of truly different stripes, many of the new president's policy measures may have been jarring. Some of these policy steps were fulfillments of commitments Clinton had made during the campaign to particular constituencies (abortion-rights activists and homosexuals), while others were the outgrowth of policy deliberations within the new administration.

Abortion Rights and Gays in the Military

On his second full day in office, Clinton signed a series of executive orders directing government agencies to undo key decisions by Presidents Ronald Reagan and George Bush that had put the federal government squarely in opposition to abortion. With the stroke of his pen, Clinton eliminated the 1988 "gag rule" prohibiting abortion counseling in federally funded family planning clinics; called for a review of the import ban on RU-486, the French abortion pill; eliminated a ban on federal funding of medical research using fetal tissue from elective abortions; and lifted the order against abortions at military hospitals overseas. While the president's actions inflamed pro-life activists around the country, they occasioned little comment from other constituencies. Many of those who oppose abortion as a fundamental right were skeptical of the Bush administration's arguments that the prospect of beneficial research involving fetuses would encourage abortion, and they strongly opposed restrictions on what health professionals may discuss with their patients. So, while Clinton was not out of step with majority opinion on this set of issues, his decisions were charting a decidedly more liberal course.

15

But public reaction to Clinton's proposal to lift the ban on homosexuals in the military was very different. Clinton had promised his gay and lesbian supporters during the 1992 campaign that if elected he would eliminate that ban. After the election, a work group began meeting to craft plans to drop the policy, and during the inaugural week, one member of that group, Rep. Barney Frank (D-MA), told report-

The economic program was in reality balanced, centrist, and fiscally responsible.

ers that plans were in place to end the ban in two steps. First, Defense Secretary Les Aspin would issue a directive saying essentially that no one could be thrown out of the service for being gay and that no one could be asked if he or she were homosexual before being accepted into the military. Aspin would then work with top military officials to develop an executive order lifting the ban.[1]

A strongly negative reaction came in quickly from every political quarter. Most conspicuous among the opponents were high-ranking military officers such as General Colin Powell, chairman of the Joint Chiefs of Staff, conservative Republican senators such as Jesse Helms (R-NC) and Daniel Coats (R-IN), and military experts in Congress such as Sam Nunn, the conservative Georgia Democrat who chaired the Senate Armed Services Committee. Their opposition was predicated on the view that the open presence of homosexuals in the services would adversely affect morale and weaken military performance. Public opinion polls soon showed that the public decidedly supported the military's view on the subject. As a groundswell of opposition to his plan grew, Clinton retreated from his original proposal and began negotiating with military leaders to formulate a compromise plan—the "don't ask, don't tell" policy that eventually was adopted.[2]

This controversy was a political disaster for the young administration. Paul Quirk and Joseph

Hinchliffe have neatly summarized the mess: "All in a single episode, he identified himself with an unpopular liberal stance on a controversial social issue; he ended up grievously disappointing his gay and lesbian supporters; and by caving in to resistance from Congress and his nominal subordinates in the military, he raised doubts about the strength of his leadership."[3]

The Stimulus Package and the Budget Plan

Clinton also staked out a liberal stance in his early economic policies. During the 1992 campaign, Clinton had been quite critical of George Bush's hands-off response to the recession, and he pledged that if elected he would get the economy moving again. Once in office, the president proposed economic policies toward that end, with two principal goals of job creation and deficit reduction. The administration's proposals involved an immediate economic "stimulus package" (an emergency multibillion-dollar spending bill involving an assortment of programs aimed at creating jobs) as well as a deficit-reduction budget plan, notable for both its spending cuts (for which candidate Clinton had done little to prepare voters) and for its assorted tax increases (especially, increased taxes on the wealthy and an across-the-board energy tax).

The political fights over the president's stimulus package and the budget proposal occupied most of the first nine months of 1993, required tremendous investments of presidential political will, and soured relations between the two parties on Capitol Hill as well as between liberals and conservatives within the Democratic Party. In the end, the economic program that passed in 1993 produced considerable deficit reduction (roughly $450 billion over five years), with major spending cuts and substantial tax increases of $241 billion (which Republicans for months thereafter labeled "the largest tax increase in the history of the country"). Although the program was in reality balanced, centrist, and fiscally responsible, it produced little in the way of political benefits for either Clinton or the Democrats on the Hill. If anything, because the final outcome was achieved through high-profile bargains and concessions (all amidst constant Republican attack and obstructionism), the public was left with the impression that Bill Clinton's stewardship of the White House had brought little change to the way Washington works.[4] Unfortunately for the president and his fellow Democrats, things were only to worsen as the policy focus shifted in September of 1993 to the health care arena, where the Clinton administration would experience its most devastating first-term setback.

Health Care Reform

If there was any policy initiative of Clinton's first term that defined the president and his administration in conventional liberal terms, it was his determination to achieve comprehensive health care reforms. However, a series of errors plagued the health care initiative. Perhaps the greatest was the ambitious scope of the initiative itself: guaranteed, affordable health care for everyone, with benefits that would meet every basic medical need. Even though there was substantial public support for the individual components of the Clinton plan, the proposal eventually foundered largely because it called for too much government involvement and was almost incomprehensible in its complexity.

Essentially, Clinton's plan aimed to provide universal insurance coverage for Americans and also to introduce new competition into the health care system to contain rising costs. The universal coverage goal was to be met chiefly by requiring businesses to provide coverage for all workers (a so-called employer mandate). The goal of increased competition was to be met by building on an already growing trend in health policy known as "managed competition," in which doctors and hospitals and insurers compete for patients. The Clinton plan was to require consumers to join large groups called "health-care alliances"—quasi-governmental entities organized by region all around the country. These large alliances would have the necessary market power to drive a hard bargain with insurance companies, thus benefiting consumers. Most doctors would have to join in "managed care" networks with hospitals and other providers in order to be competitive and have access to patients. Competition among the health care providers would improve quality and hold down costs. And in case it didn't, Clinton proposed a regulatory structure to control costs and quality. A complex network of gov-

ernment agencies would help engineer and orchestrate all these reforms.[5]

Although supporters regarded the plan as visionary, attacks upon it came from many diverse quarters. Some critics accused the White House of trying to nationalize health care and impose price controls on medical services; the insurance industry saw the plan as a competitive threat and set out to defeat it quickly with a national advertising campaign designed to unsettle voters; and small businesses rebelled against the idea of being forced to buy health insurance for workers, arguing that the cost would drive many into bankruptcy. Business owners and Republicans pointed to the employer mandate provision as proof of the president's liberal, big-government agenda.

Many saw the plan as too bold and too late in coming. The program designed by first lady Hillary Clinton's health care task force was not ready for introduction to Congress until September of 1993. The administration conceded, even as it was introducing the package, that its passage could not be achieved until the summer of 1994.

The health care proposal died a long, slow death over a period of about a year. The defeat could be attributed to many causes—excessive delay in proposing the legislation, inadequate consultation with Congress during the formulation stage, congressional fragmentation, obstruction by Republicans and organized interests, mishandling of the issue by the media, the inflated egos of Democratic committee heads, and so forth. But the central problem surely stemmed from the Clinton administration's failure to develop a responsible, incremental, and centrist approach that would be more sensitive to citizens' wariness of extensive governmental involvement. The defeat not only impaired the administration, it also emboldened the Republicans, galvanizing them in their opposition and furnishing them with material for the attacks they would mount on Clinton and the Democrats in the 1994 campaign.[6]

OTHER POLICY ISSUES AND THE 103RD CONGRESS

The attention lavished on the health care reform effort meant that other important items on the Democrats' agenda were left to languish

17

unaddressed. With the benefit of hindsight, it seems clear that the Clinton White House would have been better advised to go after a more incremental version of health care reform and to avoid letting the issue crowd other important measures off the congressional agenda.

Candidate Clinton had been adamant during the campaign about welfare reform, promising to "end welfare as we know it"—a pledge

---

Even more surprising was the failure of Congress to pass legislation cleaning up its own act.

---

also adopted by many Democratic House candidates running for the first time in 1992. The plan, eventually embodied in the Clinton welfare overhaul package offered in 1994, was to replace the patchwork of government assistance programs with a system that imposed strict limits on how long poor people could collect benefits but also helped those willing to work by providing training, tax credits, health benefits, child care, and, if necessary, a job. These ideas had broad support in the 103rd Congress; indeed, they even became the inspiration for an early, competing Republican proposal. But President Clinton had insisted (over the objections of many new House members and of Senator Daniel Patrick Moynihan, D-NY, then chairman of the Senate Finance Committee) that Congress must deal with health care reform first. The decision to postpone welfare reform meant that Democrats who had presented themselves as agents of change would be denied any accomplishment in the welfare reform column to tout in their 1994 campaigns for reelection. Welfare reform never surfaced seriously in the 103rd Congress.

At the same time, the Democrats were fumbling another important matter. During the 1992 campaign, Clinton had pledged that as president he would work hard to enact political reforms in the realms of campaign finance, lobbying, and congressional procedures. In his inaugural address, he had reminded Americans of

that pledge: "And so I say to all of you here, let us resolve to reform our politics so that power and privilege no longer shout down the voice of the people. Let us give this capital back to the people to whom it belongs."

In the early weeks of his presidency, Clinton held a meeting with Democratic congressional leaders on the subject of his political reform agenda. With respect to campaign finance reform, he received strong support from Senators George Mitchell and David Boren, longtime leaders on the issue, who wanted to capitalize on the Democrats' momentum coming out of the election. They pushed for immediate action on campaign finance reform. But Speaker Tom Foley and House Majority Leader Richard Gephardt argued for delay, even though the Speaker had publicly pledged to move early on the issue. The House leaders argued that other pressing issues should be taken up first and that it should be up to them to decide when to schedule the matter. Clinton deferred to Foley and Gephardt.[7]

The president's acquiescence to the demands of the House leaders would ultimately spell the death of campaign finance reform for the 103rd Congress. To their credit, the Senate leaders brought the issue to the floor, brokered an agreement that attracted the support of seven Republican senators, broke a filibuster, and passed a significant reform bill. But in the House, Speaker Foley refused to deal with political reform, putting off consideration of the bill until late November 1993, when it passed by an 80-vote margin in the last week of the first session. But the bill was weaker in many respects than the Senate version, and House Democratic leaders throughout most of 1994 rejected efforts to reach compromises with the Senate on stronger legislation. By the time a compromise finally was reached in the closing days of the 103rd Congress, Republicans in the Senate, giddy over the way the Democrats had shot themselves in the foot by failing to deal with the issue earlier, filibustered it to death.[8]

Much the same thing occurred with other legislative proposals to change Washington's ways. A bill to tighten controls over lobbyists was taken up by the House only in the final weeks leading up to the 1994 elections. But the bill failed to pass in the House as Republicans and conservatives successfully organized grassroots opposition to it. Perhaps even more surprising was the failure of Congress to pass legislation cleaning up its own act. Although many freshmen had made such pledges a prominent part of their campaigns, Congress failed even to enact the most moderate of proposals to achieve that goal. In the final weeks of the second session, legislative action faltered on a bill to require Congress to comply with the same federal workplace laws that private sector companies must obey. On the final day of the 103rd Congress, as it became clear the legislation would not be passed, the House adopted a resolution that would amend its rules to include much of the language of the ill-fated bill. One observer noted that the last-minute House action on the rule change was "designed to let members tell constituents they had done what they could to address a common voter complaint: that Congress imposes laws on others that it is not willing to live by. It also would let freshmen say they delivered on a key 'reform' even though more sweeping proposals to alter Congress's operations ran aground."[9]

Of course, the 103rd Congress was not without its legislative accomplishments. But most of those enactments—the Family and Medical Leave Act, the "motor-voter" registration law, the NAFTA trade agreement, an expansion of the earned-income tax credit, creation of a national service corps, the Brady gun control bill, a crime bill (with an assault weapons ban), and nearly a half-trillion dollars in deficit reduction—provided only long-term benefits for voters, with few tangible gains that could be felt by the 1994 election. And some of them, such as the Brady bill and the assault weapons ban, galvanized strong opposition from resourceful groups such as the National Rifle Association—opposition that would prove troublesome for many vulnerable freshman Democrats in the 1994 elections.

One could fairly say about the Democrats in 1993 and 1994 that their political judgment had failed them. Clinton seemed to leave behind the "New Democrat" clothes he had worn throughout the campaign, trying on instead the mantle of a liberal social engineer, at least in his most conspicuous policy endeavor, health care reform. He overreached, though there was little in the election results of 1992 to justify such a political stretch. And one could argue that neither the president nor his fellow partisans on Capitol Hill took seriously the voters'

insistence in 1992 that they reform welfare and bring change to the way Washington works. As a consequence, by the time the 1994 midterm elections came, the Democrats were exceedingly vulnerable.[10]

It's also true, of course, that the Republicans had played their hand well. Throughout the 103rd Congress, Republicans in the House and Senate struck a steady and united posture of obstruction and opposition ("principled obstructionism," as Republican strategist William Kristol termed it). As the months wore on, and especially as the health care reform measure blew up in the Democrats' face, congressional Republicans began to view the 1994 elections as an opportunity to pick up substantial numbers of seats in both chambers of Congress.

THE 1994 MIDTERM ELECTIONS AND THE REPUBLICAN 104TH CONGRESS

History was already on the Republicans' side as the 1994 elections approached: One of the most stable and persistent patterns in American electoral politics is that the president's party loses seats in midterm elections. And in some cases (1946, 1958, 1966, and 1974), the losses have been dramatic. In each of those years, the election had become "nationalized," as voters dissatisfied with the performance of the incumbent president took out their wrath on his party's congressional incumbents. Although congressional election races typically revolve around local issues, a midterm congressional election may become nationalized by a drop in presidential popularity, a sharp economic decline, a series of poorly received policy actions, or an event like the Watergate scandal that redounds to the electoral disadvantage of the president's political party. Members of the other party are poised to pounce, ready to highlight policy "mistakes" or to put negative frames on the political choices made by their opponents.

In 1994, Republican congressional candidates succeeded in nationalizing the elections with a clear theme and a clever strategy that played on the failure of Democrats to deliver on their promise to produce change. In late September 1994, Representative Newt Gingrich (R-GA) assembled over 300 Republican

19

congressional candidates from around the country on the steps of the U.S. Capitol to sign a "Contract with America," pledging that if elected they would support changes in the way Congress operates and bring to votes in the House a series of proposals long pushed by many in the GOP and deemed to have considerable appeal with voters—proposals that would, among other things, cut capital gains taxes, impose the death penalty more often, reform congressional rules, impose term limits on members of Congress, give the president a line-item veto, and provide a balanced-budget amendment to the Constitution. The "contract" was meant to cast the Republicans in favorable contrast to Democrats. The implicit message was that Republicans could be counted on to keep their word to the voters and deal with national issues that were important to voters. During the elections, Gingrich advised Republican candidates to use such words as "decay, failure, shallow, traitors, pathetic, corrupt, incompetent, and sick" in characterizing their Democratic opponents.[11]

Whatever the ultimate electoral impact of the contract itself (exit polls on election day revealed that fewer than half the voters had even heard of it), the campaign themes and strategies pursued by Republican candidates and their political allies apparently struck some responsive chord with voters. Their trip to the polls in November 1994 wrought devastation for the Democratic Party, which lost 52 House seats and 8 Senate seats. Among incumbents seeking reelection, 35 House Democrats failed to retain their seats, including some of the chamber's most prominent members, such as Speaker Thomas Foley and Jack Brooks, chairman of the Judiciary Committee. Three incumbent Democratic senators also lost their seats. By contrast, every single Republican incumbent who sought reelection to the House or Senate won in 1994. The election gave the Republicans majority control of both houses of Congress for the first time in 40 years.

Given the magnitude of the Republicans' victory, it's not surprising that the election was widely interpreted as a message that the voters disapproved of the liberal path Clinton often had steered in his first two years and that they were no longer willing to put up with Democratic legislators who ignored the public's call for fundamental changes. This was certainly the

way many Republicans interpreted the election results. The day after the election, Newt Gingrich, who would be elected by his fellow Republicans to the speakership he coveted, told reporters that the Republican triumph, like Clinton's victory four years earlier, was a public cry for change. "It's a sad comment on the Clinton administration that they had an enormous opportunity to bring about change and they failed."[12]

Revolutionary zeal was to be the most characteristic feature of the 104th Congress.

As the new 104th Congress began to take shape under Republican control, the rhetoric heard from zealous members of the new majority was of "a new American revolution." Indeed, revolutionary zeal on the part of Republicans, especially on the House side, was to be the most characteristic feature of the 104th Congress throughout the first year. House Republicans put in place a strikingly conservative leadership team to support Speaker Gingrich—Richard Armey as majority leader and Tom DeLay as majority whip. Both Texans, Armey and DeLay shared Gingrich's commitment to aggressive leadership but espoused a conservative line even sharper and more determined than Gingrich's. This triumvirate would have little trouble bringing their fellow partisans along with them: the impulse toward party unity was strong. Moreover, many rank-and-file Republicans were even more aggressively conservative than the party leaders. This was true especially among the 73 Republican freshmen, who included such firebrands as Mark Souder and David McIntosh of Indiana and John Shadegg and J. D. Hayworth of Arizona.

The Republicans wasted no time putting their stamp on Congress. Even before the members of the 104th were sworn into office, the Republican Party caucus in the House worked out changes to the chamber's committee system, eliminating several committees and subcommittees and cutting committee staffs. Several committees were renamed to suggest the fundamental changes in policy emphasis that were to come, with conspicuous swipes at urban affairs, education, labor, and protection of natural resources.[13]

Once seated, the new Congress started off with a bang, approving several of the political-reform planks in the contract, including legislation requiring Congress to abide by worker protection laws it had imposed on other employers. The House approved rules changes to reform its operations (limiting to six years the length of time a representative can be chair of a committee, requiring a three-fifths majority vote for passing income tax increases rather than the simple majority previously needed, and other changes). On the Senate side, Republicans gradually altered their rules to promote party loyalty and more power for junior members.

But there was to be no leisurely or moderate build-up toward legislative action, nor would the public reaction ultimately be what the Republicans wished. Gingrich had committed his fellow Republicans to bringing every one of the 10 items in the GOP contract to a floor vote within the first 100 days of the new Congress, so several months passed with the House operating at a brutal pace. Sessions went late into the night as members and their staffs worked 14- and 15-hour days. But as the Republicans repeatedly brought measures to a vote, only a few of them passed. And gradually the public view came to be that the Republicans were trying to do too much too quickly, taking on enormous issues without sufficient forethought or informed debate. Despite their manic efforts, congressional Republicans soon were treated to the frustrating news that 60 percent of the public felt it had been "politics as usual" since Republicans took over leadership of the House and Senate in January of 1995.[14]

To a considerable extent, however, the Republicans had only themselves to blame for the public's cynicism and the continuing sense that little was different on the Hill. The Republican-controlled House voted down the measure that would have limited the number of terms a member of Congress could serve. Apparently, term limits were a fine idea only as long as the Democrats were the majority party. This double standard was not lost on the public.

And as the weeks and months wore on, the news stories emanating from Capitol Hill only reinforced the growing popular sense that the Republicans who had positioned themselves in 1994 as populist allies of middle-class Americans were nothing of the sort. Gradually but inexorably the House Republicans cozied up to their well-heeled allies in big business, skillfully using the legislative process to load appropriations bills with riders on behalf of oil companies, chemical plants, trucking companies, meat packers, cattle ranchers, timber and mining companies, freight delivery services, and many others.[15]

The GOP's problems with the public swelled still more as it became apparent that the Republicans intended to mount an attack on the whole constellation of programs and laws that had been designed to protect the environment and public health and safety. Here again, some of the House leaders were responsible for some of the worst damage to the GOP's cause. One news report that received front-page attention provided details on the extraordinary degree to which industry lobbyists had been made full partners of the Republican leadership in shaping congressional priorities and individual bills to push back government regulations. Representative Tom DeLay (R-TX), the new majority whip and former exterminator, was well known on Capitol Hill for his eagerness to eliminate federal safety and environmental rules that he believed were excessively burdensome to American businesses. And he wasted no time pooling the resources of his office with those of business interests toward that goal. Their initial collaboration succeeded in pushing through the House a measure to put a moratorium on environmental and safety regulations.[16]

As the spring of 1995 wore on, it became apparent that DeLay and other antigovernment Republicans in the House were pushing to delay implementation of new meat inspection rules, limit the regulatory reach of the Occupational Safety and Health Administration, end retroactive corporate liability at Superfund toxic waste sites, eliminate the Department of Commerce, provide regulatory relief to businesses overburdened by the mandates of the 1990 Clean Air Act amendments, loosen mileage standards for vans and light trucks, and slash the budget of the Environmental Protection Agency, reducing its ability to regulate specific types of pollution.[17] But those conservative Republicans quickly learned that more moderate members of their own party would not support them in such endeavors. An even greater problem for them was that their attacks on regulations designed to protect the environment were alienating millions of Americans who remained strongly supportive of governmental rules aimed at protecting the environment, workers, and consumers.

Clinton positioned himself to take advantage of the Republicans' mistakes.

The antiregulatory agenda was not the only area in which congressional Republicans made serious political miscalculations. They also misstepped badly in their attacks on programs aimed at helping the poor—they tried, for example, to cut 10 percent from the funding of the program providing federal aid to schools serving low-income kids, to eliminate youth job programs, and to terminate a program assisting elderly poor people with their utility bills. These and other GOP initiatives throughout the first session of the 104th Congress alienated segments of the electorate—especially women and older Americans—whose support would be necessary in any campaign to reclaim the Oval Office.

But the Republicans' most serious miscalculations were still to come on two controversial matters—balancing the budget and controlling growth in Medicare costs. Throughout 1995, the congressional Republicans had been crafting a strategic plan to achieve a balanced budget in seven years, a goal that was of primary importance to them. The balancing would be achieved by dismantling some Great Society programs, shortening welfare eligibility, turning Medicaid into a block grant program to be run by the states, and—most important—reining in spending for Medicare, a program that long had been seen as untouchable. Gingrich and other Republican strategists had devised what they thought was a foolproof plan: In the fall they would tie their budget bill (with its spending cuts and programmatic changes) into one big legislative package along with other bills that would have to be passed at that time—stopgap spending measures and a bill to raise the debt ceiling. Their assumption was that President Clinton would lack the courage to veto such a bill, since doing so would force a controversial shutdown of the government. They also assumed that the political costs the GOP would suffer over the planned Medicare cuts would be temporary.[18]

But the Republicans' strategy backfired in a way that put all congressional Republicans on the defensive throughout the 1996 election year and that dramatically strengthened Bill Clinton's chances of holding onto the Oval Office. Whereas the president might have been inclined earlier in 1995 to strike a deal with the Republicans, by autumn public opinion polls showed that support for the Republican spending cuts was falling dramatically, with particularly negative reactions to the GOP's proposed reductions in Medicare. Consequently, the White House began to see some potential political advantage to having the president stand up to the Republicans, presenting himself to the public not as an accommodator of conservatives' preferences but as a principled protector of programs valued by the American people.[19]

Conservative Republicans could not see how rapidly things were changing and they allowed the federal government to be closed down—not once but several times in November, December, and early January. But President Clinton never capitulated. Instead, the president stood firm and, rather than finding himself the target of withering public criticism, as the Republicans had expected, Clinton found his approval ratings surging upward as he presented himself as the resolute defender of average Americans' interests—the only force preventing Medicare from being savaged in order to finance GOP tax cuts for the rich. Meanwhile, the political costs to the Republicans were extraordinary, as the public held them responsible for the "train wreck" of government shutdowns that imposed hardships on hundreds of thousands of federal workers, companies dependent on government work, and millions of Americans who were hurt by the loss of a wide range of governmental services.

So the great Republican Revolution fizzled out as the 104th Congress reached its halfway point. Public support for the conservative agenda was not sufficient to sustain it. Worse yet for the Republicans, their efforts to push that agenda had breathed new life into a Democratic president who 12 months earlier had seemed beyond political resuscitation. But Clinton's revival was not only the Republicans' doing. It can fairly be said of Clinton that by the second half of 1995, he had already set himself rolling down the road of recovery. Clinton crafted his own equivalent of a political self-help program, and in the process masterfully positioned himself to take advantage of the Republicans' mistakes.

CLINTON'S REVERSAL OF FORTUNE

The Democrats were chastened by the beating they took at the polls in November 1994, and moderate Democrats especially read the setback as a warning to the president and the party to return to centrist "New Democrat" themes and policies that Clinton had promoted during the 1992 campaign. It was clear that the president would have to focus on reoccupying the political center on issues of social and economic policy. At a White House press conference the day after the election in 1994, Clinton accepted his share of responsibility for the devastating defeats suffered by Democrats in Congress. And sending a clear signal about where on the political spectrum he henceforth would be found, Clinton called on the Republicans "to join me in the center of the public debate where the best ideas for the next generation of American progress must come." In the following months, Clinton then went on to claim that political center for himself, even as the Republicans were racing to the extreme.

Clinton's reversal of fortune obviously did not occur overnight. It was a long, slow, nonlinear process that involved fits and starts, ups and downs. But when looked at in its entirety, Clinton's comeback in 1995 and the first half of 1996 clearly had several different components, each of them important: the president found his voice, he found surer footing in his handling of foreign policy, and he found his way to the sacred center of domestic politics. In retrospect, it was a remarkable set of journeys.

Finding His Voice

One of the striking things about the Republican takeover of Congress was how thoroughly it shifted the responsibility for policy agenda-setting from the White House to Congress. Having thus been effectively sent to the sidelines in the central game of legislative policy making, Clinton understandably turned to the "bully pulpit" as an alternate arena of presidential power. Even though he is widely regarded as a skilled and poised speaker, quick on his feet and comfortable before live audiences and television cameras alike, Clinton's earlier exercises in "going public" had typically been tactical, aimed at winning support for particular pieces of legislation. He hadn't resolutely used his presidential voice as an instrument for shaping moods, discussing values, and connecting with his listeners. But with his arms pinned to his sides by the new Republican majorities in Congress, Clinton would find the power of voice.

In part, things began to change because of the tragic bombing of the Murtha Federal Building in Oklahoma City in April 1995, a blast that killed 168 people and brought grief to many others. Suddenly and ironically, the federal government was given a human face by the deaths of some who had staffed it. According to John Ellis, an occasional columnist for the *Boston Globe* and a thoughtful observer of Clinton's comeback, the dangers of political extremism thus came to seem all too real, spread as they were across the front page of every newspaper in the United States: "President Clinton seized that moment to reassert his authority and introduce the central metaphor of his reelection campaign. From that day forward, he positioned himself as an unbreakable line of defense against political extremism." And Clinton would use that metaphor repeatedly throughout the months to come, describing the Republicans' proposed budget cuts and attempts to roll back government regulations as "extreme." As Ellis noted, "It sometimes seemed in Clinton's metaphor [that] the Republican Party had become the political equivalent of the militia movement."[20]

After Oklahoma City Clinton used his voice not only to portray his Republican opponents as extreme but to speak repeatedly with conviction about the need for "common ground" in a nation split ideologically, divided economically, and torn racially. One conspicuous

23

occasion on which Clinton voiced such a theme was the day of the Million Man March in October 1995. This was an event organized by Louis Farrakhan and other African American leaders to energize their male followers as a political and social force. In his own speech that day, Clinton spoke passionately of his vision of a diverse America, steeped in tolerance, good will, and compassion. Some veteran observers considered this the best speech of his presidency to date.[21]

Finding His Footing in Foreign Policy

Whereas foreign policy issues had been primary for virtually all of his predecessors in the modern presidency, Clinton came into the White House at a time when such issues had substantially less primacy for the voters. Red-hot national security issues were eclipsed by seemingly less threatening issues of trade and the international political economy. And although Clinton had some of his most notable first-term successes on precisely those issues (with the adoption of NAFTA and GATT), foreign policy generally was not an arena in which he achieved any distinction in his first two years. Having come into office promising to focus "like a laser beam" on the economy, Clinton had seemed to pay relatively little attention to international affairs, and his administration acquired an image of drift and indecision in foreign policy, an image that reached its nadir in late 1993.

In office less than a full year at that point, the Clinton administration seemed to be fumbling badly in foreign policy. Its China policy was in disarray, with administration officials later admitting that they had erred in trying to use trade policy with Beijing as a lever for advancing human rights in China. Its posture concerning Bosnia seemed weak and spineless; having once promised to take a tough stand against Serb aggression, the administration had largely abdicated responsibility in Bosnia to the Europeans. The situation in Somalia was a horrifying mess, epitomized by the gruesome image of dead U.S. soldiers being dragged through the streets of Mogadishu. And in October 1993 came another severe blow—the humiliating spectacle of an American warship being turned around in the Port-au-Prince harbor by a disorderly mob of Haitian demonstrators. To Clinton's critics, all this was confirmation of their

worst fears—the president who had never served in the military was conducting foreign policy with a trial-and-error approach, yielding mostly errors.

But here was yet another arena in which Clinton by late 1995 would be playing the role of the "Comeback Kid," a label he had pinned on himself after the New Hampshire primary in 1992. Just as the presidential spine was stiffening over the budget battle with the Republicans, Clinton started showing more backbone in foreign policy as well. Despite public opinion polls that showed widespread opposition to the move, Clinton sent 20,000 U.S. peacekeeping troops to Bosnia. And lo, like presidents before him, Clinton discovered that public opinion rallied to his side as U.S. troops eventually settled into the mountainous Bosnian terrain. He was acting like the commander in chief many doubted he could be.

And as the presidential election year picked up steam, the Republicans had a hard time identifying foreign policy issues capable of provoking much public indignation. American intervention in Haiti had led to a significant decline in violence there; U.S. diplomatic initiatives kept a lid on a potentially explosive situation in North Korea; American initiatives had succeeded in preventing economic collapse in Mexico; Clinton's personal diplomacy with Boris Yeltsin paid off with a Russian pullback from the Baltic states and a commitment to democratic elections in the summer of 1996; and U.S. involvement in the Middle East peace process (the matter to which Secretary of State Warren Christopher had given the bulk of his attention) was helping to maintain a relative calm in the most volatile region of the globe. In short, as the election year approached, the Clinton administration had neutralized foreign policy as an issue in the presidential campaign.[22]

Finding His Way to the Center on Domestic Policy

But it was in the arena of domestic policy that the most important and redeeming moves of the Clinton White House would come in 1995 and early 1996, as the president skillfully moved to the center of the political spectrum and then went on to steal the Republicans' best issues out from under them. Nobody in the GOP could

In the spring of 1996, Clinton preempted one Republican issue after another.

credibly claim that they didn't see this coming, for Clinton was, if anything, unabashedly bold in his political theft. On January 23, 1996, while various Republicans were sloshing around New Hampshire in an effort to secure a victory in that state's primary election, Clinton delivered his nationally televised State of the Union speech, twice emphasizing a simple declarative sentence that would appear in the headlines of virtually every American newspaper the next morning: "The era of big government is over." Radiating confidence, the president stressed how eager he was to work toward a balanced budget, welfare reform, improvements in education, and the promotion of family and of individual responsibility.

This effective speech was well received by the public and was just the first preemptive strike in what would be a deft and tenacious series of maneuvers by Clinton, all aimed at positioning himself as a centrist and convincing voters that the worries of the middle class were his worries, too. Throughout the early spring of 1996, Clinton preempted one Republican issue after another: he denied recognition of same-sex marriages; he supported a repeal of the gas tax he himself had proposed in 1993; he backed the Republicans' proposal to extend a $5,000 tax credit to families of adopted children; he issued an executive order forcing states to end welfare payments to teenage mothers who quit school or move out of their parents' homes; he proposed to "mend, not end" affirmative action programs; he supported antiterrorism legislation that included new limits on death-row appeals; he repeatedly reminded voters of his strong support for anticrime and gun control legislation; he endorsed teen curfews; he extolled the virtues of school uniforms; he lamented the vulgarity and violence of modern television (and supported use of the "V-chip" to block violent or sexually explicit programming). In short, with a renewed emphasis on moral values and

political moderation, Clinton recaptured the center on cultural issues and sent a message to stressed-out, middle-class voters (epitomized by the fabled, oft-cited "soccer moms") that government needn't be big and intrusive but could be used to protect families and promote fundamental values as well as economic security.

Clinton's success in finding his way back to the mainstream of American politics was achieved in considerable measure by co-opting many of the Republicans' own best issues—a fact that profoundly exasperated Republicans. By early June 1996, Dole had taken to complaining that Clinton was plagiarizing GOP ideas on the campaign trail. Dole quipped: "We don't give out advance copies of my speeches anymore, because he'll give them before I do."[23] But by the time the Republicans had fully opened their eyes to what was happening to them, it was all over.

CONCLUSION

It's often been observed that the American political culture has a built-in predisposition toward moderation or that the American policy-making system has a structural bias toward incrementalism. But every once in a while in our political history, we're reminded of these truths in a particularly conspicuous way.

The period from 1993 through 1996 was one in which "overreach" came to seem pandemic in American politics. The malady visited itself indiscriminately on Democrats and Republicans alike, with each party reading more than it should have into the results of the 1992 and 1994 elections. Clinton overreached in 1993 with his government-laden health reform plan, and the Republicans overreached in 1995 with their four-square assault on government itself. The curious thing about overreach is that those who have contracted the affliction seem unaware of it until it has virtually disabled them. And the only apparent cure for it seems to be a good stiff cuff to the side of the head in the form of public disapproval. The size of the Republican victory in 1994 taught the Democrats that the public was not ready to embrace new exercises in big government and liberal social engineering of the sort that Clinton's health care reform proposal espoused. And later negative reaction to the Republicans' frontal

25

attack on federal programs showed that the public is more discriminating than conservative in its views on cutting back government programs.

So 1996 can well be described as the year in which both parties came to recognize that "while much has changed, much abides." The national government's safety net, while an enormous fiscal burden in this as in other democratic societies, still enjoys widespread public support, particularly when it serves the needs of women, children, and the aged. Proposals for wholesale change in an area like health care carry considerable political risk, as Clinton discovered in 1993 and as the House Republicans discovered in 1995. Incrementalism and moderation would still appear to be the preferred strategy for initiating any major policy change in this country. This strategy was evident, for example, in the passage of the so-called Kassebaum-Kennedy bill, to make health insurance coverage more secure and accessible for people who change jobs or lose their jobs.

As a result of the painful learning experiences that each party endured in the first three years of the Clinton presidency, the political climate in 1996 was one in which a centrist position on policy issues was the most valuable asset any candidate could bring to the election. For each side of the political divide, the most valuable lesson to be learned from the preceding four years of political combat was that in the American system it still pays to heed the injunction of a wise statesman from the past that "great innovations should not be forced on slender majorities."

Endnotes

1. Christine C. Lawrence, "Ban on Homosexuals to End in Two Steps, Frank Says," *Congressional Quarterly Weekly Report,* January 23, 1993, p. 187.

2. Under the policy eventually adopted, one can still be expelled from the military for being gay. But the military services are not supposed to investigate a service member's possible homosexuality, as long as he or she refrains from proclaiming or demonstrating it.

3. Paul J. Quirk and Joseph Hinchliffe, "Domestic Policy: The Trials of a Centrist Democrat," in Campbell and Rockman, eds., *The Clinton Presidency: First Appraisals,* p. 268.

4. Those interested in revisiting the 1993 battles over the stimulus package and the budget can see, for sensible accounts: Richard Cohen,

Changing Course in Washington: Clinton and the New Congress (New York: Macmillan, 1994); and Paul J. Quirk and Joseph Hinchcliffe, "Domestic Policy: The Trials of a Centrist Democrat," in Campbell and Rockman, eds., *The Clinton Presidency: First Appraisals,* pp. 268–274.

5. For a good overview of the Clinton health care reform proposal and its competitors, see *Congressional Quarterly Almanac, 1993,* Vol. XLIX (Washington, DC: Congressional Quarterly, 1994), pp. 335–347.

6. See Dan Balz, "Health Plan Was Albatross For Democrats," *Washington Post,* November 18, 1994, pp. A1, A10.

7. See Fred Wertheimer, "How Money Beat 'Change,'" *Washington Post,* October 16, 1994, pp. C1, C4.

8. Helen Dewar, "Democrats Compromise on Campaign Financing," *Washington Post,* September 29, 1994.

9. Richard Salmon, "Senate Demurs on Labor Rules, But House Acts on Its Own," *Congressional Quarterly Weekly Report,* October 8, 1994, p. 2855. Among the federal labor and civil rights laws the House resolution required the chamber to observe were the Americans with Disabilities Act of 1990, the Occupational Safety and Health Act of 1970, the Fair Labor Standards Act of 1938, and the Civil Rights Act of 1964. Salmon also notes that "left expiring on the Capitol steps were bills and resolutions . . . that were supposed to be the vehicles for a broader overhaul of congressional procedures" (Ibid.).

10. See David S. Broder, "Two Years in Office Have Washed Away Clear Image of 'New Democrat' Clinton," *Washington Post,* October 2, 1994, pp. A1, A9; and Dan Balz and Helen Dewar, "Wary of Government, Many Voters Turn to Right and Place Emphasis on Values," *Washington Post,* October 2, 1994, pp. A1, A8.

11. Noted in Clyde Wilcox, *The Latest American Revolution* (New York: St. Martin's Press, 1995), p. 46.

12. Quoted in Dale Russakoff, "Gingrich Lobs a Few More Bombs," *Washington Post,* November 10, 1994, pp. A1, A36.

13. See Guy Gugliotta, "New Priorities Reflected by GOP Nomenclature," *Washington Post,* Dec. 3, 1994, p. A4.

14. See Guy Gugliotta, "Breakneck Pace Frazzles House," *Washington Post,* March 3, 1995, P. A1; and Richard Morin and Thomas B. Edsall, "Despite Changes on Hill, Public Remains Critical," *Washington Post,* April 7, 1995, p. A1.

15. See Dan Morgan, "Industry Finds a Way Around Budget Cutters: House Appropriations Panel Proves Friendlier to Corporate Subsidies," *Washington Post,* June 26, 1995, pp. A1, A6.

16. Michael Weisskopf and David Maraniss, "Forging an Alliance for Deregulation: Rep. DeLay Makes Companies Full Partners in the

Movement," *Washington Post,* March 12, 1995, pp. A1, A8.

17. See George Hager, "As They Cut, Appropriators Add a Stiff Dose of Policy," *Congressional Quarterly Weekly Report,* July 29, 1995, pp. 2245–2248; and Dan Morgan, "A Revolution Derailed," *Washington Post National Weekly Edition,* October 28–November 3, 1996, p. 21.

18. See Adam Clymer, "Firebrand Who Got Singed Says Being Speaker Suffices," *New York Times,* January 22, 1996, pp. A1, B10.

19. See Alison Mitchell, "Toughness in Negotiating Suits Clinton, Aides Say," *New York Times,* November 2, 1995, p. B10.

20. John Ellis, "Clinton's Road to Reelection Began in Oklahoma City," *Boston Globe,* November 2, 1996, p. A15.

21. See, for example, Mary McGrory, "Our Boy Bill," *Washington Post National Weekly Edition,* October 30–November 5, 1995, p. 29.

22. Michael Dobbs, "Building Popularity on Unpopular Moves," *Washington Post National Weekly Edition,* October 28, 1996–November 3, 1996, p. 15.

23. Quoted in Jill Zuckman, "Dole Charges Clinton with Saying 'Me Too' to Republican Ideas," *Boston Globe,* June 2, 1996, p. 8.

Chapter Three

The Presidential Campaign and the New Geography of American Politics

Jerome M. Mileur

There is a new geography in American politics. Bill Clinton remade the nation's electoral map in 1992 by winning three mega-states—New York, Illinois, and California—that had come together behind a Democratic presidential candidate only once since World War II. This continental coalition, which in rough outline joins the East, Midwest, and Far West against the Deep South, Plains, and Mountain West, redefined the lines of partisan combat. In 1996, as Figure 3.1 shows, Clinton's reelection was, geographically, an almost perfect replication of his win four years earlier and, as such, affirmed the new geopolitical lines of presidential politics in the U.S. Moreover, the congressional elections of 1994 and 1996 followed a similar pattern and thus measure the depth of the new cartography.

This new geography is the latest stage in the long secular realignment of the white South from Democrat to Republican, which began in the 1920s, gained speed after World War II, and was consummated in the 1970s and 1980s.[1] It had been evident just below the surface of presidential contests since the 1960s, and has emerged in the 1990s as the culmination of this fundamental reorganization in the mass base of party politics in America. The partisan consequences of this reconstruction remain in doubt, however, and the stakes are high for both parties over the next half-dozen years—as the postelection calls for bipartisan cooperation from Republican and Democratic leaders alike attest.

EVOLUTION OF THE NEW GEOGRAPHY

The origins of this new geography trace to the intramural struggles of the Democratic Party in the 1920s and especially to the 1928 nomination of Al Smith for president. The "solid South," which had been the party's electoral base since the end of Reconstruction and critical to its success since the presidency of Thomas Jefferson, split over the nomination of an Irish Catholic for President. Al Smith represented the triumph within the party of northern, urban, ethnic forces that had been gathering strength for years from the floods of immigrants arriving in the nation's cities, but whose national ambitions had been frustrated by the Democratic Party rule requiring a two-thirds vote of convention delegates for the party's presidential nomination.

Smith's candidacy electrified immigrant and first-generation, working-class voters in the nation's major cities of the North and East, who turned out as never before to support one of their "own kind." The Democratic vote in Boston alone increased almost threefold in 1928, as Massachusetts gave a majority of its popular vote to a Democrat for the first time in the state's history and Rhode Island did so for only the third time. But Smith's candidacy also ended a half-century of rock-solid southern support for the nominees of the Democratic Party.

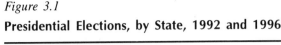

Figure 3.1
Presidential Elections, by State, 1992 and 1996

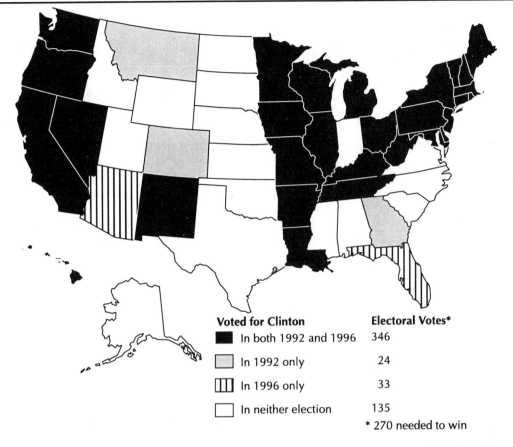

Voted for Clinton	Electoral Votes*
■ In both 1992 and 1996	346
▨ In 1992 only	24
▥ In 1996 only	33
□ In neither election	135
	* 270 needed to win

From 1880, the 11 states of the Confederacy had, with but one exception (Tennessee in 1920), voted Democratic in 12 consecutive presidential elections. In 1928, 5 voted for the Republican Herbert Hoover, turning their backs on the Catholic Smith.

In 1932, Franklin Roosevelt, while using the South and West to win the party nomination for president, won election on the base Al Smith had built: the big cities in the big states of the North. Moreover, FDR governed in the interests of this constituency. The liberal nationalism of the New Deal was alien to the states-rights conservatism of southern Democrats. In 1936, the Democrats dropped their two-thirds rule, and in the late 1930s southern Democrats joined congressional Republicans in a "conservative coalition" that repeatedly blocked New Deal and later liberal initiatives for the next quarter-cen-

tury. It also foretold the future of party politics in America.

Following World War II, race moved politically to center stage for the liberal forces who now dominated the Democratic Party's presidential wing.[2] At the 1948 Democratic National Convention, they won adoption of the first civil rights plank ever in the party platform. Rejected and feeling their way of life threatened, several southern delegations left the convention, formed the States Rights Party, and challenged the reelection of President Harry Truman. These "Dixiecrats" carried four states in the Deep South, polling 87 percent of the vote in Mississippi, 80 percent in Alabama, 72 percent in South Carolina, and 49 percent in Louisiana, while scoring in the teens in three other states and getting about 10 percent in three more. They failed to defeat Truman, but

29

the North/South split within the party was now public and would grow deeper over the ensuing years.

The schism became permanent during the presidency of Lyndon Johnson with the passage of the Civil Rights Act of 1964 and the Voting Rights Act of 1965. The North/South alliance that had defined the geography of Democratic Party politics for almost two centuries was no more. In 1964, the Deep South went to the conservative Republican Barry Goldwater, and then to the southern insurgent George Wallace in 1968.[3] In 1972, the Confederacy became solid once more for the Republican Richard Nixon and, except for Jimmy Carter in 1976, remained solid for the GOP through the 1980s. The partisan realignment of the South has been the most dramatic in American history. In 1960, Democrats held 99 of 106 U.S. House seats in the South, 79 of which had been won without opposition. They held 21 of 22 Senate seats as well. In 1997, the GOP has a 71–54 advantage in the House and a 15–7 edge in the Senate.

The defection of the South left the Democrats with only a handful of states in the Northeast and Midwest to call their own, and the party often found itself at risk on this turf. The great cities of the North were now ringed by even greater suburbs whose middle-class, quality-of-life liberalism clashed frequently with the working-class, economic, and racial liberalism of the inner cities. Moreover, the South and West were growing in population and political power at the expense of eastern and midwestern states. As the Democrats' old New Deal base shrank beneath them, the Republicans were consolidating their regional and suburban strengths. The GOP had commanded the Plains states since the 1940s, most of the West since the 1950s, the Deep South since the 1960s, and more and more of the northern suburbs after the 1960s. By the 1980s, the party had a "lock" on the electoral college, and a conservative Republican realignment seemed imminent.

As the Republicans capitalized on the new divisions in American politics after 1964, winning five of six presidential elections from 1968 through 1988, the Democrats were struggling to find any ground on which to compete for the White House. The party was in fact two parties: a more conservative one whose muscle bulged in the South, and a more liberal one whose strength was concentrated in the old Progressive states of the North from Massachusetts

to Minnesota and down the West Coast. The former preferred moderate conservatives like Jimmy Carter; the latter supported moderate liberals like Walter Mondale and Michael Dukakis. In 1992, with centrist southerners Bill Clinton of Arkansas and Al Gore of Tennessee as their na-

Clinton and Gore carved a new base for the Democrats and they worked hard to secure it.

tional ticket, it appeared that the Democrats planned to challenge Republican hegemony in the South, but instead they ran North and West in a campaign that carefully targeted states and concentrated resources accordingly.[4] In winning, Clinton and Gore carved a new base for the Democrats and, in the following four years, they worked hard to secure it.

THE 1996 CAMPAIGNS

The presidential election seemed over before it began. Bill Clinton, who entered 1995 as an embattled president, occupying a White House under siege from the first Republican Congress in four decades, ended the year as the stalwart Democrat who had fought off the conservative hordes and was ready to lead his party to triumph in 1996. The federal government shutdowns in the fall of 1995 worked to Clinton's political advantage, as public opinion judged Congress at fault. The president had also skillfully neutralized one hot-button "wedge" issue after another—crime, welfare, drugs—that Republicans had used against the Democrats through the 1970s and 1980s. The end of the cold war had removed anticommunism as an issue, while deficit reduction and "reinventing government" undercut GOP charges of big-government and free-spending liberalism. With no opposition to his renomination, a substantial war chest in the bank, a veto pen with which to define issues and show leadership, and with the presidency as his stage, Clinton from the

Table 3.1

Percent of Campaign Time Scheduled by Candidate Teams in Geographic Regions, September 5–October 20, 1996

Region	Clinton	Dole
New England[1]	12%	5%
Mid-Atlantic[2]	22%	14%
Midwest[3]	19%	27%
Border South[4]	15%	10%
Coastal South[5]	11%	22%
Plains West[6]	2%	1%
Mountain West[7]	7%	9%
Pacific West[8]	12%	13%

Source: Compiled from various print and electronic media reports of candidate schedules. "Team" refers to candidates and their spouses.

1. Connecticut, Massachusetts, Maine, New Hampshire, Vermont, and Rhode Island.
2. Delaware, D.C., Maryland, New Jersey, New York, and Pennsylvania.
3. Illinois, Indiana, Iowa, Michigan, Minnesota, Ohio, and Wisconsin.
4. Arkansas, Kentucky, Missouri, Tennessee, and West Virginia.
5. Alabama, Florida, Georgia, Louisiana, Mississippi, North Carolina, South Carolina, and Virginia.
6. Kansas, Nebraska, North Dakota, Oklahoma, South Dakota, and Texas.
7. Arizona, Colorado, Idaho, Montana, Nevada, New Mexico, Utah, and Wyoming.
8. Alaska, California, Hawaii, Oregon, and Washington.

outset of 1996 could focus solely on the November election and concentrate all of his assets and resources on it.[5]

The Republicans, on the other hand, were faced with a contest for their presidential nomination. Many prominent Republicans, from Dan Quayle to Colin Powell, dropped out as candidates, leaving Senate Majority Leader Bob Dole as the front-runner and thus the target for all the other GOP hopefuls. Dole's failures in previous bids for the presidency, as well as his early stumbles in the 1996 race for the nomination, did little to erase concerns within the party about his candidacy. Though he recovered and had the nomination in hand by the end of March, the campaign was low on cash and unable to mount a vigorous late spring/early summer challenge to Clinton. By the time of the Republican National Convention in July, the president had opened a double-digit lead on Dole, who narrowed the gap dramatically dur-

ing the party's week in San Diego, only to see it widen again after the August Democratic convention in Chicago. Faced with a popular, well-funded, politically astute incumbent, Dole and his running mate, Jack Kemp, entered the fall campaign against formidable if not insurmountable odds.

The Clinton-Gore Campaign

In 1992, the Clinton-Gore campaign was a whirl of activity. From the New York-to-St. Louis bus trip following the Democratic National Convention to the election eve rally in Little Rock, the two challengers stumped daily, often in several states, mainly those key to the success of their new continental strategy. In 1996, the campaign was more cadenced, less frenetic, and less expansive, as the candidates, especially President Clinton, made fewer appearances. Coming out of the Democratic convention with solid poll leads in New York, Illinois, and California, as well as other "swing" states like New Jersey, the Clinton campaign was able to focus on a few targets of opportunity, like Florida, but for the most part, concentrated once again on the states that comprised the party's new geographical base.[6]

In 1992, then-governor Clinton often appeared tired on the stump, his voice raspy and almost failing at times. In 1996, President Clinton appeared always fresh, vigorous, and full-throated. All of his campaign appearances were carefully scripted and targeted, with an emphasis on large, well-planned media events, not quick-hit, airport-type press conferences. The president entered the campaign with strong approval ratings for his performance in office, and the plan was that he would be optimistic, stress moral values, promise action on narrow issues, and avoid grand visions for the future. He would, like Ronald Reagan in 1984, stand for reelection as "the president," not run as a mere aspirant—a strategy clearly designed both to avoid the pitfalls of a campaign and to use the prestige of the White House as a defense against the "political" thrusts of an ambitious opponent.

The Democratic campaign followed the same geopolitical strategy it had in 1992, though seemingly with somewhat greater discipline. There was no eleventh-hour rush to campaign in long-shot states in the hope of an upset that would enhance an electoral college win for Clinton and Dole. Table 3.1, which summarizes campaign visits by region through mid-October, shows that the Democratic "team" (Hillary Clinton and Tipper Gore were active campaigners) made few forays into the Plains states and, except for Arizona, few into the Mountain West. In the Coastal South, the focus was mainly on Florida, with some attention to Georgia and Louisiana and little elsewhere.

The reelection campaign had begun with solid Democratic leads in New York, Illinois, and California, and until the final weeks of the campaign, when California became a battleground, mainly for Congress, these states received some but not extensive attention. All of them, however, had gotten special attention during the four years of Clinton's presidency. In New England, the states with U.S. House and Senate elections drew campaign visits, as did most of the Mid-Atlantic states, though most effort there went into New Jersey and Pennsylvania, where the Republicans were mounting their biggest challenges. Likewise in the Midwest and Pacific West, the Democratic campaign followed congressional races, waging the fight more broadly in Ohio and Michigan, where the GOP was running hardest, and in Washington, where the opportunity to pick up House seats seemed good.

In the closing weeks, with a Clinton-Gore win seemingly secure, the Democratic campaign, like the Republican, shifted to a fight for control of Congress. An increasingly negative GOP campaign, coupled with charges of campaign finance irregularities, frustrated Democratic efforts to regain control of the House and led to a late surge by Ross Perot that once again denied President Clinton 50 percent of the popular vote.

The Dole-Kemp Campaign

Bob Dole was a man of the Senate, a consummate broker of legislative deals, not an ideologue, whose skill lay in finding common ground, not in sharpening differences. His three decades in Congress hardly fit him for the role of an anti-Washington outsider, nor did he aspire to it. His senatorial votes comprised a record that, while consistently conservative, was not simply so, reflecting instead the shifting importance of issues within and between the par-

ties since the late 1960s. Dole's Senate years were also often at odds with the imperatives of the campaign, nowhere more so than in his call for a massive tax cut after a career as a budget balancer.[7]

Dole's campaign mirrored the man. Its planning seemed more like that for a legislative session, built around particular moments and tactical opportunities, calculations suitable to getting disparate bills through Congress, but without integrating themes, coherent images, or an overall strategic plan. Over the summer, the campaign progressed from Dole's Senate retirement to the promise of an economic plan to the naming of a vice president to the convention, while the public portion—the candidate speaking to the voters—seemed almost an aside. To be sure, the shortage of campaign money limited Dole's access to television, but paid TV is not the only way to frame campaign issues. And the Dole campaign failed to devise or, as in declining an invitation to address the NAACP convention, to take advantage of opportunities.

The problem of strategy for the campaign was clearly conceptual, as quarrels over message and geography continued well past the party convention. Two maps were considered, both drawn in reaction to the new geography of presidential politics. They assumed that most of the South, Plains, and Mountain West were relatively safe for the GOP and presented a strategic choice between going East or going West. These alternatives were understood to entail different messages: an eastern strategy, centered on the suburbs, required a positive appeal, stressing Dole's record and character; a western strategy, aimed at voter anger, required going negative, focusing on issues like immigration reform and affirmative action.[8] In the end, the campaign adopted a more centrist strategy, concentrating heavily on the north/south tier of states from Michigan to the Gulf of Mexico.[9] Through mid-October, after the second debate, the Dole campaign, as Table 3.1 indicates, pursued an eastern strategy. It was selective in the states it targeted: New Jersey and Pennsylvania in the Mid-Atlantic region; Ohio, Michigan, and to a lesser extent Illinois in the Midwest; Kentucky and Missouri among the Border states. Save for Connecticut, New England was ignored, as were Wisconsin and Minnesota in the Midwest, and West Virginia in the Border South. The Plains states, the Coastal South, ex-

Table 3.2

1996 Popular and Electoral College Vote for President by Region Compared with 1992

Regions	% of Total Vote, 1996			% Change in Vote, 1992–1996				Electoral Vote	
	Clinton	Dole	Difference	Region	Clinton	Dole	Perot	1992	1996
Solid Democrat									
New England[1]	57.9	31.8	+26.1D	−12.5	+13.3	−12.6	−61.6	35D–0R	35D–0R
Mid-Atlantic[2]	55.6	35.8	+19.8D	−12.8	+ 1.3	−13.0	−54.0	87D–0R	87D–0R
Likely Democrat									
Pacific West[3]	52.8	39.0	+13.8D	−11.7	+ 2.6	+ 6.1	−67.9	76D–3R	76D–3R
Midwest[4]	50.4	39.8	+10.6D	−11.5	+ 3.2	− 4.4	−56.6	89D–12R	90D–12R
Competitive									
Border South[5]	48.9	42.6	+ 6.3D	− 8.1	− 3.7	+ 2.7	−48.4	41D–0R	41D–0R
Likely Republican									
Coastal South[6]	46.6	46.1	+ 0.5D	− 2.3	+ 7.9	+ 0.9	−52.3	22D–76R	34D–64R
Mountain West[7]	43.8	47.2	− 3.4D	− 7.5	+ 9.4	+13.4	−66.0	20D–30R	17D–33R
Solid Republican									
Plains West[8]	41.9	49.9	− 8.0D	− 9.8	+ 5.8	+ 8.9	−67.9	0D–57R	0D–57R

Source: Congressional Quarterly Weekly Report, November 9, 1996, corrected in Midwest and Pacific West with state election division final counts.

1. Connecticut, Massachusetts, Maine, New Hampshire, Vermont, Rhode Island.
2. Delaware, D.C., Maryland, New Jersey, New York, Pennsylvania.
3. Alaska, California, Hawaii, Oregon, Washington.
4. Illinois, Indiana, Iowa, Michigan, Minnesota, Ohio, Wisconsin.
5. Arkansas, Kentucky, Missouri, Tennessee, West Virginia.
6. Alabama, Florida, Georgia, Louisiana, Mississippi, North Carolina, South Carolina, Virginia.
7. Arizona, Colorado, Idaho, Montana, Nevada, New Mexico, Utah, Wyoming.
8. Kansas, Nebraska, North Dakota, Oklahoma, South Dakota, Texas.

cept for Florida and Georgia, and the Mountain West, save for Colorado, saw little or nothing of Bob Dole or Jack Kemp.

After the second debate, when no breakthrough was made, the Dole campaign shifted to the western strategy, going negative and focusing on California, a state in which Dole had trailed badly from the outset but in which there were a number of incumbent House Republicans in close races.[10] In the final two weeks of the campaign, Dole's attacks, aided by questions about Democratic Party fund-raising, began to cut into Clinton's lead, and in the final week of the campaign, highlighted by Dole's 92-hour non-stop sprint to the finish line, undecided voters broke 47–35 percent for Dole.[11] Erosion in support for the president also bene-

fited Ross Perot, which both helped GOP congressional candidates and held Clinton under 50 percent of the vote. There was, however, no point in the fall campaign when the Republican efforts seemed to threaten the president's reelection or to change in any way an outcome that had seemed fixed from the beginning.[12]

THE NEW GEOGRAPHY OF PARTY COMPETITION

Bill Clinton won reelection, carrying 31 states plus the District of Columbia, with 379 electoral votes to Bob Dole's 159. It was a night of firsts: the first Democrat reelected since Franklin Roosevelt (only the third to win con-

Table 3.3

Changes in Party Control, Congress and the States, by Region, 1994–1996

| | Congress | | | | | | Governors | | | State Legislatures | | | | | |
| | House | | | Senate | | | | | | House | | | Senate | | |
Region	Dem	Rep	Chnge	Dem	Rep	Chnge	Dem	Rep	Chnge	Dem	Rep	Chnge	Dem	Rep	Chnge
Solid Democrat															
New England[1]	18**	4	+4D	6	6	—	2**	3	+1D	5	1	+1D	5	1	+1D
Mid-Atlantic[2]	39	35	+2D	6	4	—	2	3	—	2	3	—	2	3	—
Likely Democrat															
Pacific West[3]	38	31	+5D	5	5	+1R	3	2	—	2½	2½	+1½D	2	3	+1R
Midwest[4]	44	43	+6D	8	6	—	1	6	—	3½	3½	+2½D	3	4	—
Competitive															
Border South[5]	15	16	+2R	4	6	+1R	2	3	+1R	5	0	—	5	0	+1D
Likely Republican															
Coastal South[6]	31	51	+1R	6	10	+1R	3	5	—	5	3	+1R	6½	1½	—
Mountain West[7]	4	20	+2Rl	5	11	+1D	2	6	—	2	6	+½D	1	7	—
Solid Republican															
Plains West[8]	18	27	+3R	4	8	—	1	5	—	2	3##	—	2	3##	—

Source: National Journal, November 9, 1996, adjusted for Texas runoffs, December 10, 1996.

1. Connecticut, Massachusetts, Maine, New Hampshire, Vermont, Rhode Island.
2. Delaware, D.C., Maryland, New Jersey, New York, Pennsylvania.
3. Alaska, California, Hawaii, Oregon, Washington.
4. Illinois, Indiana, Iowa, Michigan, Minnesota, Ohio, Wisconsin.
5. Arkansas, Kentucky, Missouri, Tennessee, West Virginia.
6. Alabama, Florida, Georgia, Louisiana, Mississippi, North Carolina, South Carolina, Virginia.
7. Arizona, Colorado, Idaho, Montana, Nevada, New Mexico, Utah, Wyoming.
8. Kansas, Nebraska, North Dakota, Oklahoma, South Dakota, Texas.
** Independent elected.
Nebraska state legislature is nonpartisan.

secutive terms since Andrew Jackson) and the first Democrat in over a century to win without carrying at least one house of Congress. Clinton finished with just over 49 percent of the popular vote, joining Grover Cleveland, Woodrow Wilson, Harry Truman, and John Kennedy as the party's "minority" presidents since the Civil War.[13]

The geography of the Clinton victory, as Figure 3.1 shows, was almost identical to that of 1992. He won 29 states for a second time, as well as D.C., lost 16 for a second time, while only 5 states switched sides in the two elections: Colorado, Georgia, and Montana, for Clinton in 1992, went to Dole in 1996, while Arizona and Florida, Republican in 1992, were Democratic in 1996. The continental coalition

forged by Clinton in 1992 held in 1996, as New York, Illinois, and California continued to be centers of gravity for state constellations in the Northeast, Midwest, and West that form the Clinton political universe.

By reinforcing and deepening his 1992 win, President Clinton established a new electoral college calculus in presidential politics, a calculus that beviled the Dole campaign in 1996 as they debated East versus West as a campaign strategy. Table 3.2 details the impact of the 1996 election on the new regional divisions, and while it in no way suggests that a Democratic "lock" has replaced that of the Republicans on the electoral college in the 1980s, it does make clear that the GOP lock is broken beyond repair. Table 3.3, which reports party

There was no point when the Republican efforts changed an outcome that had seemed fixed from the beginning.

control in Congress and the states, portrays a new universe for American politics, whose partisan orbits, while currently in place, are not secure.

The Democratic Sun

The northeastern states, as Table 3.2 illustrates, are the most Democratic region in the country. The Democrats won all 122 Northeast electoral votes in 1996, shutting the Republicans out for the second election in a row. Support for the Democrats is strongest in New York and the southern New England states, but it is impressive throughout the entire region.

President Clinton won big in New England, receiving over 50 percent of the popular vote in all six states, averaging almost 58 percent. Bob Dole did best in New Hampshire, where he took 40 percent of the vote, but could claim only 35 percent in Connecticut, 31 percent in Maine and Vermont, and less than 30 percent in Massachusetts and Rhode Island. Moreover, despite a drop in voter turnout in all of New England—single digits in Massachusetts and New Hampshire, double digits elsewhere, President Clinton increased his total popular vote from 1992 in all six states, while the GOP total decreased in all of them.

Clinton's popular vote also topped 50 percent in all of the Mid-Atlantic states except Pennsylvania. Voter turnout was down in all of these states; nonetheless, the president's popular vote totals increased in New York, New Jersey, and Delaware, where his campaign made inroads into the suburban vote. The most dramatic Democratic gains were in New Jersey, home to many Reagan Democrats, where Clinton's popular vote increased by 11 percent over 1992, while the GOP vote dropped by 20 percent. The poorest Democratic performance was in Pennsylvania. The president carried the Keystone State with 49 percent of the vote, a point below 1992, while

Dole won 40 percent to improve slightly on Bush's showing four years earlier.

Democratic strength in the Northeast, especially New England, is evident in elections other than that for president. The party picked up 6 U.S. House seats in 1996 to gain a 57–39 advantage in the region, and retained its 12–10 majority in Senate seats. The Democrats also have majorities in 14 of the 22 state legislative chambers, but despite adding a chief executive in 1996, it controls only 4 of 11 governorships in the region (1 is an independent).

The Democratic Stars

If the Northeast is the brightest constellation in the new Democratic universe, the Pacific West and Midwest are the constellations that make it a political heaven. The Democrats repeated their electoral college success in both regions, winning 165 of its 180 electoral votes, losing as in 1992 only Alaska and Indiana. President Clinton won more than 50 percent of the vote in both the Midwest and Pacific West, while Republican Dole averaged less than 40 percent in both. The Democrats also picked up 11 seats in the U.S. House, captured 3 lower houses in state legislatures, and tied for control in 2 others. The Republicans, however, added an upper chamber in Iowa to give them control of a majority in both areas to go with their command of 9 of 13 governorships.

With its 54 electoral votes, 20 percent of the total needed for election, California has become the great prize in contests for the presidency—and more so in the new geography of American politics. In 1992, Bill Clinton became only the second Democrat since Harry Truman in 1948 to win the Golden State, and whatever the policy inconsistencies of his first term, there was no wavering in his political attention to California—a state he visited 29 times during his first four years in the White House. Capitalizing on a large and Democratic Latino vote, Clinton won the state easily with 51 percent of the vote to 38 percent for Bob Dole, a showing that helped switch three House seats for the Democrats as well.

Clinton won by an even larger margin in Washington, 31–56, increasing his popular vote margin by about 30 percent. The Democrats also gained a House seat, but the president's coattails were not long enough for other Democratic House challengers, two of whom lost very close races to Republican incumbents. In Oregon, Clinton won with 47 percent of the vote, below his average both nationally and in the region, and was unable to hold a Democratic seat in the Senate, which the Republicans reclaimed despite Bob Dole's getting only 37 percent of the popular vote.

In the Midwest, Clinton increased his support. Illinois led the way, giving the president 54 percent of its vote to 37 percent for Dole. Clinton carried Minnesota and Michigan by about 15 percentage points, Wisconsin and Iowa by 10. In Ohio, he won by 6 points, 47–41, but his popular vote margin tripled over 1992. Voter turnout was down across the Midwest, but the rising Democratic tide lifted Clinton's popular vote totals between 3 and 7 percent in all states except Illinois. The Democrats also won majorities in the lower houses of state legislatures in Michigan and Illinois and tied for control in Indiana, where they also retained the governorship.

The Nebulae

The Border South, home to Bill Clinton and Al Gore, has been solid in support for its native sons and important in their gaining decisive electoral college wins. In their presidential runs, the Clinton-Gore team has twice had easy double-digit wins in Arkansas and West Virginia, comfortable 7- to 10-point wins in Missouri, but narrow 1- to 4-point victories in Kentucky and Tennessee. In actual votes, support for the Democrats was down in all of the five states in 1996 by almost 4 percent overall, whereas the Republican vote increased by about 3 percent across the region. GOP gains were greatest in Missouri, where Dole's vote was almost 10 percent higher than that of George Bush, while Clinton's shrank by about 3 percent. Of the Border states, only West Virginia is reliably Democratic; the Republicans are competitive in all the others.

This pattern carries over into congressional and gubernatorial elections. In 1996 the Republicans gained seats in both branches of Congress, picking up House seats in Kentucky and Missouri and a Senate seat in Arkansas. The Republicans also gained a 3–2 edge in governorships in the Border states by adding West Virginia to those they hold in Arkansas and Ten-

nessee. In state legislatures, however, the story is different. By regaining control of the upper house in Tennessee, the Democrats now have majorities in both chambers in all five states.

The Republican Stars

The Coastal South has tended to vote Republican in presidential elections since the 1960s, while the Mountain West has been reliably Republican since the 1950s. They remain predominantly Republican, but in the 1990s, the Democrats have enjoyed successes in both. Three states in these regions—Louisiana in the Coastal South, Nevada and New Mexico in the Mountain West—voted Democratic in both 1992 and 1996, while five others have divided their electoral votes between the two parties in these elections. In the 1970s and 1980s, the Mountain West regularly gave all of its electoral votes to the GOP and the Coastal South did much the same except in 1976, but the Republicans have held only two-thirds of that vote in the 1990s. Still, these regions remain among the most Republican in the nation.

The Coastal South, all states of the old Confederacy, is home to great numbers of white voters who transferred allegiance from Democrat to Republican and keyed GOP presidential victories in the 1970s and 1980s. In the 1980s, with the exception of Georgia in 1984, these states gave all of their electoral votes to the Republicans. President Clinton has made inroads into the Coastal South, carrying Louisiana twice, Georgia in 1992, and Florida in 1996, where Hispanics voted more heavily Democratic. The wins in Florida and Louisiana swelled Clinton's share of the popular vote across the region to a half-point more than Dole, but when these two states are not counted, Dole beat Clinton by a 52–41 margin in the others.

The Coastal South is of course home to the Republican leadership in Congress: House Speaker Newt Gingrich from Georgia and Senate Majority Leader Trent Lott from Mississippi. In 1996, the GOP added a House seat in Mississippi and two in Alabama, but lost two in North Carolina. The Republicans also gained a U.S. Senate seat in Alabama. The GOP holds a 5–3 advantage in governorships, but the Democrats remain in control of most state legislatures.

In the Mountain West, a number of the smaller states—Idaho, Utah, and Wyoming—are reliably Republican. New Mexico has been comfortably Democratic in the 1990s, but the other four states in the region have been battlegrounds in presidential contests, with four percentage points or less regularly separating winner from loser. The Democrats carried four states in the region in 1992, three in 1996 yet the Republicans still collected almost two-thirds of the electoral votes both times. In 1996 both parties increased their vote totals across the region, but the GOP added three voters to every two for the Democrats.

For offices other than the presidency, the Mountain West is heavily Republican. The GOP picked up U.S. House seats in Montana and Utah, giving them 20 of the region's 24. They lost a Senate seat in Idaho, but retain an 11–5 advantage in that body. Six of the region's eight governors are Republican, as are both houses in six of the eight state legislatures. There is divided party control in Nevada, the Democrats breaking a tie to win a majority in the lower house in 1996, while only New Mexico has a Democratic majority in both chambers of the state legislature.

The Republican Sun

Since Barry Goldwater captured the Republican presidential nomination in 1964, the South has been the big story, as it underwent a massive political conversion that moved it dramatically from Democratic to Republican in national politics. But through it all, it has been the Plains West that has been most reliably Republican. Since 1940, the tier of four states from North Dakota south to Kansas has voted Republican in every presidential election except 1964. Since 1980, Oklahoma and Texas have joined in their allegiance to the GOP. In 1996, as in 1992, the region gave all of its 57 electoral votes to the Republicans, as Kansan Bob Dole polled almost 50 percent of the vote across the region, defeating President Clinton by double digits in Kansas and Nebraska and by 5 percent or more in all the other states except South Dakota.

Republicans also occupy five of the region's six governorships and have majorities in both houses of the state legislature in three of the five states with partisan bodies, Nebraska having a nonpartisan state legislature. Since the

1930s, the Plains states have been the bedrock of Republicanism and remain that. While not as rich in electoral votes as the Democratic base in the Northeast, the Plains West has added electoral muscle as Texas and Oklahoma have moved into its orbit.

CONCLUSION

The 1990s have been years of political transformation for the nation, as the political issues and partisan alignments of the last half century—New Deal, cold war, and 1960s alike—pass into history. Both political parties have struggled to locate themselves advantageously in this new world of American politics. Both have known success. Both have known failure. Neither can be sure that the ground beneath them is solid. For in times like these, when the mass base of the electorate has come unstuck, no longer held together by the old partisan glues, governing is the key to the future. With Democrats in the White House, Republicans commanding Congress, and the electorate more or less evenly divided between them, both parties are well positioned to compete for this future.

In times like these, however, when parity defines the party battle, the natural instinct of the partisan, as the last decades of the nineteenth century illustrate, is toward caution.

The South has moved dramatically from Democratic to Republican in national politics.

There is much to be lost, and the risks of action are clearer than the potential gains. Accordingly, the chorus of bipartisan cooperation heard after the 1996 elections was singing a song of caution. Will the Clinton campaign's narrow-gauge proposals and centrist ideology—the president's "Small Deal," as one wag put it—be sufficient to rally partisan and public to the Democratic cause? Will the Republican Party's abundance of ideology—its conservative factions—accommodate the imperatives of building a majority coalition?

The midterm elections in 1998 afford the next opportunity for the parties to explore the new world of American politics. Control of Congress will again be at issue, but more importantly, so will many governorships in the East, Midwest, and West, most held presently by the GOP. Winning those seats assures the victorious party a major role in congressional redistricting after the U.S. Census in 2000. Moreover, the constitutional ineligibility of the president for another term levels the playing field for the next contest for the White House. How will the parties contest these elections? The answer to that question is as much conceptual as it is tactical.

The public works project urged most often by President Clinton in 1996 was the building of a bridge to the twenty-first century. Politically, the project poses questions of engineering: Where are the footings secure enough in the new terrain of American politics to support the structure, and how is it to be designed? Neither party presently has a certain blueprint, but we can be confident that their draftsmen will be hard at work over the next four years.

ENDNOTES

1. Partisan realignment in the South has been extensively documented. See Alexander P. Loomis, *The Two-Party South* (New York: Oxford University Press, 1984); Earl Black and Merle Black, *Politics and Society in the South* (Cambridge: Harvard University Press, 1987) and *The Vital South: How Presidents Are Elected* (Cambridge, MA: Harvard University Press, 1992); Robert H. Sevansborough and David M. Brodsky (eds.), *The South's New Politics* (Columbia: University of South Carolina, 1988); and Nicol C. Rae, *Southern Democrats* (New York: Oxford University Press, 1994).

2. For an analysis of politics in this era in terms of the presidential and congressional wings of the parties, see James MacGregor Burns, *The Deadlock of Democracy: Four-Party Politics in America* (Englewood Cliffs, NJ: Prentice Hall, 1963).

3. The new conservatism of the GOP in the 1960s and the party strategy to win the South is well documented. See Kevin P. Phillips, *The Emerging Republican Majority* (New Rochelle, NY: Arlington House, 1969); Mary C. Brennan, *Turning Right in the Sixties: The Conservative Capture of the GOP* (Chapel Hill: University of North Carolina Press, 1995); Robert Alan Goldberg, *Barry Goldwater* (New Haven: Yale University Press, 1995); and Dan T. Carter, *The Politics of Rage: George Wallace, the Origins of the New Conservatism, and the Transformation of American Politics* (New York: Simon & Schuster, 1995).

4. Jerome M. Mileur, "The General Election Campaign: Strategy and Support." In *America's Choice: The Election of 1992* (Guilford, CT: Dushkin, 1993), pp. 45–60.

5. John F. Harris, "The Keys to the White House," *The Washington Post National Weekly Edition,* November 11–17, 1996, p. 10.

6. David S. Broder, "Wary of the Garden Path," *Washington Post National Weekly Edition,* September 9–15, 1996, p. 12.

7. Blaine Harden, "The Changing Value of Dole's 'Word,' " *Washington Post National Weekly Edition,* November 4–10, 1996, p. 12.

8. *Newsweek,* November 18, 1996, p.109.

9. Dan Balz, "Threading the Needle, State by State," *Washington Post National Weekly Edition,* September 30–October 6, 1996, p. 10.

10. Blaine Harden, "Bob Dole's Garbled Message," *Washington Post National Weekly Edition,* November 11–17, 1996, pp. 8–9.

11. *Time,* November 18, 1996, p. 35.

12. Richard Morin and Mario A. Brossard, "So Did the Campaign Accomplish Anything?" *Washington Post National Weekly Edition,* November 25–December 1, 1996, p. 10.

13. The Democrats' "majority" presidents since 1860 are Franklin Roosevelt, Lyndon Johnson, and Jimmy Carter. Samuel J. Tilden won 51 percent of the vote in 1876, but lost the presidency to Rutherford B. Hayes in an Electoral College "deal" that also ended Reconstruction in the South.

Chapter Four

The 1996 Congressional Elections

John S. Jackson III

The 1996 congressional campaigns were presented by both parties as a referendum on the past. The Democrats couched their appeals in terms of a referendum on Speaker Newt Gingrich, the Republican congressional majority, especially in the House, and the Contract with America. They attempted to tie every Republican opponent faced by a Democratic congressional candidate to Gingrich and the ideological "extremists" who the Democrats contended had taken control of the Republican Party. Since Gingrich and the Republican majority in the Congress had become fairly unpopular by the summer and fall of 1996, this appeared to be the most promising overall strategy the Democrats had for taking back control of the majority in either the House or Senate. And, the Democrats enjoyed whatever benefits their congressional candidates could accrue from running on the same ticket with President Bill Clinton. Since President Clinton maintained a steady lead over Senator Dole in the polls throughout the election, Democratic congressional candidates did not need to distance themselves from the president and first lady Hillary Rodham Clinton as they had in 1994. In fact, according to two of the most important predictors of Democratic success in congressional elections in 1996—the performance of the economy and President Clinton's job approval ratings—their chances for picking up seats in both the House and Senate should have been very good.[1]

The Republican strategic challenge was to expand the time frame considered by the voters in their decision making. Whereas the Democratic candidates wanted the public to focus on the 104th Congress and the prior 18 months under Republican control in the Congress, Republican strategists wanted to include the prior years of Democratic control of the House and the Senate. The Republicans wanted to talk about the Clintons' health care proposal, the excesses of the "welfare state," the programs from Lyndon Johnson's Great Society that had allegedly failed, and what George McGovern would have done if he had been elected president in 1972. Whether the voters' collective memories extended that far back is uncertain, but it is clear that the Republicans wanted to take them back much farther than the previous 18 months.

Political science literature offers a more theoretical perspective on the election events of 1996. Morris Fiorina and other observers who have emphasized the concept of "retrospective voting" would easily have recognized both parties' strategic presentations of their major campaign appeals.[2] Unfortunately, the theory does not provide an entirely clear answer as to *which* retrospective, a long view or a short view of recent history, is more likely to sway the voters' decisions. Each retrospective had some validity and something to recommend it as the superior interpretation of the stakes involved in the 1996 congressional elections.

DIVIDED GOVERNMENT

What both parties *did* implicitly agree on, although they avoided acknowledging it publicly,

Table 4.1

Divided vs. Unified Government in the United States since the End of World War II

	1946–48 Truman	1949–51 Truman	1952–54 Eisenhower	1955–60 Eisenhower	1961–68 JFK/LBJ	1969–76 Nixon-Ford	1977–80 Carter	1981–88 Reagan	1989–92 Bush	1993–94 Clinton	1995–96 Clinton	1997–98 Clinton
Divided	☐			☐		☐		☐	☐		☐	☐
Unified		☐	☐		☐		☐			☐		

was that the 1996 elections were also heavily influenced by the voters' evaluations of the American separation of powers system and its corollary of divided government that had prevailed in so much of the recent past. By 1996 what had been an aberration in earlier American history had become almost the norm in American politics. In the 42 years between the start of Dwight Eisenhower's first term (1953–1954) and the second half of Bill Clinton's first term (1995–1996), the United States had experienced 26 years of divided government. Since 1960, only Presidents John F. Kennedy (3 years), Lyndon Johnson (5 years), and Jimmy Carter (4 years) had avoided having at least one house under the control of the other party during their term of office.

However, Kennedy, Johnson, and Carter as Democrats were plagued during all or part of their tenure in the White House with a coalition of Republicans and other conservatives (mostly southern Democrats) that frustrated their legislative agendas on a number of issues. One could argue, then, that even these three presidents had to some extent been hampered by the separation of powers system. Lyndon Johnson, in the 1965–1966 era, was the only Democratic president with a real working legislative majority coalition that he could mobilize to pass controversial legislation. Jimmy Carter from 1977 through 1979 and Bill Clinton in 1993 and 1994 could sometimes muster Democratic legislative majorities in the face of determined Republican opposition, but only with the expenditure of much political capital. Ronald Reagan in the first two years of his first term and for a short period at the start of his second term presents something of a special

case. Because of his perceived popularity and his landslide victories, and with the help of conservative Democrats, Reagan was able to muster legislative majorities for the tax cuts of 1981, the defense buildup of 1981–1982, and the Tax Reform Act of 1986, even though he

The American system has been marked by deep divisions between the legislative majorities and the president.

faced a nominal majority of Democrats in one or both houses of Congress at those times.[3] In general, the American system in the last half of the twentieth century has been marked by deep divisions between the legislative majorities and the president—no matter what the partisan combinations. The foremost question going into the 1996 election season was whether divided government would continue at least until 1998 and probably into the next millennium.

During the summer and fall of 1996 it was unclear exactly what verdict the American voters might render on divided government and its effects on policy making in the United States. There is very little evidence in the voting behavior research that directly indicates behavior by the voters that aims at exhibiting a desire to create or maintain divided government, so that one branch can more effectively check the other. Instead, the effects of weakened political party identification, the power of incumbency—especially the incumbents' name recognition and fund-raising advantages—and an increased willingness to vote a split ticket have consistently produced this unintended consequence.[4] On the other hand, when explicitly asked by pollsters and researchers whether they approve of one party controlling the White House and the other party controlling Congress, substantial pluralities and occasional majorities say "yes."[5] Unlike academics, voters are not hobbled by the desire to achieve some sort of policy consistency across all branches of American government. The so-called "responsible parties model," which would have one party control both the legislative and executive branches and then be held responsible for the policy-oriented consequences, has always had more academic than popular appeal.[6] In the recent past we had party unity under the Democrats in 1993–1994 and divided government in 1995 and 1996, and there is very little evidence that the American people were conscious of the difference.

DEMOCRATIC AND REPUBLICAN CONGRESSIONAL STRATEGIES

Against this backdrop the Democrats and the Republicans adopted two opposite scenarios for the general election. The Democrats generally believed that President Clinton would be reelected. They also realized that they faced an uphill battle to recapture either the House or the Senate. As we will see, the objective electoral facts were against their taking majority control of the Congress. Thus, the Democratic congressional candidates had to run against Newt Gingrich and his followers in Congress without explicitly advocating the benefits of a Democratically controlled Congress. This required a delicate balancing act. Democratic congressional candidates in 1996 tried to reverse the local versus national focus of the 1994 elections. In 1994 the Republicans had tried to "nationalize" the vote by linking each Democratic congressional candidate directly to President Clinton. By contrast, the congressional Democrats wanted to talk about their service to their constituents and their pork barrel successes—to localize their races. Incumbents traditionally try to run on their record of casework, service to the district, and success in pork barrel politics, and Democrats in 1994 pursued this classic strategy. As we now know, many of them lost their seats in the Republican revolution in Congress that year. Republican congressional candidates enjoyed marked success in nationalizing the issues and personalities of the 1994 contests.

In 1996 the Republican congressional candidates were faced with exactly the opposite challenge from their 1994 campaigns. Many of them implicitly believed that Senator Dole was likely to lose the presidential race, since the polls consistently told that story. On the other hand, they could advocate their own candidacy as the best way to achieve such long-term policy ends as welfare reform, a balanced budget, anticrime measures, and term limits, which they believed were popular. If they were incumbents, the Republicans also wanted to continue their positive records in congressional casework, and they could tout the local benefits of their party's being in power. At least implicitly, Republican congressional candidates could play on fears of an unbridled Bill and Hillary Clinton leading the country to liberal destruction if the Democrats regained control of both houses of Congress. As the season wore on and Dole's campaign failed to ignite, the congressional Republicans became more and more open in their appeal to stay in office as a check on Bill Clinton's purported liberalism. Thus, for Republican congressional candidates, divided government could be seen as an advantage.

American voters are not particularly concerned with building a government, as voters in a parliamentary system often are. Instead, Americans select the presidential candidate they prefer and, in a separate set of decisions that are related for some and quite unrelated for others, they choose House and Senate candidates. That appears to be precisely the record of the 1996 elections. At the outset of the 1996 elections, it was clear that both objective data and subjective assessments gave the advantage to Republicans in maintaining control of the House and the Senate. Thus, it was not surprising to discover that when all the votes in all the congressional races were finally counted, the Republicans had done precisely that.

Table 4.2

Midterm House and Senate Election Results: 1994 to 1996 Net Seat Losses by the President's Party

Year	House	Senate
1946	−55	−12
1950	−29	−6
1954	−18	−1
1958	−48	−13
1962	−4	+3
1966	−47	−4
1070	−12	+2
1974	−48	−5
1978	−15	−3
1982	−26	+1
1986	−5	−8
1990	−8	−1
1994	−52	−8

Source: Adapted from John S. Jackson III and William Crotty, *The Politics of Presidential Selection.* HarperCollins, 1996, p. 154. Original data adapted from Rhodes Cook, "A Touch of Fear in the Air as 1994 Campaign Begins," *Congressional Quarterly Weekly Report,* December 11, 1993; Karlyn Bowman and Everett Carll Ladd, "Gauging the 1994 Vote," *The American Enterprise,* January–February, 1995, pp. 101–104, p. 3408; Harold W. Stanley and Richard G.

THE OBJECTIVE DATA REGARDING THE CONGRESSIONAL RACES IN 1996

The erosion of Democratic majorities in Congress actually started in 1992 when, despite Bill Clinton's election, the Democrats lost 9 seats in the House and 1 seat in the Senate. And, of course, Democrats in 1996 faced the disastrous consequences of their landslide losses in the off-year elections of 1994, when they gave up 52 seats in the House and 8 seats in the Senate. Since the end of World War II, one of the best-documented patterns in American politics has been that the president's party *invariably* loses seats in the "off-year" or midterm elections. However, for perspective it should be noted that between 1946 and 1994 the *average loss* for the president's party was 26 seats in the House and 3.9 in the Senate. This is why the 52 seats lost in the House and the 8 seats lost in the

Senate in 1994 were nearly unprecedented and so devastating to the Democrats. The only off-year election loss of comparable magnitude was the Democrats' loss of 55 House seats and 12 Senate seats in 1946.

The 1992 and 1994 congressional election results left the Democrats in a weakened condition.

On the other hand, the 1946 Democratic losses were immediately recouped in 1948 when the Democrats won 75 House seats and 9 Senate seats in tandem with Harry Truman's narrow reelection victory. Indeed, in 1948 the Democrats reestablished majority control over both branches of the Congress, and after that they lost control only intermittently (House and Senate 1953–1954; Senate 1981–1986) until the revolution of 1994. In fact, by 1994 the Democrats had held the House for so long that only one incumbent Democrat, Representative Sidney Yates of Illinois, could remember ever having been in the minority. In some quarters the Democrats had begun to act as though the natural order of things were for the Democrats to have majority control of the Congress. Some of their leaders, such as minority leader Richard Gephardt of Missouri, have now ruefully admitted that in 1994 Democrats in the Congress had grown somewhat complacent and a bit arrogant. This complacency may have affected some of their followers as well. Certainly the low turnout among the Democratic Party's core constituencies in 1994 added to their defeat. At any rate, the Democrats' 1994 defeat was the second worst in post–World War II history for an off-year election (see Table 4.2). The 1992 and 1994 congressional election results left the Democrats in their most weakened condition since Franklin Roosevelt had constructed the New Deal coalition in the 1930s. The election of 1994 especially provided the crucial backdrop against which the 1996 congressional campaigns were played out.

THE POTENTIAL FOR REALIGNMENT AND REPUBLICAN RESURGENCE

Both 1992 and 1994 served as "wake up calls" for the Democrats and their allies for 1996. For example, the labor unions mobilized early for the 1996 elections, since they had seen some of their most cherished policies and values put in jeopardy by the 104th Congress. Big labor was reported to have spent approximately $35 million on the 1996 elections in an attempt to help President Clinton and the Democrats in Congress. Many activist women's groups also mobilized very early to help women candidates, most of whom were Democrats. The Reverend Jesse Jackson and several prominent African American leaders promised to help mobilize the minority community for the 1996 battle. On the Republican side, the Christian Coalition, the National Rifle Association, and various right-to-life groups vowed early on to mobilize their followers to ensure continued Republican control of the Congress. The National Chamber of Commerce promised to match the labor unions' $35 million with a war chest of their own donated predominately to Republicans. In short, while the labor unions' commitment of big money to congressional Democrats drew the most media attention, the campaign finance battle and the grassroots mobilization battle were probably won by the Republicans.

The party system was reshaped in the first half of the 1990s, and the old order has passed. The shape and nomenclature of the emerging system is not yet clear, although it is clear that the party system has changed fundamentally. The problem for the Democrats in 1996 was that their base had been eroding for years through a secular realignment or dealignment, and they had not yet assembled a winning coalition to replace the crumbling New Deal coalition. In the early 1990s the labor unions were at a modern low point in terms of the proportion of the total work force who were union members. Minorities in urban areas were not registered and voting in percentages comparable to such Republican core constituencies as the Christian Coalition and the pro-life forces. Most importantly, the once "Solid South," which sent a Democratic majority to Congress from almost every southern state for three-quarters of a century

after the Civil War, was changing drastically. The nonminority southern congressional districts were shifting inexorably from moderate Democratic to conservative Republican.

The Republicans in predominantly white districts in the South had been handily electing members of the House in the 1980s and early 1990s. Several southern states also had two Republican senators by the end of the 1994 elections. The only places in the South where Democratic members of Congress were predictably reelected was in the "majority-minority" districts anchored in the southern cities, and those districts were under challenge in the Supreme Court. The secular realignment of the white South from Democratic to Republican presidential and congressional candidates is one of the most important political changes in American history.[7] While Clinton and Gore proved that it was possible for Democratic presidential candidates to break the Republicans' so-called electoral college lock, the portents for changing the congressional majority markedly favored the Republican Party in the South. The Democrats simply had not reconstituted a new nonminority coalition to replace the Roosevelt coalition, which was clearly irretrievable by 1996. All of these long-term megatrends worked against the Democrats' potential for retaking the Congress even in a year that held some promise because of the Clinton tide.

There were other more immediate factors in the congressional races, and most of those also worked in favor of the Republicans' holding their majority. As the work of Gary Jacobson has so succinctly shown, the outcomes of the congressional races are partially determined one or two years before the actual campaigns.[8] The candidates who challenge an incumbent must decide whether to run long before the filing deadlines, and the same is true for those who will run in open-seat contests. And the quality of the candidates recruited to run can be a major factor in deciding the outcomes. From spring to fall of 1995, the Republicans were still flush with their victory of November 1994. Speaker Newt Gingrich and his "Contract with America" were still riding high. Bill Clinton's political fortunes had not yet turned around, and the chances for Democrats to regain control of the Congress, or even to be competitive in the close races, appeared unpromising. Consequently, most observers credited the Republicans as recruiters of high-quality congressional candidates going into the 1996 races.[9]

The Republican campaign committees—the Republican National Committee, the National Republican Congressional Committee, and the National Republican Senatorial Committee—were also well organized and could be expected to provide campaign money, indirect contributions, and staff expertise to congressional candidates. Paul Herrnson has cogently demonstrated that such "Capitol Hill committees" for both parties have become increasingly active and efficient as brokers of campaign assistance for congressional candidates.[10] Nevertheless, Herrnson and other experts consistently rate the Republicans as better organized and better financed than their Democratic counterparts. Thus, the assistance of the national party forces was likely to give an edge to the Republicans.

THE PROSPECTS FOR THE DEMOCRATS

This is not to suggest that the Democratic congressional candidates had no advantages going into the 1996 contests. President Bill Clinton's expected strong candidacy seemed to provide a boost for most Democratic candidates. The president's poll numbers solidified in the summer of 1996 in the wake of the Democratic National Convention and his lead held steady from then on, between 10 and 20 percent over Senator Dole. As November 5 drew closer, the media and the commentators increasingly came to focus on the congressional races and what effect a big Clinton victory might have on the close contests. Some commentators even speculated that a strong pro-Clinton tide could sweep in a new Democratic majority in the Congress. Indeed, the Republican National Committee late in the campaign began airing commercials in selected congressional districts urging people to vote for the Republican candidate for Congress as a counterweight to Clinton in the White House. The fact that these ads effectively abandoned the Dole presidential bid did not go unnoticed. Even vice presidential candidate Jack Kemp took the rather unusual step of blasting his fellow Republicans for publicly writing off Dole's presidential campaign so early.

Whether the Republican appeal to ensure a continuation of checks and balances by continuing divided American government was effective is hard to demonstrate. The various public opinion poll soundings through the summer and fall congressional races revealed the following anomalous results regarding voters' claims about their congressional voting intentions:

1. The generic question "do you plan to vote for the Democratic or the Republican candidate for Congress in your District" consistently yielded a small Democratic advantage.[11]
2. When voters were asked whether they wanted the *Democrats* to control both the White House and the Congress, a clear majority rejected this version of unified government.[12]
3. When voters were asked whether they wanted the *Republicans* to control both the White House and the Congress, they responded "no" by wide margins.[13]

Thus, the venerable American concepts of separation of powers and checks and balances have taken such a hold in the American political culture that we have apparently come to accept divided government as the best guarantee against abuse of power by one party. In fact, a political culture that exhibits ever-increasing levels of political distrust toward elected officials and alienation from the political system might also be expected to show high levels of comfort with divided government. This was the backdrop for the 1996 congressional elections.

THE 1996 ELECTION RESULTS: WHAT HAPPENED AND WHY

The 1996 election results, when aggregated at the national level, had a curiously status-quo quality. After all the thousands of hours of television commercials had faded, after the millions of dollars were spent, after all the hundreds of speeches were delivered, after all the candidates went home to await the results, and the votes were counted, not much had really changed in the basic contours of American politics. Those basic contours had been set in 1992 with the election of Bill Clinton to the presidency and in 1994 with the takeover of the House and

Table 4.3

House Turnover, 1962–1996

Year	Retirements*	Defeated in Primary	Defeated in General Election	Total Turnover**
1962	24	12	22	67
1964	33	8	45	91
1966	22	8	41	73
1968	23	4	9	39
1970	29	10	12	56
1972	40	12	13	70
1974	43	8	40	92
1976	47	3	13	67
1978	49	5	19	77
1980	34	6	31	74
1982	40	10	29	81
1984	22	3	16	43
1986	40	3	6	50
1988	23	1	6	33
1990	27	1	15	45
1992	65	19	24	110
1994	48	4	34	86
1996	50	2	21	74

Source: CQ Monitor, November 7, 1996. *Election 1996: Analysis and Profiles of New Members.* Washington, D.C.: Congressional Quarterly, Inc., p. 19. Reprinted by permission.

*Includes retirees and those running for other offices.

**Also includes open seats due to deaths and resignations.

Senate by the Republican Party for the first time since 1952. The 1995–1996 period was the first time since Harry Truman in 1946–1948 that a Democratic president had faced a Republican majority in Congress. In 1948, though, the aggregate vote outcome immediately changed the temporarily divided government that the 1946 split decision had produced. In 1948 Harry Truman won a narrow presidential victory, and the Democrats regained a majority in the House and Senate. There was some talk among Democrats that the 1996 results would be like those of 1948, with unified government reestablished after the 1994 Republican victories in Congress. But the numbers were all against them. Of the 13 Senate incumbents retiring, 8 were Democrats, and 29 of the 50 House incumbents retiring or seeking other office were Democrats. The Democrats had more open seats in the South than did Republicans; they had a less successful candidate recruiting season; and the twin advantages of incumbency and campaign spending differentials were with the Republicans in Congress in 1996.

The aggregate results of the 1996 elec-

We have come to accept divided government as the best guarantee against abuse of power by one party.

tions produced a level of continuity with 1994 that is remarkable. As Table 4.3 indicates, when it was all over the Republicans had maintained their control of the U.S. House of Representatives by a 228 to 206 margin (total members include 1 Independent who usually votes

Table 4.4

Senate Turnover, 1962–1996

Year	Retirements*	Defeated in Primary	Defeated in General Election	Total Turnover**
1962	4	1	5	10
1964	2	1	4	7
1966	3	3	1	7
1968	6	4	4	14
1970	4	1	6	11
1972	6	2	5	13
1974	7	2	2	11
1976	8	0	9	17
1978	10	3	7	20
1980	5	4	9	18
1982	3	0	2	5
1984	4	0	3	7
1986	6	0	7	13
1988	6	0	4	10
1990	3	0	1	4
1992	7	1	4	12
1994	9	0	2	11
1996	13	1	1	15

Source: CQ Monitor, November 7, 1996. *Election 1996: Analysis and Profiles of New Members.* Washington D.C.: Congressional Quarterly, Inc., p. 9. Reprinted by permission.

*Includes retirees and those running for other offices.

**Also includes open seats due to deaths and resignations. The total does not include freshmen appointed soon after the election to replace senators who died or resigned to take other office, such as Pete Wilson, R-CA, in early 1991, or Walter B. Mondale, D-MN, in late 1976.

with the Democrats).[14] Thus, the 1996 House results produced a modest Democratic Party gain of only 8 seats. Total turnover was 74 seats, counting all retirements from the House (50), those defeated in the primaries (2), and those defeated in the general election (21). Both the aggregate turnover rate and the total defeated in the general election were down considerably from the 1992 and 1994 results (see Table 4.3).

On the Senate side, the Republicans actually scored a net gain of 2 seats, for a 55 to 45 advantage in the 105th Congress. As is evident from Table 4.4, the total turnover of 15 in the Senate in 1996 was relatively high by recent standards; however, this turnover was driven mostly by 13 retirements, the largest number of voluntary retirements from the U.S. Senate in more than three decades. In fact, only 2 incumbents, both Republicans, lost in either a primary or a general election. The Republican defeated in the primary was Senator Shiela Frahm of Kansas, who had just been appointed to take the seat vacated by former Senator Bob Dole, who gave up his seat to campaign full-time for the presidency. Republican Larry Pressler of South Dakota was the only senator of either party defeated in the general election. The elections of 1994 and 1996 were the first since before Franklin Roosevelt's New Deal realignment of the parties in which the Republican Party's candidates won two consecutive majorities in the House.[15] In addition, these elections produced two consecutive victories in which the Republicans' total congressional vote exceeded the Democrats' total. In 1994 the Republican congressional candidates outpolled the Democrats by an astounding 5 million total votes. In 1996 the Republicans' total national margin was reduced to a mere 300,000 vote advantage, but it was clearly enough to continue their control of the House and to expand their control of the Senate. If one examines only the results of the congressional elections in 1994 and 1996, it would appear that long-term secular trends had finally produced the Republican conservative realignment that had been predicted at least since Kevin Phillips's influential *The Emerging Republican Majority* was published in 1969.[16] Nevertheless, with Bill Clinton taking 49.2 percent of the popular vote and winning an electoral college landslide of 379 to 159 votes, the results of 1996 were more complicated than a simple party realignment thesis could explain. At best we have a sort of truncated realignment under way, in which the results are staggered across many races in different parts of the country, and there is change in a pro-Republican direction in some parts of the nation and in a pro-Democratic direction in other parts. For instance, the Republicans continue to do very well in the white South, where they won a clear majority of the House votes, 53 percent according to *Congressional Quarterly*.[17] In addition, Republican congressional candidates did well in the Rocky Mountain states and some of the farm states of the Plains, where Dole won. By contrast, the Democrats held their own or actually picked up seats in the East, the Northeast, and the industrial Midwest.[18] These are also the states where Bill Clinton and Al Gore ran well. In short, there may well be a secular realignment evident in these results, and they may produce the new American party system predicted by political scientists for the past three decades.[19]

NATIONAL VERSUS LOCAL FORCES

The 1994 results seemed to disprove Tip O'Neill's adage that "all politics is ultimately local." In some ways, all politics in 1994 were ultimately national, and the Democrats took a beating. We witnessed a reversal of roles in 1996 from 1994 on the national versus local focus of most congressional campaigns. The Republicans wanted a local focus and an emphasis on casework and service. The Democrats wanted to nationalize the focus in 1996—to conduct a nationwide referendum on Newt Gingrich, the House Republican majority, Medicare, fears for Social Security, foreign policy,

and the budget battle. When it was all over, each party could claim some success for its strategy. The Democrats gained a handful of seats in the House and defeated a few first-term Republican House members. The GOP, on the other hand, scored a net gain of one in the Senate.

The Republicans had made the congressional elections of 1992 and 1994 into referenda on the size and scope of government. They had argued successfully for major reductions in the size of government and in the tax burden. That is a fine symbolic issue, but when it comes to specific cuts that hit real people's pocketbooks, voters are not so dedicated to those budget cuts, and they tend to be skeptical of the more enthusiastic Republican budget cutters.

In 1996, then, the Democrats had to make a positive case for government and for the programs and policies that enhance community and quality of life for all. In Mancur Olson's terms, they had to make the case for "collective benefits" over "selective" or individual benefits such as the tax reductions that the GOP favors.[20] The Democrats, and especially President Clinton, were able to do that on such issues as the environment, Medicare, and education during the 1996 campaign.

TOWARD THE FUTURE

What remains to be seen with the 105th Congress is which model of recent White House/congressional decision making will prevail in 1997–1998. In December 1995 and January 1996, one distinctive form of executive/legislative conflict prevailed when the budget disagreements proved to be intractable. The "nonessential" functions of the federal government actually came to a halt. Federal offices closed in Washington, D.C., and across the nation, as the Gingrich/Dole–led Republican majority in Congress fought with Bill Clinton over the 1997 budget. This was the logical product of divided government: leaders of both parties stood on principle, refused to compromise, and jockeyed for any political advantage that could be milked from the situation.

On balance, it was a showdown that most analysts now believe Clinton won. His facing down Gingrich and Dole over budget priorities and his ability to control the terms of the debate gave Clinton new standing in the eyes of many

Americans. The confrontation was the launching pad for his successful reelection campaign.

Republicans in Congress sensed that they had lost public support in the showdown. Accordingly, by the summer of 1996, many were in a mood to move some legislation in order to claim credit with their voters. Thus, Clinton was able to gain some concessions on the Welfare Reform Act of 1996; Senator Edward M. Kennedy (D-MA) was able to work with Senator Nancy L. Kassebaum (R-KS) on a modest health care plan; and the Republicans gave up the fight to stop a minimum wage increase. A beaming Clinton signed all these bills in White House Rose Garden ceremonies. At several ceremonies, Democratic and Republican sponsors of the legislation, as well as symbolic beneficiaries of the act being signed, looked on approvingly.[21] With the fall campaign well under way, a different model for the 105th Congress had been demonstrated. That is, even before the 1996 election a sense of "bipartisanship" showed that some legislation could move as a result of a desire to compromise on the part of both Clinton and the Republicans in Congress.

The remaining question is whether the 105th Congress will predominantly follow the deep partisan conflict model of December 1995 and January 1996, or the more compromise-oriented model of executive/legislative relations of August–September 1996. Most Americans probably prefer the compromise-oriented model over the deeply partisan model that prevailed in the middle period of the 104th Congress. President Clinton and the Republican leaders in both Houses of Congress will have to decide how much to hold out for their pet policy objectives and how much to seek bipartisan compromise in the 105th Congress.

THE DOCTRINE OF RESPONSIBLE PARTY GOVERNMENT IN
1994–1996

These two models of executive/legislative relationships resemble the two dominant party models described by political scienctists. The "responsible parties" school of thought emphasizes programs, principles, and ideology. A willingness to compromise, to do whatever it takes

to get at least part of a legislative agenda enacted is associated with the traditional "pragmatic parties" model.[22]

One way to ameliorate the more baneful effects of divided government, the theory holds, is through the unifying effects of cohesive political parties. The doctrine of responsible parties holds that parties should have platforms in both a programmatic and a philosophical sense. They should campaign on principles and programs, explaining clearly to the American people what they propose to do once elected. After an election, the party should strive to keep its campaign promises. The Republican Party's 1994 Contract with America under the leadership of House Speaker Newt Gingrich is a recent example of a party's attempt to follow a systematic philosophy of government and to run on a platform of policy steps that are taken once the party is elected.[23]

Most Americans probably prefer the compromise-oriented model over the deeply partisan model.

The theory further holds that once the party has introduced the requisite policy measures, it can then be held accountable in the next election, which becomes a referendum on how well the party has produced in office.

Here, of course, is where the theory breaks down in the 1994–1996 example. Republicans in the House took great pride in the contract—at least at first. They trumpeted their accomplishment of bringing all its major provisions to a vote within the first 100 days—as promised. Some 1996 candidates ran on such popular planks as a balanced-budget amendment. But by November, the public was much more likely to hear about the Contract with America from Democrats as an attack on Republican congressional candidates and any ties they might have to Speaker Newt Gingrich.

What went wrong with the responsible parties model in the 1994–1996 era? First, although the Republicans controlled both the

House and Senate, they were far from unified on several features of the contract. The Senate either modified or defeated several of its provisions, with the most notable casualty being the balanced-budget amendment, which fell one vote short in the Senate. And the term-limits amendment did not even make it out of the House.

More importantly, the Republican majorities in both the House and the Senate had to contend with the Democrat in the White House. During his negotiations with the Congress in 1995–1996, Bill Clinton bargained, persuaded, cajoled, and threatened in order to win at least a partial victory on each issue. He wielded the veto or threatened one on several occasions, very effectively modifying the Republican agenda. In fact, his budget negotiations leading to the federal government's shutdown in November and December of 1995 and again in January and February of 1996 were the beginning of the political comeback that made Bill Clinton the first Democrat since Franklin Roosevelt to win a second term.

THE CONSEQUENCES OF DIVIDED GOVERNMENT

Two quite different schools of thought have emerged in political science about the effect of divided government. The older approach holds that American government is fractured vertically by separation of powers and horizontally by federalism. James Madison did his constitutional chores well, and the structural features of American government make it almost impossible for any dictatorial powers to be vested in one person or even one body. But those same constitutional fractures make it difficult to move policy in a coherent manner through the entire political system. In the twentieth century we have come to rely on strong, activist presidents who pursue policy mandates they see emerging from definitive electoral victories. These mandates provide the driving force for setting a direction and an agenda that will appeal to a majority in Congress and win endorsement in the courts. In the absence of such direction, the policy process moves in fits and starts, usually incrementally. Even in periods of unified government, it is often difficult to tackle the big issues on the nation's agenda because

the president and Congress have different constituencies and different electoral timetables that condition their strategies. Thus, divided government further exacerbates what is already a fragmented and disjointed policy-making process. In this view, the normal structural impediments to making policy are overlaid with deep partisan conflict that makes it even harder to develop public policy and move it through the political system in a coherent attack on the nation's problems.[24]

Legislative gridlock and constant political buck-passing are the natural concomitants of divided government, according to this negative evaluation. The president blames the Congress and the Congress blames the president for inaction on the nation's ills. The deadlock between Republican Presidents Ronald Reagan and George Bush and the Democratic majorities in Congress over the nation's annual budget deficits and mounting public debt in the 1981–1992 era are exhibit A for this approach. Ronald Reagan's "supply side" theory of budgeting held that the federal government could cut taxes, build up defense, and still balance the budget. After only a feeble effort to cut domestic spending, according to David Stockman, head of the Office of Management and Budget in Reagan's first term, the administration simply abandoned further spending reductions.[25]

The result was an enormous expansion of the federal deficit throughout the Reagan and Bush years. That annual deficit and accumulated federal debt have come to define federal policy in the 1990s. The major growth in the federal budget during the 1980s and early 1990s was interest on the debt. The single major item on the public agenda in the Clinton era has been how to address the deficit, and even an activist president like him has been limited to advocating small programs and incremental changes. Big-ticket items like national health care have been out of reach. Despite the fact that he has been out of office for almost a decade, Ronald Reagan's legacy lives on in the form of the budget deficit.

The second and more positive school of thought holds that divided government is intrinsically little different from unified government in terms of how policy is made and problems addressed. This view is most closely associated with the names of Morris Fiorina and David Mayhew,[26] both of whom have researched the

Ronald Reagan's legacy lives on in the form of the budget deficit.

policy impact of divided government. Both acknowledge the structural impediments that separation of powers and federalism create for policy making, as well as the fragmentation and incrementalism inherent in Madison's model of American government. Where they part company with the negative evaluation is in their assessment of how much gets done in public policy during eras of divided government compared to those of unified government. Fiorina and Mayhew contend that there are few indicators of systematic policy change differences between periods of divided and unified government.

The 1996 election results promise to continue divided government at least through 1998. If the presidential party loses seats in Congress, as usual, in 1998, we will have divided government until the twenty-first century. Now that Democrats have won the White House twice in a row, Republicans have won control of Congress in two successive elections, and divided government has been the rule rather than the exception for almost three decades, some fundamental political norms may have changed in ways that political science cannot yet describe, let alone explain. It is clear, however, that at the end of the century, the American party and political systems continue to evolve in compelling ways.

ENDNOTES

1. Gary C. Jacobson, *The Politics of Congressional Elections,* 3rd ed. (New York: HarperCollins, 1992), pp. 148–162.
2. Morris P. Fiorina, *Retrospective Voting in American National Elections* (New Haven: Yale University Press, 1979); Alan I. Abramowitz, "Economic Conditions, Presidential Popularity and Voting Behavior in Midterm Congressional Elections," *Journal of Politics* 47 (February, 1985), pp. 31–43; Gary C. Jacobson and Samuel Kenell, "National Forces in the 1986 U.S. House Elections," *Legislative Studies Quarterly* 15 (February 1990), pp. 72–85.
3. Charles O. Jones, *Separate but Equal Branches*: *Congress and the Presidency* (Chatham, NJ: Chatham House, 1995); Jeffrey H. Birnbaum and Alan S. Murray, *Showdown at Gucci Gulch: Lawmakers, Lobbyists, and the Unlikely Triumph of Tax Reform* (New York: Random House, 1987).
4. Gary C. Jacobson, *The Electoral Origins of Divided Government* (Boulder, CO: Westview Press, 1990).
5. A *New York Times*/CBS News poll, October 20, 1996, found that 48 percent of the respondents said they preferred a Republican Congress to balance a Democratic president, while 41 percent favored a Democratic Congress and a Democratic president. A Pew Research Center poll published the same month showed 60 percent favoring the presidency being controlled by one party and the Congress by the other.
6. E. E. Shattschneider, *Party Government* (New York: Holt, Rinehart & Winston, 1942); Austin Ranney, *The Doctrine of Responsible Party Government* (Urbana, IL: University of Illinois Press, 1954); John K. Whitehead and Jerome M. Mileur, eds., *Challenges to Party Government* (Carbondale, IL: Southern Illinois University Press, 1992).
7. Earl Black and Merle Black, *Politics and Society in the South* (Cambridge, MA: Harvard University Press, 1987); Earl Black and Merle Black, *The Vital South: How Presidents Are Elected* (Cambridge, MA: Harvard University Press, 1992).
8. Jacobson, *The Politics of Congressional Elections,* chapter 3.
9. Juliana Gruenwald and Deborah Kalb, "Quick Democratic Comeback in House Faces Obstacles," *Congressional Quarterly Weekly Report,* February 24, 1996, pp. 454–458.
10. Paul S. Herrnson, *Party Campaigning in the 1980's* (Cambridge, MA: Harvard University Press, 1988); Paul S. Herrnson, *Congressional Elections: Campaigning at Home and in Washington* (Washington, DC: CQ Press, 1995).
11. Results of a poll by the Pew Research Center published in the *Southern Illinoisan,* Carbondale, IL, October 4, 1996, p. 1.
12. Ibid.
13. Ibid.
14. Tobias Ball et al., "This Time, Voters Rejected Upheaval in Favor of the Status Quo," *Congressional Quarterly Monitor* 32 (November 7, 1996), pp. 3–9.
15. Rhodes Cook and Deborah Kalb, "Though Vote Margin Is Thin, GOP Outpolls Democrats," *Congressional Quarterly*: from CNN/Time Web site, All Politics: The States (November 25, 1996).
16. Kevin Phillips, *The Emerging Republican Majority* (New Rochelle, NY: Arlington House, 1969).
17. Cook and Kalb, "GOP Outpolls Democrats."
18. Ibid.

19. Walter Dean Burnham, *Critical Elections and the Mainsprings of American Politics* (New York: W.W. Norton, 1970).

20. Mancur Olson, *The Logic of Collective Action* (Cambridge, MA: Harvard University Press, 1965).

21. "House Republicans Stray from 'Contract' Terms," *Congressional Quarterly Weekly Report,* July 6, 1996, pp. 1929–1933; "As Lawmakers Head to Recess, Gridlock Yields to Frenzy," *Congressional Quarterly Weekly Report,* August 3, 1996, pp. 2163–2164.

22. Schattschneider, *Party Government,* 1942; Ranney, *The Doctrine of Responsible Party Government,* 1954; White and Mileur, *Challenges to Party Government,* 1992.

23. Newt Gingrich, Richard Armey et al., *Contract with America* (New York: Times Books, 1994).

24. James L. Sundquist, "Needed: A Political Theory for the New Era of Coalition Government in the United States," *Political Science Quarterly* 103 (Winter 1988), pp. 613–635.

25. David Stockman, *The Triumph of Politics: Why the Reagan Revolution Failed* (New York: Harper & Row, 1986).

26. Morris Fiorina, *Divided Government* (New York: Macmillan, 1992); David Mayhew, *Divided We Govern* (New Haven: Yale University Press, 1992).

Chapter Five

Communication Strategies in the 1996 Campaign

Jarol B. Manheim

Perhaps fittingly for the last election of the twentieth century, communication strategy in the contest of 1996 was a confluence of three different realities—one each from the 1970s, 1980s, and 1990s—each driving the choices of a different candidate. Bob Dole was a prisoner of positivity, haunted by the specter of his 1976 performance in the vice presidential debate and by his years as Richard Nixon's partisan hatchet man. For Bill Clinton, 1996 was really 1984, and he was Ronald Reagan, headed for a second term. Ross Perot was an evocation of ego, secure in the certainty that 1996 was really 1992 and that he—and he alone—could build on his remarkable performance the last time around.

STRATEGIES PAST AND PRESENT

In 1996 the Republican Party had anticipated solidifying its hold on Congress, recapturing the White House, and beginning the conservative revolution in earnest. But somewhere between the Contract with America (or, as Democratic wags termed it, the Contract *on* America) and the coming of the millennium, the revolution was derailed. Most observers point to the shutting down of the government in 1995 as the critical moment.

The shutdown itself was, in the long view of Republican rhetoric, a logical and highly symbolic step. By the time Richard Nixon ascended to the presidency in 1968, it had been nearly two decades since the Republicans had dominated Capitol Hill, and every indication was that the Democrats were in control for the

duration. During the Nixon administration, the party came to the conclusion that it might never again obtain a congressional majority if it simply fielded 435 individual House candidates and 33 or 34 individual Senate candidates each year. What was needed was a unified campaign effort built around a unifying and enduring theme—a theme for the ages. What might that theme be?

The Republican rallying cry— Get Big Government Off Our Backs—still echoes.

The polls held the answer. The polls showed—in a unified and enduring way—that citizens all across the country had great confidence in their own representatives but at the same time held Congress itself in contempt. The key, then, was to run, not against individual incumbents, but against the institution of Congress. And that is what the Republicans began to do. Over a period of years they built a political campaign machine the likes of which the country had never seen—a bevy of professional political operatives with the skills and, thanks to an effective fund-raising operation, the resources to develop, test, and implement an assault on Capitol Hill. Many of the assault troops are still in the vanguard of Republican strategists today, and their rallying cry—Get Big Government Off Our Backs—still echoes.

There followed two decades of attacks on big government in general and Congress in particular. Some of the attacks, as during the first Reagan campaign, occurred at the presidential level, but the bulk of the heavy lifting was done by literally hundreds of congressional "wannabees" toiling in states and districts from Florida to Alaska. At first, it was a difficult message to carry, but over time that changed. And by 1994 the Republicans had achieved their first congressional majority in some 40 years.

There is an old saying that you should be careful what you wish for because you might get it. In 1994 the Republicans put themselves in the ironic position of controlling the very institution they had spent many years deriding. Once the euphoria had passed and the need to consolidate their gains became evident, they found they had only two choices. They could continue their campaign of attacking the government, or they could become the government's stewards. In 1995 they made a choice. They closed the government down for days at a time, fully expecting that it would not be missed by citizens across the country.

Victims of their own rhetoric, they guessed wrong. And 1996 was the year the Republican Party—through its presidential candidate—paid the price for that error.

All of this history and all of this conflict was captured in the party's 1996 presidential candidate, Bob Dole. When he was a young senator from Kansas during the Nixon years, Bob Dole had served as chairman of the Republican National Committee, a role in which he was the chief voice of partisanship. His sardonic manner and quick tongue fit the job well, but the job itself—his first nationally prominent role—permanently shaped his persona in the public mind. That image was solidified in 1976 when, as Gerald Ford's running mate, Dole used the vice presidential debate to blame Democrats for all the wars of the twentieth century and even to castigate the League of Women Voters for scheduling the debate itself on a Friday night, when most Americans would be attending high school football games. Polls at the time suggested his performance might have been responsible for the ticket's narrow loss.

Bob Dole still carried that baggage in 1996, and he was also smart enough to see that the government shutdown had discredited the long-running party line among key voters. He knew that he—especially he—could not run a negative campaign and win. But Bob Dole was also the Republican champion, and to him fell the campaign machine that had shaped so many successes in the past and that was still committed to slash-and-burn rhetoric. The ensuing conflict within Republican ranks, which burst into public view in October when the candidate and his advisers struggled over the wisdom of going negative, encapsulated the continuing competition among alternative communication strategies and presaged the outcome. Bob Dole "couldn't" go negative, and when he eventually did, the results were predictable.

Ross Perot, of course, fared no better. Perot had been the political *Wunderkind* of 1992—the outsider whose "infomercials" created a new style of political advertising, whose use of Larry King and other talk show hosts was the essence of the strategy of circumventing journalists while retaining the appearance of cooperating with them, and whose nascent third-party movement captured nearly one-fifth of the presidential vote nationwide.

Perot entered 1996 having moved to institutionalize what was now termed the Reform Party, and having promised that its presidential nomination would be open to any aspirant. Richard Lamm, former governor of Colorado, made the mistake of believing Perot, only to discover that the party mechanism had been rigged to benefit its founder.

Having secured the nomination, Perot selected a more articulate vice presidential candidate than he had in 1992 and set out to replicate his campaign. But immediately, he ran into problems. Where his infomercials had been unique in 1992 and easy to place on television, in 1996 they were old news and programming time was harder to come by, though he did manage to spend $2 million buying network time on election eve. Where he had made news by relying on the talk shows in 1992, by 1996 the tactic was not deemed newsworthy. And where he had used the presidential debates in 1992 to greatly bolster his candidacy, in 1996 he found himself excluded from them altogether. Ross Perot, it seems, was not the only one to have learned the lessons of 1992.

All told, Perot's candidacy was a nonstarter. There were many things that made 1996 different for the Reform Party's candidate. But one of the most important was something that stayed the same—his communication strategy. In sum, Perot appears simply not to have realized that campaign communication is an evolving art.

Finally, there was the winner in 1996—Ronald Reagan. Oh, he looked like Bill Clinton, and he sounded like Bill Clinton, and he appealed to the constituency that was Bill Clinton's. But from the perspective of communication strategy, Clinton's was, as one analyst termed it, a "Reaganesque" performance.

Reagan was the last president of either party to successfully achieve reelection. Bill Clinton's great insight was to use "the Gipper's" playbook. He stayed on theme—which changed from 1992's "It's the Economy, Stupid" to 1996's "Building a Bridge to the Twenty-First Century." He took credit for the country's prosperity. He asked Ronald Reagan's quintessential question: "Are you better off today than you were four years ago?" And above all, he stayed positive, going so far as to praise Senator Dole's character even as the senator was attacking his. The contrast between Clinton's elastic smile and Dole's dark visage gave cartoonists a field day and voters an important nonverbal cue. Small wonder, then, that in the final week of the campaign Clinton even appropriated the defining slogan of the 1984 Reagan effort, telling voters in San Antonio, Texas, and elsewhere, "It's morning in America." [1] After perhaps 3,647 references to bridge-building in a mere three months, the change was probably welcomed. As in 1984, the playbook produced a big win.

Though the candidates and their messages play a central role in every presidential campaign, they do not operate independently of history, their advisers, or their party organizations. If the election of 1996 tells us anything, it tells us that. Accordingly, if we are to understand fully the role of communication strategy and media in 1996, in addition to examining the candidates and their strategies, we must look at the political infrastructure within which those strategies are framed and implemented. For it is that infrastructure, and not the candidates, that endures and that will shape the politics of the new century. As always, past is prologue.

THE NEWS DOCTORS

Back in the 1960s, television was just beginning to emerge as the medium of choice for news and public affairs information among the American people. Indeed, it was not until that decade that television sets were sufficiently widely distributed among the population that the medium could be seen as potentially influential. Television journalism was still strongly influenced by the values and styles of print journalism. Indeed, virtually all of the medium's journalists came to their respective newsrooms from previous employment with one or another newspaper or magazine, or from television's electronic cousin, radio.

Television is far more effective at conveying emotions than it is at conveying rational arguments.

The differences between television and these other media are of two principal types. The first is psychological. Research has shown that, when they watch television, people tend to let the medium set the pace of communication and define the content and context of the message. In fact, because television messages go by so quickly and cannot be recalled (leaving aside the more recent advent of in-home video recording), the medium controls the interpretation of the message to a much greater degree than does print. And because television messages are so complete, providing no opportunity for individual viewers to fill in blanks in the images that the medium creates, television messages are much more likely than those of radio—which requires the listener to paint a picture in his or her own mind—to produce a relatively uniform understanding of the message across a large and diverse population, like that of the voting public.

And there is one more important psychological difference. Precisely because of the pacing and comprehensiveness of the television image and the fact that it is received without stimulating the viewer to do any individual thinking about the message, television is far more effective at conveying emotions and very simple messages than it is at conveying rational arguments and complex ideas.

The second set of differences between television and other mass media is economic. Put most simply, by comparison to radio or print media, television production is extraordinarily expensive. It requires a great deal of complex equipment, consumes vast amounts of electrical power, and employs entire classes of technicians whose jobs have no parallel in the other media.

In the American economy, this high cost of production is covered by the sale of advertising (or its public-television equivalent, corporate and foundation underwriting). This in turn means that television programs are expected to attract sizable audiences, so that the sales staffs can sell advertising time to corporations at a rate that covers costs and produces a profit. As a general rule, the bigger the audience for a given program, the higher the rates that can be collected for advertising aired during that program, and the higher those rates, the more profitable the enterprise. There is pressure, then, on the producers of television programs to design those programs to have maximum appeal to the prospective audience, pressure that is not unique to television, but that is, nevertheless, much more intense in this medium.

The newsroom is not immune to that pressure. And in fact, news is very profitable. All of the major networks have historically made money on their news reporting, and for many local stations, the local evening news program is the single largest profit center of the entire operation. But not all newsrooms are equally profitable, and therein lies the tale.

Beginning in the mid-1960s, there emerged a group of media consultants—they came to be known as "news doctors"—whose expertise was grounded in what was then emerging as a substantial body of research-based knowledge about how people process information from the mass media and about other related aspects of human psychology, and whose sensitivities were principally economic. In other words, these consultants understood the importance of a client station's gaining a competitive edge in the race for advertising dollars, and they had a

plan for using the newly emerging knowledge of television's influence on its viewers to help their clients.

Hired first by several local stations affiliated with the ABC network and Westinghouse Broadcasting, stations that had in common their last-place standing in their respective local news markets, the news doctors devised a new form of television news—some might say the first form of news that was designed expressly for the medium—which came to be known as the "eyewitness" format. It is the style of presentation that we see today on nearly every channel—heavy on graphics, live-action film or video, human drama, personalities, and interplay among a cast of several anchorpersons. But what is commonplace today was innovative in an era when the national news lasted 15 minutes, and local news perhaps twice that, all read in great seriousness from printed text or teleprompter by one, or in the case of NBC's groundbreaking *Huntley-Brinkley Report,* two white male talking heads. And its effect was galvanizing. In virtually every instance, the station with the new eyewitness style of news leaped from last to first in its market.

Success like that does not go unnoticed, and it was not long before station after station, and eventually network after network, learned the lessons of the new format. Hard news was softened by bringing to the fore the effects of events on *people* ("Your parents have been kidnapped and brutally killed. Your three-month-old daughter has been thrown from a train and maimed. Tell me . . . how does it feel?"), and story selection was changed to increase the emphasis on human rather than institutional news. Dramatic video became more important than solid background reporting. A pretty face and a reassuring voice came to outweigh journalistic experience. Even Dan Rather took to wearing sweaters rather than those formal old coats and ties. And anchormen and *-women* all across America laughed and joked their way through the nightly horrors to communicate one simple message to their audiences: "The world is a nasty place, but we still like each other, and we still like you. So tune in tomorrow."[2]

And tune in people did, and still do. The success of defining news in television's own terms has continued. And as the broadcasting industry has gone through changes of ownership that have typically placed in control corporate executives devoted much more to profit values than to news values, the pressure on newsrooms to produce programming that emphasizes entertaining the audience more than informing it has moved television journalism much more toward good television and much less toward good journalism in the traditional sense. So it is that many people in the audience have come to view Larry King or Oprah Winfrey as journalists, and *Inside Story* or *Unsolved Mysteries* as news.

Hold that thought.

THE SPIN DOCTORS

At the same time that these news doctors were initiating changes in the style and substance of television news, a similar group of political consultants, whom we'll call "spin doctors" even though that term actually has a more specialized meaning, using the very same body of developing research on media use and effects, began to play a central role in determining strategy for the conduct of political campaigns, first at the presidential level, then in more and more state and local races. But where the news doctors' goal was to maximize the audience for a given station or network news program and thereby increase profits, the spin doctors set out to *build electoral coalitions* by using their specialized knowledge of the media to develop campaign messages that would appeal to particular segments of the voting public, then targeting those messages to maximize their desired effects and to minimize the collateral damage that would occur if the wrong message reached the wrong voter. Like the news doctors, spin doctors came to rely more and more on symbolic and emotional messages, less and less on detail and reason.

It's morning in America; I feel good. Willie Horton is out on parole; I feel threatened. The message is there, but it is a message of a particular kind, one that conveys feelings, but not one that engages the mind of the viewer. It is, in effect, eyewitness campaigning.

Though there are many things one could point to in characterizing the trends in political advertising—and campaign messages in general—over the last several election cycles, the one that has attracted the most attention

from scholars and journalists alike is the rise of negativity.

It is an enduring trait of human nature that we are prone to exaggerate the significance of our own times and experiences precisely because they are our own. The emergent concern about negative campaigning is a case in point. Historically, candidates for public office in the United States have been charged with remarkable regularity since the earliest days of the republic with sexual misconduct, lack of patriotism, physical ugliness, and sheer stupidity. If even half of these charges had validity, it is a wonder we have managed to muddle through all these years. Still, by more recent standards, there was, especially in elections through 1988, a sharp upswing in the attention to such themes, and that upswing caught the eyes of journalists and voters alike. In part, it was a function of Republican challengers' attacks on Congress and government, in part the tit-for-tat responses of Democratic incumbents. But either way, electoral politics in the United States had gotten ugly.

Post-Watergate journalism, with its tendency toward distrust of all public figures and their policies, contributed significantly to this trend, if in no other way than generating a context of public expectations that emphasized the negative. But in the electoral arena, a primary force toward negativism was the theme selection for the ever-more-invasive campaign advertising.

Historically, there have been several reasons that campaigns have employed such messages. For one thing, negative ads are fun to do and fun to view. They add an element of entertainment to an otherwise dreary exercise. For another, they are excellent vehicles for energizing voters who are already committed to a candidate. They get people revved up. Third, they can sometimes force the opponent onto the defensive and give the campaign momentum and control of the agenda for a period of time. But perhaps most important of all, they make news.[3]

Essentially, there are two classes of media in a political campaign: paid and free. Paid media include such things as advertisements or bumper stickers. Free media—some consultants use the term "earned" media—take the form of news coverage or other media appearances. From the perspective of the campaigners, the advantage of paid media is the amount of control they exercise over the shape, timing, and placement of the message. The disadvantage is that such messages are generally recognized by prospective voters as nothing more than campaign propaganda. As a result, paid media have low credibility and limited persuasive effect. In contrast, free media have high credibility—the messages assume the credibility of the deliverer, typically a more or less respected journalist, and of the showcase, a news or other program or journal that the voter has independently chosen to read, hear, or view—but are controlled by persons outside the direct influence of the campaign. In other words, the campaigners have the most effective control over the least effective media, and the least effective control over the most effective media.[4]

By more recent standards, electoral politics in the United States had gotten ugly.

As a result, much of the increase in sophistication of political campaigns in recent years has taken the form of evolving strategies for "managing" free media messages by manipulating journalists and news organizations. And negative advertising has played a central role in this management for a reason that we have already seen: Negative advertising meets the criteria of "newsworthiness" established by the news doctors. It is inherently dramatic, personal, conflict-driven, and interesting. It is news.

The model of "going negative" that is uppermost in the minds of consultants is the "Daisy" spot run by Lyndon Johnson against Barry Goldwater in 1964. In it, a young girl is plucking petals off a daisy and counting up to 10. The camera zooms in on her eye, and as the voiceover shifts to a metallic-sounding missile countdown, the screen fills with a hydrogen bomb explosion. There is but one choice, says Lyndon Johnson—to live or to die. That ad was run only once, but was then repeated many times in news accounts and analyses until everyone saw it, and everyone had a chance to attach to it the credibility of a favorite journal-

ist. It did not matter that the ad was decried; it mattered that it was repeated. The lesson was straightforward: negative advertising has a multiplier effect to the extent that it is sufficiently outrageous to make news.[5] By 1988, when much of the news coverage of the campaign centered on various controversial television advertisements, this ethic had come to define not only political advertising, but the general strategies of political campaigning. The year 1988, however, may have been the last in which emblematic television advertising defined a presidential campaign.

CONTRA-INDICATIONS

Two things happened after the 1988 election that altered this trend. First, journalists began to give more than lip service to their contributory negligence in the drive toward negativity. Second, more and more members of the public, whose tolerance for inane messages was being tested, reached the saturation point. The first countertrend was instigated largely by influential journalist David Broder, who undertook a personal campaign to encourage his colleagues to be more responsible in their election coverage.[6] The second became the basis for Ross Perot's broadly based challenge to the two-party dominance of presidential elections in 1992, and for the all-party clamber for the high ground in 1996.

For his part, Broder challenged the news media not merely to repeat negative advertising, but to explicate it. His newspaper, the *Washington Post*, for example, was one of several in 1992 that regularly dissected campaign messages to identify underlying facts and strategies. *USA Today* published a weekly "People's Press Conference" in which the campaigns responded to questions from readers, while the *Los Angeles Times* set its film critic to analyzing the campaign as a theatrical performance. And even the television network newscasts gave at least lip service—though at times little more—to reducing their reliance on sound bites and increasing their substantive analysis of the candidates and their programs. In the words of ABC News anchor Peter Jennings, "We'll only devote time to a candidate's daily routine if it is more than routine. There will be less attention to staged appearances and sound bites designed exclusively for television."[7] As perhaps befits a political campaign, the performance was somewhat less than the promise.

Though truth-box journalism had only a limited impact in 1992, by 1996 it was clearly one of the factors that led candidates and their advisers to rethink the virtues of going negative. By "deconstructing" virtually every new ad that came along, journalists simply took this incentive away from the campaigners. In addition, following the lead of Fox Television, most television networks with the exception of ABC took a tentative step toward the European model of campaigning by setting aside small segments of free air time for the major presidential candidates, although most observers did not judge this experiment successful.[8]

In 1996, two of every three presidential campaign dollars were still spent on electronic media (a combined $66 million for the Clinton and Dole campaigns by mid-October).[9] And there were clear strategies at work. Clinton, for example, aired an emotional endorsement by the father of Polly Klaas, a 12-year-old girl who had been murdered, while the Republicans, having given up on Dole's chances by late October, began running ads calling for the election of a Republican Congress to keep from giving President Clinton a "blank check."[10] But for the second time in a row, no single advertisement emerged to define the campaign. Strategy had moved on.

For its part, the public by 1996 had had about all it could take of negativism. The government shutdown of 1995 had communicated to voters, in a way that rhetoric could not, their dependence on at least some federal institutions. But beyond that, the general disillusionment with politics that had begun in the Vietnam/Watergate era was taking its toll. Bob Dole and Bill Clinton both knew it, and both tried to respond. But Clinton's advisers seemed to understand this shift in public opinion better than Dole's, and only he succeeded.

THE FUTURE HEALTH OF THE BODY POLITIC

With all these news doctors and spin doctors, you'd think the body politic would be healing. But the fact is that the patients served by these doctors are the media and the candidates, not the voters. The only thing the public has going for it here is not that it is a patient, but that it is *im*patient. We know from long experience that campaigners will do whatever they think will win them votes. And we know that, at least until 1996, the conventional wisdom among political professionals has been that voters would accept—would *respond to*—the most trivial, meaningless, negative, and demeaning messages in campaign media. So that is what they provided.

But in 1996 voters expressed their anger and frustration. When the public had a real chance to express itself, what it expressed was a general, systemic outrage at the state

---

One candidate adjusted and did well, one tried to adjust but failed, and one never understood the game at all.

---

of political dialogue. One candidate adjusted and did well, one tried to adjust but failed, and one never understood the game at all.

Presidential politics in the coming century will continue to evolve as new media and new messages come into play. But old strategies and old messages will continue to shape and frame future contests for years to come. There is no escape from history. Perhaps that is the real "bridge to the twenty-first century."

ENDNOTES

1. Peter Baker, "Clinton Reads Reagan's Script," *Washington Post* (November 3, 1996), p. A31.

2. Jarol B. Manheim, *All of the People, All the Time: Strategic Communication and American Politics* (Armonk, NY: M.E. Sharpe, 1991), pp. 30–47. For a case study that illustrates these points, see Gwenda Blair, *Almost Golden: Jessica Savitch and the Selling of Television News* (New York: Simon & Schuster, 1988).

3. L. Patrick Devlin, "Contrasts in Presidential Campaign Commercials of 1988," *American Behavioral Scientist* (1989), pp. 389–414. For a characterization of the types of negative advertising, see Montague Kern, *30-Second Politics:*

Political Advertising in the Eighties (New York: Praeger, 1989), pp. 93–112.

4. Manheim, op. cit., p. 55.

5. Ibid, p. 57.

6. David Broder, "Five Ways to Put Some Sanity Back in Elections," *Washington Post* (January 14, 1990), pp. B1, B4.

7. Howard Kurtz, "Media Alter Approach to Campaign Coverage," *Washington Post* (September 11, 1992), p. A10.

8. Howard Kurtz, "Campaign for Free Air Time Falls Short of Organizers' Goals," *Washington Post* (October 31, 1996), p. A17.

9. "Public and Party Money Behind Clinton and Dole," *Washington Post* (November 5, 1996), p. A17.

10. Howard Kurtz, "An Emotional Pitch for Clinton," *Washington Post* (October 22, 1996), p. A11; and Dan Balz, "GOP Stresses Division of Power in Ad," *Washington Post* (October 27, 1996), p. A24.

Chapter Six

Public Opinion Polls and Public Opinion in the 1996 Election

Kenneth M. Goldstein[1]

Imagine for a moment that you are a modern-day Rip Van Winkle. You fall into a deep sleep after the 1988 election and awake on November 6, 1996. Being an avid follower of American politics—and knowing nothing of the Internet—you immediately check the newspaper for election results. You learn that less than half of us decided to vote, that the president was reelected to a second term, and that the opposing party has retained control of Congress. Most likely, none of this would surprise you very much. After all, the 1980, 1984, and 1988 elections all yielded divided government, with voter turnouts hovering just above the 50 percent mark.

The surprise comes, however, when you discover that the divided government is comprised of a Democratic president elected in 1992 and a Republican Congress elected in 1994. You are also surprised to learn that there was a fellow named Ross Perot involved in both elections. He won only 8 percent of the vote in 1996, but garnered almost one in five votes (19 percent) in 1992, keeping the president from winning a majority of the ballots cast in either of the two elections. You also learn that the 49 percent turnout represents a sharp decline from the 1992 election, when the three-decade-long decline in turnout had been reversed and 55 percent of the voting-age population had cast their ballots.

As a "political junkie," you may also be disappointed to discover that the presidential election was relatively unsuspenseful. Despite hundreds of millions of dollars in campaign expenditures, 752,891 television commercials, and countless speeches about bridges to various epochs, public opinion about the presidential

Public opinion about the presidential race solidified early and remained steady for virtually the entire campaign.

race solidified early and remained steady for virtually the entire campaign. In fact, of the over 200 publicly released surveys conducted from the first of January 1996 through election day, not a single one showed Bob Dole in the lead.

According to the polls, Dole got a minor—and short-lived—bounce after the Republican convention, and GOP voters seemed to come home toward the end of the race, but in general the race was extraordinarily stable. Clinton's support stayed around the 50 percentage-point mark, Dole's support lingered around the 35 percentage-point mark, and Ross Perot fell below the 10 percent mark early in the year and never rebounded. Individual polls did show

Table 6.1

Final Results of Preelection Polls for President

Poll	Clinton	Dole	Perot	Difference
CBS/*NYT*	53	35	8	18
Pew Center	52	39	9	13
ABC News	51	39	7	12
Harris	51	39	7	12
NBC/*WSJ*	49	37	9	12
USA Today/Gallup	52	41	7	11
Hotline Battleground	45	36	8	9
Reuters/Zogby	49	41	8	8
Actual	**49**	**41**	**8**	**8**

Source: PoliticsNow (http://www.politicsnow.com) and survey organization press releases.

some movement from week to week, and even from day to day, but as I will discuss later, this may say more about polling methodologies than about true changes in voter attitudes.

In an effort to explain to Rip—as well as to other less sleepy observers of American elections—how public attitudes influenced the election outcome, this chapter asks three questions. One, what can explain the decline in turnout? Two, what factors led to Bill Clinton's stable lead and comfortable victory over Bob Dole? And three, why did most public opinion polls show Clinton's lead as being even bigger than the final tally?

To examine both the nature of public opinion and how it was measured, this chapter is divided into three parts. First, I will cover issues related to the quality of the polls and how we gauge public opinion. Second, I will discuss the nature of some of the fundamental factors that typically influence presidential elections. Finally, I will mention various puzzles posed by the low turnout in the 1996 election.

POLLS, POLLS, AND MORE POLLS

At first glance, finding survey data on the 1996 election does not appear to be a problem.[2] Hundreds of national surveys were conducted in the months preceding the election, four daily national tracking polls were in place throughout September and October, and a national exit poll of over 16,000 voters was conducted on election day. Still, even with this plethora of public polls, as-

sessing the state of public opinion in the 1996 election is no easy task, primarily because the quality of the available data is questionable.

For example, the election day exit polls—conducted by Voter News Service, a consortium of the five television networks and the Associated Press—are often cited as a source of information on the attitudes and composition of the electorate. The exit polls, however, suffer from some serious biases. As they have done in past elections, exit polls overstated Democratic candidates' shares of the vote in the 1996 election.[3] And, according to exit polls, 17 percent of the 93 million voters who cast their ballots in the 1996 election (or approximately 16 million voters) had postgraduate education.[4] However, the most recent Bureau of the Census reports indicate that fewer than 12 million Americans have postgraduate education.

Turning to the preelection telephone polls conducted by the popular press, all predicted that Bill Clinton would be reelected. In fact, not a single publicly released survey taken in 1996 showed Bob Dole in the lead. Still, there was considerable variation in the margin of victory that each poll predicted in its last survey, and some of the results were outside the margin of simple sampling error. Table 6.1 shows the final survey predictions for the presidential race for eight major polls.

Most preelection surveys also overstated the share Democrats would receive of the total House vote. Table 6.2 shows the final survey predictions of House votes in seven surveys conducted just before election day.

Table 6.2

Final Results of Preelection Polls for House Candidates

Poll	Democrat	Republican	Difference
CBS/*NYT*	47	41	6
Pew Center	48	44	4
ABC News	53	42	11
NBC/*WSJ*	43	41	2
USA Today/Gallup	51	43	8
Hotline Battleground	40	39	1
Reuters/Zogby	38	41	−3
Actual	**50**	**50**	**0**

Source: PoliticsNow (http://www.politicsnow.com) and survey organization press releases.

In a provocative column penned just after the election,[3] Everett Carll Ladd argued that the performance of the polls constituted an embarrassment to the profession. He went so far as to recommend that a commission much like the

---

Republican missteps during the budget battle gave Clinton the opening he needed.

---

one set up after the 1948 "Dewey beats Truman" election be established to examine what happened in 1996. Whether or not surveys from the popular press were any more or less accurate than in past years is certainly of interest to scholars and other consumers of survey research. More problematic for scholars, however, are the often mysterious ways in which the different polls are conducted and weighted.

For instance, since prospective voters who are easy to reach may have different attitudes from those who are more difficult to contact, proper callback procedures to reach hard-to-get respondents are crucial. Most major polls claim to follow rigorous callback procedures.[5] But the short durations of most of these polls (some only two days), make proper callback procedures impossible. Tracking surveys, which combine nightly results into two- or three-day rolling averages by dropping the oldest day's sample, do allow pollsters to attempt

many callbacks. In fact, one of the most accurate of the tracking polls, the Battleground Poll, attempted at least three callbacks on every number. Other tracking surveys, such as the one conducted by ABC News, attempted virtually no callbacks.

In fact, much about the methodological practices of media polls remains unclear, and the information that scholars require to evaluate the quality of a poll is often treated as proprietary. Survey organizations do report their sample sizes and the possible variance in their results due to sampling error. But other sources of nonrandom error—weighting schemes, callback procedures, time of interview, length of study, sample quality—may have a far greater influence on the accuracy of results. Different methods of conducting surveys and weighting data justifiably concern many scholars.[6]

The polls did provide us with useful information despite their shortcomings, but perhaps 20 rather than 200 surveys would have been sufficient. Measures of public opinion consistently told us that Clinton was leading, that perceptions of the economy were positive, and that interest in the campaign was low.

PUBLIC OPINION AND THE VOTE FOR PRESIDENT

Why did a comfortable plurality of those who did vote choose Clinton? This basic inquiry is really two questions: What attitudes or beliefs were the most important to individuals in making their personal voting decisions, and what

Table 6.3

Party Identification and Voter Choice in 1996

Party	Clinton	Dole	Perot
Democrat (40%)	84%	10%	5%
Republican (34%)	13%	80%	6%
Independent (26%)	43%	35%	17%

Source: Voter News Service.

factors were the most important in deciding the election?

The work of several political scientists suggests which factors are most important to individual voter choices. I will review their theories and then discuss how attitudes were distributed on 1996 polls as well as how these attitudes influenced the election outcome.

Party Identification

One theory argues that party identification is a long-term psychological attachment that shapes a wide variety of beliefs and behaviors. In particular, self-described party identification is highly correlated with voters' choices in most elections.

Based on information from the Voter News Service exit poll, Table 6.3 shows the relationship between self-described party identification and reported vote in the 1996 election. It tells a simple story. More registered voters were Democrats than were Republicans, and Democrats were more loyal to Clinton than Republicans were to Dole. Fur-

thermore, Clinton won the votes of a plurality of independents.

The origin of these partisan attachments has become a source of much controversy in the study of public opinion and electoral behavior. The debate centers around this question: Does party identification cause people to act in certain ways and to hold particular beliefs, or do those actions and beliefs cause individuals to identify with a particular party?

Some observers consider party identification to be akin to a religious bond that is inculcated early in life and endures as a person ages.[7] They are supported by studies that demonstrate the stability of party identification at the individual level.[8] Other scholars, however, have argued that party identification is not so much a long-term orientation as a running tally of evaluations of the party.[9]

My own view is that while party identification can be influenced by short-term factors, it is one of the most stable independent variables and is a powerful predictor of political attitudes and political actions.

As Figure 6.1 shows, the Democratic advantage in party identification has fallen over the last 30 years. The graph also illustrates how the number of Americans identifying with one of the two parties has dropped and the number professing to be independents has increased. Still, Democrats do hold an advantage over Republicans, and most Americans do identify with one of the two major political parties.

To help ascertain the role played by party identification in the 1996 election, Table 6.4 shows the results of several major polls conducted by telephone, as well as the Voter News Service (VNS) exit poll.

John Zogby, who directed the Reuters survey, observed:

Table 6.4

Party Composition of Election Poll Respondents

Poll	Democratic	Republican	Independent
Pew Center Preelection	37%	28%	29%
Pew Center	36%	34%	29%
Postelection CBS/*NYT*	39%	31%	29%
Reuters/Zogby	34%	34%	32%
VNS Exit Poll	40%	34%	27%

Figure 6.1

Party Identification 1960–1992

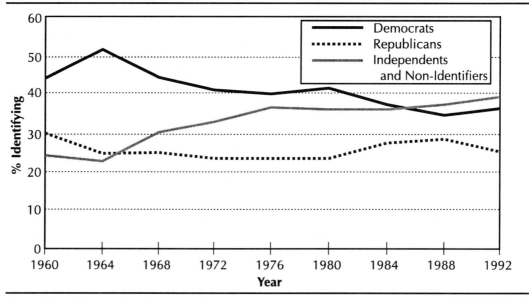

Source: National Election Study Cumulative File.

This is the portion of our business that is art. I feel that, in addition to the hard data that we collect, since Republicans control 32 governors' mansions, more state legislatures than do the Democrats, the mayoralties of most of the nation's major cities, and are competitive in congressional elections, it is reasonable to assume that, despite a lack of enthusiasm for their presidential candidate, there are still approximately the same amount of Republicans as Democrats.[10]

The fact that the Reuters tracking survey pegged each candidate's proportion of the vote to the percentage point, while the CBS/*New York Times* and Pew Center for the People and the Press surveys overstated Clinton's vote and understated Dole's, suggests that Reuters' estimation of party identification in the electorate was more accurate.

The Democratic advantage in party identification obviously did not guarantee a Clinton victory. If the advantage had that effect, the Republicans would not have won five out of the last eight presidential elections. Republican victories in presidential races in the face of Democratic advantages in partisanship can be explained partly by higher voter turnout and greater candidate loyalty among GOP partisans.

But there are also short-term factors that influence both partisans and independents.

Presidential elections are referenda on the incumbent. Prominent among the short-term factors that influence voters' assessments of the president and presidential elections are public perceptions of the state of the economy. Incumbents benefit when the public perceives that the economy is robust. When the economy is strong, the public is likely to have a favorable opinion of the president. On the other hand, incumbents suffer when times are bad.[11]

Public Perceptions of the Economy in 1996

According to the CBS/*New York Times* poll, in 1992, three out of four voters rated the nation's economy as fairly bad (39 percent) or very bad (36 percent). In 1996, however, only a little over one in four voters rated the economy as fairly bad (21 percent) or very bad (6 percent). Similarly, 34 percent of those polled in October 1996 thought they were better off than they had been four years ago, while only 16 percent thought they were worse off. In 1992, only 22 percent thought they were better off, while 36 percent thought they were worse off.

Figure 6.2

Clinton's Job Approval Ratings, March 1995–July 1996

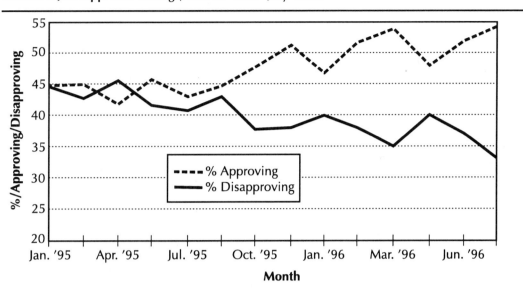

Source: CBS/*New York Times.*

According to exit polls, the 33 percent of Americans who thought their family situation was better than it had been four years ago voted for Clinton. Those who perceived their family's financial situation as worse than it had been four years ago voted for Dole. Likewise, according to the VNS exit poll, over half of those who voted (52 percent) believed that the national economy was in good condition, and they voted for Clinton by a margin of two to one. The little over one in three (36 percent) who thought the economy was not in good shape voted for Dole.

These results are typical of the findings from other polls. In 1996 Americans felt better about the state of the national economy as well as their own family's economic well-being than they had in 1992. Perceptions that the economy was weak in 1992 hurt George Bush and perceptions that the economy was strong in 1996 helped Bill Clinton.

Clinton's Job Approval Ratings

Evaluations of the incumbent's job performance are highly correlated at the aggregate level with the state of the economy and America's position in the world, and at the individual level with party identification. Still, measures of general feelings toward the incumbent often provide in-

dependent information and can be important in explaining presidential elections. Figure 6.2 shows the CBS News/*New York Times* measurement of Clinton's job approval ratings from May 1995 to July 1996.

This graph shows a clear turning point for Clinton in the summer and fall of 1995. At that time, Clinton and the Democrats won the battle over whether the GOP budget would be framed as reducing the deficit and saving Medicare or as slashing Medicare to fund a tax cut for the wealthy. Using paid media and their interest-group allies, the Democrats put the Republicans on the defensive and positioned themselves to use Medicare as a campaign issue in the 1996 campaign.

More generally, Republican missteps during the budget battle and government shutdowns gave Clinton the opening that he needed. Standing up to the Republican Congress and taking advantage of public fears over Medicare cuts was one of the main ways that Clinton raised his approval ratings and positioned himself to benefit from the positive perceptions of the economy. The turnaround was striking. Not only did Clinton's numbers go up, but approval of the GOP Congress and of Newt Gingrich, in particular, plunged. Figure 6.3 shows the drop in Gingrich's approval ratings.

Figure 6.3

Gingrich's Job Approval Ratings

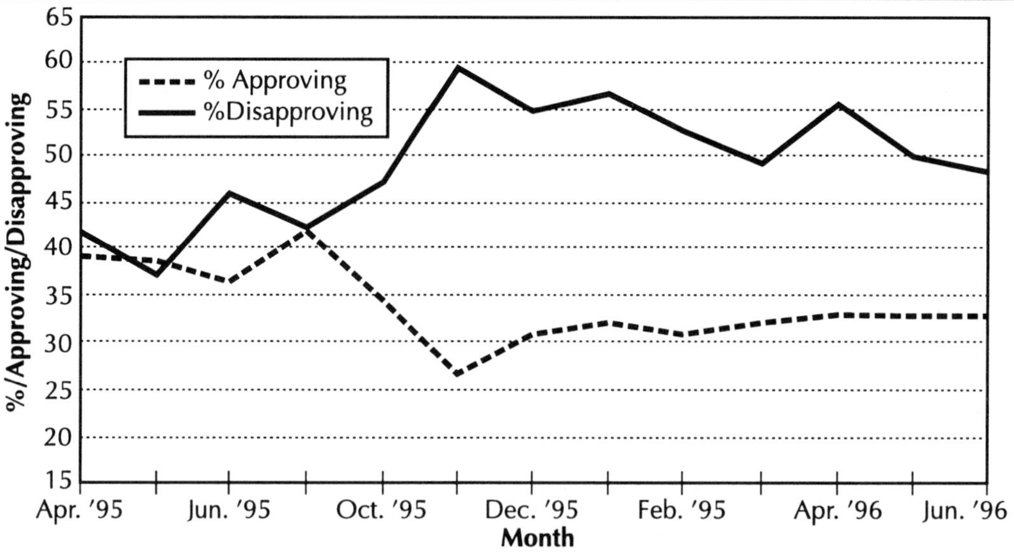

Source: PoliticsNow (http://www.politicsnow.com).

Personal Traits

Attitudes about personal characteristics of an incumbent—whether the individual is seen as honest, trustworthy, or empathetic—can also often affect vote choices. According to the VNS exit poll, a majority of voters did not believe that Clinton was honest and trustworthy (54 percent to 42 percent) or that he was telling the truth about Whitewater and other matters under investigation (59 percent to 33 percent). These results were consistent with other surveys taken both before and after the election. For example, according to the last preelection survey by CBS News and the *New York Times,* voters split evenly on the question of whether Bill Clinton could be trusted to keep his word as president (48 percent thought he could not be trusted, while 46 percent thought he could). According to a Pew Center preelection survey, registered voters believed that Bob Dole was more honest and truthful than Clinton by a margin of 42 percent to 26 percent. On other traits, however, Clinton had an advantage over Dole. According to the same Pew Center preelection poll, registered voters believed that Clinton was more likely to use good judgment in a crisis (46 percent to 37 percent), was more personally likable (66 percent to 20 percent), and was more empathetic (46 percent to 31 percent).

Conventional wisdom has it that Clinton's victory demonstrated that questions about his character and trustworthiness did not matter. That is, likability and competence won out over trustworthiness. Nevertheless, some observers believe that doubts about Clinton's character had considerable influence on the election outcome. Perceptions about the economy decided the race, but doubts that voters harbored about Clinton may have reduced turnout and denied the president a more decisive mandate.

Forecasting models of the presidential election that rely heavily on economic indicators indicated that Clinton would win by a greater margin than he actually achieved. Since observers agreed that the Dole campaign was not particularly effective, it is plausible that last-minute media attention to alleged improprieties with Democratic fund-raising and enduring voter doubts about his character cost Clinton and the Democrats a larger victory.

The Gender Gap

Women viewed Clinton in a more positive light than did men. This trend is consistent with another big story from the 1996 campaign—the difference in voting patterns between men and women. Although the magnitude of the gap and the proportion of each sex captured by the two candidates differs from poll to poll, most surveys indicated that voting patterns were significantly different.

According to VNS exit poll figures shown in Table 6.6, men split their votes evenly between Bob Dole and Bill Clinton (44 percent to 44 percent), while women chose the president by almost a three-to-two margin (54 percent to 38 percent). In the Pew Center survey, Dole won the votes of men by 8 percentage-points (44 percent to 36 percent), while Clinton won the votes of women by 19 percentage-points (53 percent to 34 percent).

The VNS poll also revealed that Dole won the votes of white men 49 percent to 39 percent and lost those of white women 49 percent to 43 percent. Among white voters in the Pew Center postelection survey, Dole won men by 16 percentage-points, and Clinton won the votes of women by 9 percentage-points (47 percent to 38 percent). This gender gap raises interesting questions for both political scientists and GOP strategists. [Editor's note: See Chapter 9 for more on these questions.]

THE TURNOUT PUZZLES

Scholars have taught us much about the basic characteristics of those who do and do not participate in the political process. Wealthier, more educated, more partisan, and more powerful individuals, as well as those facing fewer registration and voting barriers, will be the ones most likely to vote.[12] However, a major puzzle persists. Rising levels of education and less burdensome registration laws should induce higher turnout.[13] Examining the time period from 1960 to 1988, Steven Rosenstone and Mark Hansen estimated that increases in the educational level of the electorate and the easing of voting registration laws should have increased turnout by 4.6 percentage-points. Instead, as Figure 6.4 illustrates, turnout actually declined by 13 percentage-points in this period.

Some observers, including Rosenstone and Hansen, have argued that a decrease in political mobilization by the parties is the primary culprit for the decline in turnout. Others, such as Warren Miller and J. Merrill Shanks, have argued that different socialization experiences among different generational cohorts can ac-

Table 6.5

Gender Gap in the 1996 Election

	Clinton	Dole
VNS		
Men	44	44
Women	54	38
Pew Center		
Men	36	44
Women	53	34

count for the drop. Still others, such as Paul Abramson and John Aldrich or Ruy Teixeira, have argued that declines in partisanship and efficacy or connectedness to society can explain why turnout has fallen over the last four decades. Although each of these explanations has considerable merit, none seems to be a full explanation.

Moreover, while scholars continue to struggle with this familiar puzzle, we have now

I would argue that attitudes specific to particular elections influence turnout.

added the new mysteries of the sharp increase in turnout between 1988 and 1992 and the sharp decrease between 1992 and 1996. Suffrage laws, socioeconomic factors, and long-term political attitudes have not varied enough to explain the election-year-to-election-year changes we have just witnessed. In fact, the decline in turnout in 1996 occurred despite the passage of the National Voter Registration Act, which mandated that citizens be allowed to register to vote at motor vehicle and other government offices.

Who Cares?

I would argue that short-term attitudes specific to particular elections influence turnout. For example, Table 6.6 shows levels of turnout from 1960 to 1992 for those National Election Study

Figure 6.4

Turnout in Presidential Elections, 1960–1996

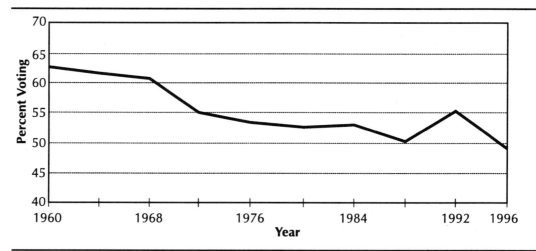

Source: Paul Abramson, John Aldrich, and David Rohde, *Change and Continuity in the 1992 Elections,* 1994, Washington, DC: Congressional Quarterly Press, p. 102; 1996, VNS estimate.

(NES) respondents who told interviewers that they were very much interested in the current campaign and those who said they were not much interested.

As Table 6.6 illustrates, more interested citizens have consistently shown higher turnout rates. Using NES data from 1964 to 1988, Stephen Nichols and Paul Beck estimated that with other socioeconomic and sociopsychological characteristics of voters held constant, citizens who were more interested in a campaign were 34 percent more likely to cast a ballot. Looking specifically at 1992, Nichols and Beck found that citizens who were interested in the election were 15 percent more likely to vote.[14]

Since interest in a campaign may influence who votes, we will look next at how interest in campaigns has changed over time.

As Figure 6.5 shows, in the high-turnout elections of the 1960s, some 4 in 10 citizens reported being very much interested in campaigns (38 percent in both 1960 and 1964, and 39 percent in 1968). In the lower-turnout elec-

tions of the 1980s, only 3 in 10 citizens (30 percent in 1980 and 28 percent in both 1984 and 1988) reported that they were very much interested in the campaigns. This pattern was reversed in the 1992 election, where once again about 4 in 10 people (39 percent) reported being very much interested.

Although we do not yet have comparable data on interest in the 1996 campaign, a number of measures suggest that interest was lower than it had been. For example, reported viewing of the presidential debates was sharply lower in 1996 than in 1992. In fact, the ratings for the final Clinton/Dole debate were the lowest of any televised presidential debate in history.

Data from various public opinion polls also suggest that interest in the 1996 campaign was lower than it had been four years earlier. In preelection polls, the Pew Research Center for the People and the Press (formerly the Times Mirror Center for the People and the Press) asked likely voters how closely they had been following the presidential elections. In

Table 6.6

Percentages of Voters in Presidential Elections, 1960–1992

	1960	1964	1968	1972	1976	1980	1984	1988	1992
Not Interested	61.3	62.3	52	50.8	47.8	43.6	50.4	39.9	43.4
Very Interested	92.4	87.6	87.5	85.9	85.2	89.5	89.2	90.5	90.3

Source: National Election Study respondents.

Figure 6.5

Interest in Presidential Campaigns, 1960–1992

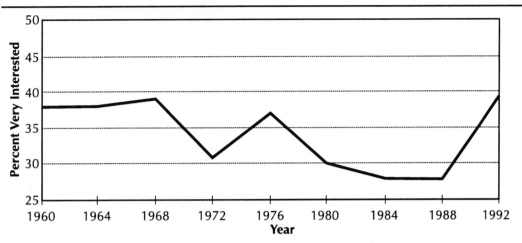

Source: National Election Study Cumulative File.

1996, just one in three (34 percent) of likely voters reported that they were following very closely, while in 1992, over half (55 percent) had given a "very closely" response. In 1988, 43 percent of likely voters had reported following the campaign very closely.

Similarly, the CBS News/*New York Times* survey asked how much attention voters were paying to the presidential campaign. In 1992, more than two in three probable voters (68 percent), questioned in the days before the election, said they were paying a lot of attention to the campaign. In 1996, less than half (48 percent) gave a similar response.

Implications

Although President Clinton won by a decisive margin, he did not win a majority of the vote, and the Democrats did not regain control of Congress. Could a higher turnout have meant a larger mandate for Clinton and given the Democrats control of the House of Representatives? The total House vote was a virtual tie (50.3 percent for the Republicans to 49.7 percent for the Democrats). In fact, so many races were close that 14,000 more Democratic votes in the right districts would have given the Democrats control of the House.

In fact, preliminary evidence suggests that Clinton's margin and the Democrats' chances in the House did suffer because of the low turnout.[15] In two major polls, Democrats seem to have suffered when pollsters screened out nonvoters.

Fourteen thousand more Democratic votes in the right districts would have given them control of the House.

CONCLUSION

Even had they been so inclined, there was little that Bob Dole and his strategists could have done to win the presidency in 1996. Put another way, a younger, more articulate Bob Dole running a perfect campaign still probably would not have won this election. Why? As this chapter has shown, a Democratic-leaning electorate, voters' positive perceptions of both the state of the national economy and their own economic well-being, and the absence of war or a threat from abroad put the fundamental advantage on Clinton's side. Furthermore, he waged a long and skillful campaign, putting Republicans on

69

the defensive about Medicare and tying Dole to the unpopular Gingrich. Nevertheless, a disinterested electorate, low turnout, and lingering doubts about Clinton's character left him without the mandate that he—and a number of political scientists—expected.

ENDNOTES

1. I would like to thank Cheryl Arnedt of CBS News, Lori Gudermuth of the Tarrance Group, and Claudia Deane of the Pew Research Center for the People and the Press for giving me some of their insight and some of their data on the 1996 election. A grateful thank you also goes out to Paul Freedman for his helpful suggestions.

2. The biannual National Election Studies typically provide the best and most comprehensive source of data on public opinion and electoral behavior in the United States. The NES conducted a study during the 1992–1994–1996 election cycle and is poised to teach us much about who voted and why. Unfortunately, NES data from the 1996 election were not available in time for this chapter.

3. See Everett Carll Ladd, "The Pollsters' Waterloo," *Wall Street Journal,* November 19, 1996, p. A22, and Richard Morin, "A Blown Call in N.H., A Lead Missed in Va.," *Washington Post*, November 7, 1996, p. A30.

4. The VNS exit poll data used in this chapter are those reported in the November 9, 1996, edition of the *National Journal.*

5. See Stephen Voss, Andrew Gelman, and Gary King, "Preelection Survey Methodology," *Public Opinion Quarterly,* Spring 1995, 98–132.

6. Exceptions include the CBS/*New York Times* polls, which are archived at the ICPSR, and the Pew Center polls which are made available on request.

7. See Warren Miller and J. Merrill Shanks, *The New American Voter,* 1996, Cambridge, MA: Harvard University Press.

8. See Philip Converse and Gregory Markus, "The New CPS Election Study Panel," *American Political Science Review,* 73: 32–49, and M. Kent Jennings and Gregory Markus, "Partisan Orientations Over the Long Haul," *American Political Science Review,* 78:1000–1018.

9. See Morris Fiorina, *Retrospective Voting in American National Elections,* 1981, New Haven: Yale University Press.

10. "Ahead of the Curve." John Zogby Group news release, November 6, 1996.

11. See Robert Erickson, "Economic Conditions and the Presidential Vote," *American Political Science Review,* 83:567–573; Morris Fiorina, op. cit.; and Edward Tufte, *Political Control of the Economy,* 1978, Princeton University Press.

12. See Paul Abramson and John Aldrich, "The Decline of Electoral Participation in America," *American Political Science Review,* 76:502–521; Ruy Teixeira, *The Disappearing American Voter,* 1992, Washington, D.C.: Brookings Institution; Ray Wolfinger and Steven Rosenstone, *Who Votes?* 1980, New Haven: Yale University Press; and Steven Rosenstone and Mark Hansen, *Mobilization, Participation, and Democracy in America,* 1993, New York: Macmillan.

13. See Richard Brody, "The Puzzle of Political Participation," in Anthony King, ed., *The New American Political System,* 1978, Washington, DC: American Enterprise Institute.

14. See Nichols and Beck, "Reversing the Decline: Voter Turnout in the 1992 Election," in Herbert Weisberg, ed., *Democracy's Feast,* 1995, Boston: Chatham House.

15. See Michael Kagay, "Experts See a Need for Refining Election Polls," *New York Times,* December 15, 1996.

Chapter Seven

Running at the Margins: Third Parties and Mightabeens

Frank B. Feigert

If there is a given about our electoral system, it is that there will almost always be candidates who might have won, but did not run, and third parties that had no hope of winning. This was no less the case in 1996. We were presented with a great many possibilities of both types. But we can dispose of one category immediately.

THE "MIGHTABEENS"

This term refers principally to those in the two major parties, although they often speak with overtones of third-party candidates. These include retired General Colin Powell, considered by many the foremost potential challenger to President Clinton, whether he ran as a Republican or on a third-party ticket. In at least one survey, Powell led Clinton by as much as 15 percent before he declared himself a noncandidate for the GOP nomination.[1] With Bob Dole trailing Clinton in the polls as early as October 1995, Republicans were of course eager to find a suitable challenger, one who could bring luster to the ticket and excitement to the electorate. Such a person seemed to be Powell, as he demonstrated a high level of popularity in general, as well as in polling trial heats against Clinton. Despite these polls and efforts by many party insiders to get General Powell to commit, he would not do so. Nor would he commit to accepting their nomination for vice president, al-

General Colin Powell demonstrated a high level of popularity.

though he did occasionally campaign for Dole as well as eventually address the convention. Ross Perot, then engaged in the petition efforts to get his newly formed Reform Party on the ballot, consistently referred to the need for a "world-class" candidate for his party, and, other than himself, he might have been referring to General Powell. Yet, like so many other scenarios, this was not to be, as Powell declared himself a Republican and, citing family concerns, took himself out of consideration for nomination by either the Reform or Republican Parties.

Could Powell have won, as either a Reform or a Republican standard-bearer? There seems little doubt that he could have done much better than did Mr. Perot. Certainly it is reasonable to assume that he might have been given a place in the presidential debates, a venue that was denied Mr. Perot by the Commission on Presidential Debates. However, we don't know how well the general might have performed on the campaign trail. His real exposure to the American public was largely through and by the media, campaigning not for votes but to

71

promote his book.[2] These ostensibly "nonpolitical" appearances may have made him all the more attractive, at least for a time.

Had he declared himself a candidate for the GOP nomination, Powell would have had substantial difficulty running on a Republican platform that called for an end to affirmative action and to the abortion option. Having declared himself a success story of affirmative action, and having favored a woman's right to choose, he would have been anathema to the GOP's conservative wing.

Pat Buchanan was another potential third-party nominee. Once again showing a strong appeal to conservatives within the Republican Party, he won the Iowa caucuses and, in the early GOP primaries, narrowly won New Hampshire, later coming in a distant second in South Carolina.[3] Having lost his earlier impetus, and as it became more evident that Dole would be the nominee, Buchanan took the public position that, if Dole were to weaken the party's opposition to abortion, he himself might run as a third-party candidate.[4] After his obvious failures in later Republican primaries, Buchanan seemed to encourage such speculation, despite his frequent denials.

Buchanan might have had substantial appeal as a third-party candidate. Beyond his base of support among Christian conservatives, he also had a populist appeal based on economic nationalism, having opposed NAFTA and the feared export of American jobs, as Ross Perot had. But despite an offer of backing from the United Taxpayers Party, Buchanan's candidacy remained a "mightabeen" in 1996. However, he appears to be willing to make yet a third successive run for the Republican nomination in 2000.

In the search for other candidates, there was also speculation about two retiring Democratic senators, Bill Bradley (NJ) and Sam Nunn (GA). Both had expressed dissatisfaction with President Clinton's policies. For Bradley, these issues were the president's views on such economic matters as Social Security and Medicare. Nunn had particularly opposed Clinton's "don't ask, don't tell" policy on gays in the military, among several defense-related questions. However, Bradley and Nunn ultimately campaigned for Clinton in their home states, closing ranks with their fellow Democrats.

THIRD PARTIES IN THE ELECTION

For some time now, there has been considerable support for the view that the two-party system does not provide sufficient choice for American voters. On the one hand, there is the school of thought that holds that the major parties are too much alike in purpose and programs—the "no-choice" school of thought espoused by, among others, Theodore Lowi.[5] This is in sharp contrast to the "ideological gridlock" view that points to the irreconcilable differences between Republicans like Ronald Reagan and House Speaker Newt Gingrich (GA), and such liberal Democrats as President Clinton and Senator Edward M. Kennedy (MA). The election of 1996 provides us with an opportunity to see what the parties, the candidates, and the electorate made of these two views.

Ross Perot and the Reform Party

If Ross Perot's 1992 candidacy demonstrated anything at all, it was that a substantial portion of the electorate was dissatisfied with "politics as usual." In this way, Perot was part of a long tradition of "dissident heroes," such as Theodore Roosevelt (1912), Robert La Follette (1924), Henry Wallace (1948), George Wallace (1968), and John Anderson (1980).[6] Such dissatisfaction has been variously attributed to politicians' failure to address such issues as budget balancing, deficit reduction, and Social Security and Medicare entitlements; conventional candidates and their conventional parties; and negative campaigning. Whatever the reason, having received almost 20 percent of the popular vote in the first election since 1960 to garner increased voter participation (55 percent in 1992 versus 50 percent in 1988), Perot seemed to symbolize a new direction for American politics.

As usual, there was no shortage of minor parties in 1996. Indeed, in addition to Democrats and Republicans, there were 43 parties and 19 announced presidential candidates registered with the Federal Election Commission on the ballot in one or more states.[7] However, Perot and his Reform Party were clearly the foremost of these, if only because of his 1992 performance—the best third-party showing since Theodore Roosevelt's Bull Moose or Progressive Party in 1912.[8]

Despite his loss in 1992, Perot was constantly visible as the 1996 election approached. An outspoken critic of NAFTA,[9] he also fretted publicly about Medicare and Medicaid.[10] With numerous appearances on such "free media" programs as CNN's *Larry King Live*, he essentially played the role of the nation's pamphleteer and critic-at-large.[11] He conducted a "National Issues Convention" in Dallas in 1995, inviting ordinary citizens to attend and political figures of both parties to make presentations on how they would address the nation's concerns. Republicans seeking their party's 1996 presidential nomination, including Dole, Buchanan, and several others, willingly appeared. In fact, they seemed eager for the endorsement of a man whose 1992 performance suggested that he could influence the 19 million voters who had supported him in the 1992 election.

The Reform Party itself was a Perot creation, growing out of United We Stand America, an organization founded by Perot in 1993 "as a research and educational organization that would study domestic problems and find ways to press for economic and government reform in Washington."[12] Interestingly, the two parties coexisted, at least temporarily.[13] Headquarters and personnel were shared, to the point that telephone operators answered with a neutral "Information Center."

Like a Lamm to the Slaughter

In the continuing search for a possible Reform nominee other than Perot, one potential candidate neither flinched nor declined. An ex-governor of Colorado, Richard Lamm had moved from being an intimate of President Clinton's to being his critic, parting company with the president on issues similar to those Perot had raised. His position on these issues closely paralleled Perot's, and in July Lamm announced his candidacy for the Reform Party's nomination for president.[14]

Perot announced his own candidacy the following day, and then staged a two-part Reform Party convention. The first phase met in Long Beach, California, just prior to the GOP convention in San Diego, in an apparent ploy to distract media attention away from Bob Dole's nomination. A week before the Democratic convention in Chicago, the Reform Party met again, this time in Valley Forge, Pennsyl-

vania. The two would-be nominees were introduced to cheers, a platform was drafted and passed, and the delegates went home to vote, along with other Reform Party members, by mail. But among the many party members who did not receive ballots were Mr. Lamm and his family! To no one's surprise, Perot was announced the winner of the nation's first national party mail-in nomination ballot, by 65 percent to 35 percent.[15]

Perot In and Out of the Campaign

Unlike 1992, when early polls had shown Perot favored by a plurality of voters shortly after announcing his candidacy, no such "bounce" occurred in 1996. Perot's support remained relatively flat in most polls, scarcely rising above 5 percent until the election, when he received about 8 percent.

Perot's support remained relatively flat, scarcely rising above 5 percent.

His public appearances were comparatively few and far between, and he commanded far less attention from the media than he had four years earlier. He did purchase time, principally on the cable networks, for 30-minute "infomercials" similar to those he had used in 1992. Eventually these and others appeared on the major broadcast networks as well, in the closing days of the campaign. But his exclusion from the presidential debates was a major blow. The Commission on Presidential Debates followed a set of guidelines for inclusion, the most important of which was whether or not a candidate had the potential to win the election, carry a state, or influence the outcome in a state. By any of these tests, Perot's inclusion in the 1992 debates was justified. But with 1996 polls in most states showing him with single-digit support, and with strong opposition coming from the Dole camp, he was excluded and further marginalized. Perot's response was typical—he suggested that if the test for inclusion were whether or not a candidate could win,

Table 7.1

Third-Party Appearances, 1992 and 1996

Office	Third Party				
	Perot/Reform	Libertarian	New Alliance	Natural Law	Green
States on Presidential Ballot					
1992	51	51	40	29	–
1996	51	51	–	44	22
Senate Seats Contested					
1992	1	21	3	5	2
1996	5	17	–	17	2
Districts on Congressional Ballot					
1992	4*	124	5	24	14
1996	20	156	–	157	5
States on Gubernatorial Ballot					
1992	–	3	3	1	–
1996	–	6	–	3	–

Sources: For 1992 congressional and gubernatorial figures, *CQ Almanac, 1992* (Washington, D.C.: Congressional Quarterly, Inc., 1993), pp. 35A–43A. For 1996 congressional and gubernatorial figures, *CQ Weekly Reports* (November 9, 1996), 3250–3257. For 1992 presidential figures, Emmet T. Flood and William G. Mayer, "Third-Party and Independent Candidates," in William G. Mayer (ed.), *In Pursuit of the White House: How We Choose Our Presidential Nominees* (Chatham, N.J.: Chatham House, 1995), Table 9.4, pp. 296–297. For 1996 presidential figures, http://www.fec.gov/96fed/pballots.htm (October 18, 1996).

*Since Perot ran without an explicit party designation for 1992, the figures include candidates affiliated in any way with Perot. Hence, the number may be understated.

Dole was the one who should have been excluded! While three-fourths of poll respondents said they believed he should have been included in the debates, there was no surge in public support for him.

What were the effects on the election of the Reform Party and Perot's presence? Perhaps because he was excluded from the debates and maintained a relatively low profile in the campaign, Perot did not have a positive impact on voter participation levels in 1996. Many observers had speculated that the higher turnout in 1992 was partly attributable to Perot's maverick candidacy, which raised interest in the tight election race.

Similarly, post-1992 analyses typically held that Perot might well have cost President George Bush his reelection, given his vote share of 19 percent and the fact that Bush had lost by only 5 percent. Republicans had feared the same outcome in 1996, and there was an abortive last-minute attempt by the Dole campaign to persuade Mr. Perot to drop out of the race and endorse the Republican candidate. The attempt failed, but Perot apparently had virtually no effect on the outcome in any case. Exit polling shows that had he not been in the race, his supporters would have been divided fairly evenly between Clinton and Dole.[16]

Other Third Parties

As usual, minor parties were active and on the ballot in many states, offering no shortage of candidates for president and lesser offices. Typically, they fared quite poorly, drawing fewer than 5 percent of the voters in most races. The rare exceptions occurred when only one major-party candidate ran, which gave voters the chance to express their dissent by supporting a third-party choice.

Table 7.1 indicates the problems confronted by third parties in 1992 and 1996. Only Perot's Reform Party and the Libertarian Party were on the presidential ballot in all states plus the District of Columbia. The Libertarians generally ran candidates for more offices in 1996 than they had four years earlier. The Natural

Law Party showed a surprising increase in its ballot appearances from 1992, and was as active as the Libertarians in seeking candidates for lesser offices. Party, whose presence, especially in California, had caused some disquiet in the Clinton camp, backed Ralph Nader, who chose not to campaign. Neither he nor other third-party candidates performed well, drawing only small proportions of the vote for virtually all offices.

THE NEAR FUTURE FOR THIRD PARTIES

As in 1992, Perot ran without significant accompaniment, with few candidates for other offices running on the same ticket. Despite his frequent statements that "This isn't about me, it's about you, the American people," in most places the third-party choice was Ross Perot, and Ross Perot alone.

However unknown their presidential candidates may have been, the Libertarian and Natural Law parties fielded many more candidates in more states than did the Reform Party for the offices of senator, governor, and representative. Indeed, the Libertarians fielded a candidate for the House in all districts in 10 states: Alabama (7), Delaware (1), Kansas (4), Michigan (16), Mississippi (5), Missouri (9), Nevada (2), Oregon (5), Vermont (1), and Wyoming (1). And, the lesser-known Natural Law Party did the same in four states: Hawaii (2), Iowa (5), Nevada (2), and South Carolina (6). If candidates for offices below the presidential level suggest something of organizational strength, then these minor parties may have more of a future than does Perot's Reform Party. Of course, it is another thing entirely to achieve sufficient legitimacy and visibility to attract a vote approaching that of Perot in 1992, the recent high-water mark for third parties. Clearly, the minor parties have a long road ahead of them if they are to achieve even a modicum of success.

It is also clear that Mr. Perot and what is essentially "his" party have substantial problems ahead. If it is to last and become an enduring part of the political scene, the Reform Party must develop an organization that does not revolve around one man who controls the purse strings and insists on being the presiden-

tial candidate in every race. For all intents and purposes, there was *no* Reform Party national organization prior to and immediately following the 1996 election. Rather, it was a collection of state organizations funded largely by Mr. Perot, with the assistance of federal matching funds he received by virtue of his 1992 performance. For the next election, the party qualifies to have federal funds for primaries, its convention, and its general election campaign. But Richard Lamm, invited by Mr. Perot to sit on the party's steering committee, has "ruled out joining a proposed Reform Party steering committee because its membership would be limited to Mr. Perot, two Perot allies, and Mr. Lamm. . . . 'I don't want to join a steering committee that is 3:1. . . . Ross Perot can no longer be the commander in chief of the army,' Mr. Lamm said."[17]

One source of potential strength for a third party is a single issue that is sufficiently compelling for would-be voters to divert a large number of them from the major parties. Such an issue might drive a wedge between either major party and its existing base of support. It could involve either public policy or party direction. For example, while the Christian Coalition plays a significant role in the GOP's nomination process and controls many state

Religious or economic conservatives might be provoked into leaving the Republicans and forming a new third party.

party organizations, its views may be incompatible with those of more traditional economic conservatives who have historically anchored the party. Either wing of the party—religious or economic conservatives—might at some point be provoked into leaving the Republicans and forming a new third party.

Another way in which minor parties might achieve greater strength is by changes in state election laws to allow mutual endorsements of candidates. Ten states now allow this, most notably New York, where the Conservative and Liberal Parties have achieved greater influence by endorsing candidates of other parties, usually Democrats and Republicans. Under this "fusion" process, in which *all* votes for a candidate are added, regardless of party, third or minor parties can achieve greater recognition and legitimacy by providing the winning margin for a major-party candidate. Conversely, the withholding of such an endorsement is a way of exerting some influence over the major party's nominations, a tool that has made New York's third parties much more visible than they might otherwise be.

In the absence of significant wedge issues and state election law changes, most third parties are likely to remain in the background, interesting artifacts of a pluralist democracy and its discontents.

ENDNOTES

1. David Winston, "Poll Track," http://www.electionline.com/polltrack/archive/ptan1109.htm (November 9, 1995).

2. Colin L. Powell, *My American Journey* (New York: Random House, 1995).

3. Richard L. Berke, "Changing Direction: Dole Easily Beats Buchanan to Win in South Carolina," *New York Times* (March 3, 1996), p. 1; Richard L. Berke, "Dole, Sweeping 8 Primaries, Calls for Party to Unite," *New York Times* (March 6, 1996), p. 1.

4. Jerry Gray, "Hinting at Third-Party Run, Buchanan Steps Up Attack on Dole," *New York Times* (May 5, 1996), p. 21.

5. For example, see Theodore J. Lowi, "The Time Is Ripe for the Creation of a Genuine 3-Party System," *The Long Term View*, 2 (Spring, 1994), pp. 13–16. For a review of the difficulties facing third parties, see Emmet T. Flood and William G. Mayer, "Third-Party and Independent Candidates: How They Get on the Ballot, How They Get Nominated," in William G. Mayer (ed.), *In Pursuit of the White House: How We Choose Our Presidential Nominees* (Chatham, NJ: Chatham House, 1995), chap. 9.

6. Clinton Rossiter, *Parties and Politics in America* (Ithaca, N.Y.: Cornell University Press, 1960), pp. 4–5; Frank B. Feigert,"The Ross Perot Candidacy and Its Significance," in William Crotty (ed.), *America's Choice: The Election of 1992* (Guilford, CT: Dushkin, 1993), chap. 7.

7. Http://www.fec.gov/96fed/pballots.htm (October 18, 1996).

8. Feigert, *op. cit.*, p. 86.

9. Ross Perot, *Save Your Job, Save Our Country: Why NAFTA Must Be Stopped—Now!* (New York: Hyperion, 1993).

10. Ross Perot, *Intensive Care: We Must Save Medicare and Medicaid Now* (New York: HarperCollins, 1995).

11. See also his *Economy in Crisis: The Need for a Strong Dollar and A Balanced Budget* (New York: Summit, 1996); *Preparing Our Country for the Twenty-first Century* (New York: HarperCollins, 1995); *Not for Sale at Any Price: How We Can Save America for Our Children* (New York: Hyperion, 1993).

12. Ernest Tollerson, "The Independents: Ex-Perot Volunteers Say Reform Party Is Using Old Tactics to Change the System," *New York Times* (August 10, 1996), p. 11.

13. Membership figures for United We Stand America have been closely held. However, internal estimates show the following: original national membership: 1,379,500–1,600,000; at end of 1994: 275,900–320,000; at end of 1995: 55,180. Source: Personal communication from Jack Koenig, former Illinois Director of UWSA, October 4, 1996.

14. Ernest Tollerson, "Third Party: Lamm, Ex-Governor of Colorado, Seeks Reform Party's Nomination," *New York Times* (July 10, 1996), p. 1.

15. R. W. Apple, Jr., "Perot Begins His Campaign: Vows to End 2-Party System as He Recalls His '92 Themes," *New York Times* (August 19, 1996), p. 1.

16. "National Exit Poll Results for Presidential Race," http://www.electionline.com/exitpolls/1996/nationale (November 5, 1996).

17. Ernest Tollerson, "Breather for Reform Party Is Giving Way to Discord," *New York Times*, November 24, 1996, p. 20.

Chapter Eight

The Year of More Women

Janet K. Boles

In the midst of the media attention to 1992 as "the year of the woman," women activists asked wryly, "Does this mean we just get one?" Subsequently, 1994 was declared "the year of the angry white male" in the wake of the off-year election. And in 1996, as a record number of women candidates were nominated and elected to the House of Representatives, this and related stories about women in public office were ignored by the media. Mary Landrieu (D-LA) and Susan Collins (R-ME) won open seats in the Senate with little national publicity. And Loretta Sanchez (D-CA) received a media blitz only after she had quietly defeated one of the loudest voices in the House, Republican presidential candidate Robert Dornan (R-CA).

The election of 1996 was not what women's groups had expected. No woman was seriously considered as a candidate for the national Republican ticket. A massive female voter mobilization project was followed by the lowest turnout since 1924. Neither abortion nor affirmative action served as a wedge issue, as had been anticipated. Instead, the slogan used by the National Organization for Women (NOW), "Newt Happens When We Don't Vote," best captured the leading catalytic force underlying the women's vote in 1996.

Yet arguably women were as central to the 1996 election story as they had been in 1992. The so-called "First Lady War" between Hillary Clinton and Elizabeth Dole was a topic of widespread fascination and did not always play out in the expected directions. And once again the gender gap took center stage in campaign coverage and candidates' strategies, but with a difference. Unlike in past years, the gap did not dramatically disappear late in the campaign. It held at around 11 percentage points and, for the first time in American voting history, a majority of women and a plurality of men voted for different presidential candidates, finally fulfilling former NOW president Eleanor Smeal's 1984 prediction that women would elect the next president.[1] At a minimum, the massive gender realignment that was envisioned by the National Woman's Party with the adoption of women's suffrage in 1920 had become a possibility.

THE DUELING FIRST LADIES

By March 1996, it had become evident that either Hillary Rodham Clinton or Elizabeth Dole would serve as America's first lady from 1997 to 2000. This represented a historic moment in that, for the first time, graduates of two of the nation's premier law schools, Harvard (Dole) and Yale (Clinton), and two highly accomplished career women were involved. Objectively, the two women were more alike than they were different. But politics are about conflict and contrasts and, accordingly, each was portrayed as offering a very different vision of the role of first lady. As communications scholar Kathleen Hall Jamison observed, "If Hillary is Lady Macbeth, Elizabeth Dole is Cinderella."[2] (Ironically, it was Dole, not Clinton, who was regularly caught during the campaign wiping her hands with towelettes after shaking hands with voters.)

Like Queen Elizabeth II, Hillary Clinton could justifiably complain about a run of horrible years. Having been involved in a variety of consecutive White House ethical inquiries and bearing much responsibility for the failure of the administration's national health care plan, she may have relished the critical eye cast upon Mrs. Dole by the media during the 1996 campaign. Mrs. Clinton read of possible conflicts of interest involving Elizabeth Dole's stock investment portfolio and noted the negative comments about Dole's blood-red lipstick and nail polish, her three-inch spike heels, and her appearance on the Jay Leno show in biker gear. Furthermore, Mrs. Dole was cautioned not to make a husband 12 years her senior seem doddering by finishing his sentences during joint interviews. And, for the first time in Robert Dole's career, the media focused closely on his failed first marriage and an extramarital affair. In contrast, Hillary Clinton emerged in 1996 as the author of a best-selling book on families and children and as the caring mother of a 16-year-old daughter often described in the media as stylish and self-assured. Elizabeth Dole, meanwhile, was left to explain why she had remained childless after her marriage to Bob Dole at age 38. Painful as such competitive image tactics undoubtedly were to both of these professional women, they may be the new ground rules for potential first ladies.

Although the conventional wisdom is that the wives of presidential candidates do not affect voter decision making, one analysis of the National Election Study data for 1992 found that both Barbara Bush and Hillary Clinton had separate identifications from those of their husbands with the voters and that these had moderate implications for the way people voted.[3] Further, despite the fact that Barbara Bush was far more warmly perceived by the voters than were her husband and the Clintons, Hillary Clinton's positive impact on the vote was larger. Equally intriguing, voters opposed to women's equality reacted negatively to both women; this would suggest that highly conservative and traditional voters—a core Republican constituency—object to any public role for women.

Nevertheless, the Republican Party in 1996 viewed Elizabeth Dole as a strong asset to the campaign, presenting her as the "anti-Hillary" who would return to her job at the American Red Cross after the election and not be in charge of health care policy. And at one point, she was even considered possible as Bob Dole's running mate. The Dole campaign concluded that there might be a debate between the two potential first ladies, an idea that 54 percent of the electorate supported.[4] A formal invitation

from the University of Toledo for such an event was refused by Elizabeth Dole, however.

Contrary to some perceptions, Hillary Clinton in the period 1993 to 1996 was a popular and widely admired first lady. She was viewed as an above-average leader by 36 percent of the public (11 points higher than Bill), as smarter than Bill (by 18 points), qualified to be president (by 47 percent of the public), and trailed Barbara Bush by only 3 percentage points as embodying the ideal first lady.[5] Most impressive, both the president and the first lady topped Gallup's list of the most admired men and women in the world in 1993 and 1994. In 1995, Hillary Clinton finished second to Mother

Competitive image tactics may be the new ground rules for potential first ladies.

Teresa on this list by 2 percentage points. Only in 1996 did Mrs. Clinton's approval ratings slip below those of her husband, as majorities came to believe that she had done something illegal or unethical relating to Whitewater and the FBI files and that she was lying about these matters. She remained popular with women, liberals, young people, Democrats, and those of moderate incomes but was especially unpopular with Republican men. The Voter News Service (VNS) exit polls, for example, found that those holding favorable views of Hillary Clinton (49 percent) roughly equaled those holding unfavorable views (47 percent).[6]

Elizabeth Dole was perceived more favorably by voters than was Hillary Clinton in polls taken during the campaign and was preferred as first lady. Despite a high-profile career as a cabinet officer in both the Reagan and Bush administrations, she was unknown to many voters; an April 1996 Gallup poll indicated that 27 percent had no opinion of her and 11 percent said they had never heard of her. The margin of the voters' preference for Dole as first lady was slim, ranging from 1 percentage point in a poll taken in August to the 50 percent to a 43 percent preference found in the VNS exit polls.[7]

And, given a choice of sitting next to any of the four national-ticket couples or the Perots on an airplane trip, respondents in a September poll preferred the Clintons by 35 percent versus 23 percent for the Doles.[8]

ABORTION, AFFIRMATIVE ACTION, AND SCANDAL

GOP insider Tanya Melich's much-publicized attack on the Republican Party's movement during the Reagan and Bush years to adopt the religious right's agenda on women,[9] combined with the ever-present gender gap that favors the Democratic Party, led Republican strategists in 1996 to craft approaches for recapturing the women's vote. In contrast, the Democratic Party was well positioned to appeal to female voters. The 1996 Democratic Presidential Voter Guide, prepared by the Democratic Task Force of the National Women's Political Caucus, listed 43 accomplishments of the Clinton administration, including economic opportunities for families, reproductive care, health care, education and training, crime, and appointments. In fact, Clinton had named six women to his cabinet and female appointees had made up 42 percent of all appointments.

The most obvious Republican tactic was to appeal to women's moralistic tendency by raising the issue of Clinton's character. And a 1995 Democratic poll had shown that the president was indeed vulnerable; parents with children at home strongly supported Dole and associated Clinton with extramarital affairs and drug use. In anticipation of GOP spot ads on these topics, the Clinton campaign filmed responses on school uniforms, assault weapons, and V-chips.[10] However, a Gallup poll taken in February 1995 indicated that most Americans did not view either extramarital affairs (67 percent) or the Whitewater affair (61 percent) as a factor in evaluating Clinton's ability to serve as president.[11] Both Dole and Perot hit character hard in the closing days of the campaign. However, the harsh social policies of the Republican Congress appear to have applied a coat of Teflon to a formerly Velcro president, and the attacks had no real impact.

The Republicans viewed affirmative action as a wedge issue that could give Democrats even greater problems with angry white males and split the traditional Democratic coalition of minorities, Jews, and working-class whites. Dole, who had previously supported affirmative action, cosponsored a bill to terminate it as federal policy. Support for this bill and California's Proposition 209 were a part of the Republican platform, while the Democratic platform promised merely to mend, not end, affirmative action. This latter position came closest to mirroring public opinion. A plurality of voters approved of the way Clinton was handling affirmative action in 1995; a September 1996 *Washington Post* poll found that only 30 percent of voters were worried that affirmative action programs were being abused. Observers also noted that Republican leaders were themselves split on the issue, with Republican governors in Massachusetts, New Jersey, and Ohio and Colin Powell favoring affirmative action. Nor was the issue ever effectively framed as a combined gender and race issue, rather than exclusively racial, even though polls indicated that women still perceived problems with economic opportunity.

Abortion is unambiguously a women's issue, particularly in view of research that suggests that abortion is developing as a realigning issue for women as an electoral bloc and that in 1992 many pro-choice Republican women voted for Ross Perot, not for George Bush.[12] The Republican Party was constrained by prominent pro-choice leaders, by a 1993 poll that showed that 43 percent of their own activists favored abortion rights, and by indications that Republican primary voters and Americans generally wanted the pro-life plank out of the platform.[13] In contrast, a Democratic poll of its supporters found solid 84 percent support for legal abortion.

The Republican platform contained a strong pro-life statement, but it also included a section acknowledging that party members differ on a variety of unnamed issues. New to the platform was a promise to ban a late-term procedure termed "partial-birth abortion." A May 1996 Gallup poll had found that 57 percent of those surveyed supported this ban,[14] which had been vetoed by Clinton, and Republicans saw another wedge issue to capture the majority of voters who support some government restrictions on abortion. President Clinton, perhaps reassured by a poll that found that 80 percent of the public did not consider Dr. Henry Foster's performance of abortions as a disqualifying factor to his serving as surgeon general, presented his veto as a compassion issue to save women's health and future reproductive chances. Or as former congresswoman Patricia Schroeder (D-CO) put it: "I've had enough of this [male legislative focus on] the fetus, the fetus, the fetus. They never talk about the woman, the woman, the woman."[15]

THE GENDER GAP: WHERE EVERY ISSUE WAS A WOMEN'S ISSUE

Even though abortion, affirmative action, and scandals neither opened nor closed the gender gap in 1996, this gap (conventionally defined as the difference between the proportion of men and women who support a particular candidate) was a staple of campaign coverage and strategy from November 1994, when an 11 percentage-point gender gap was dubbed "the revolt of the angry white male," to November 1996, when an identical gap of 11 points reelected Bill Clinton.

It is assumed that men and women voters have always diverged in their choices of candidates; since the development of scientific polling, we know this to be true. However, this gender gap was not noted until 1980 for several reasons. The differences were small, and majorities or pluralities of both sexes tended to support the same candidates. The gap did not consistently favor either of the major parties. And women voted in smaller numbers and proportions than men. Since 1964, women, a majority of the voting-age population, have cast more votes than men in presidential elections. And since 1980, women have had a slightly higher voter turnout. Beginning in 1980, women have consistently favored the Democratic Party, and the gender gap has become larger, ranging in previous presidential elections from 8 points in 1984 to 4 points in 1992. The women's rights movement deliberately publicized the gender gap as a strategy first for ratification of the Equal Rights Amendment and then to encourage the choice of a female Democratic vice-presidential candidate and support for feminist issues.[16]

Beginning in 1980, the media have generally covered the gender gap in terms set by the feminist movement. More rigorous examinations by political scientists, however, have

Since 1964, women have cast more votes than men in presidential elections.

found only weak support for this interpretation. In some years, women are more feminist and pro-choice, but men and women generally do not diverge on traditional women's rights issues. Instead, the gender gap appears to be driven by: (1) women's greater economic vulnerability that leads them to support the welfare state more strongly; (2) the greater salience of "compassion" issues (such as environmental protection, homosexuality, AIDS, child care, the elderly) to women; (3) women's greater aversion to conflict and force (such as war, the death penalty, gun ownership); and (4) the different concerns of men and women about the economy (that is, women base their votes on their perceptions of others' problems with the national economy, while men focus on perceptions of their own personal economic situations.) In the past, much of the gender gap has been attributed to the distinctive views of single, young, and college-educated women.

Media coverage of the gender gap and campaign strategies to reach women in 1996 were far more sophisticated, complex, and nuanced than in previous elections. There was a clear break with the view that the gender gap is linked to feminist issues. And the women's vote was presented as several votes driven by different issues; the omnipresent "soccer moms," the wives of the anxious white males, professional women, and housewives were to be approached differently. In their enthusiasm to cover a "big" story, the media sometimes defined the gender gap as the sum of the differences in support for the two candidates found among men and women, a method that served to double the gender gap.[17] In exasperation, the National Women's Political Caucus (NWPC) issued a report that concluded that the gap was in danger of being blown out of proportion.[18]

Certainly, there was also the "bad" and the "ugly" in coverage. Some suggested that the Democratic Party had become feminized into the "Mommy Party" of education and health care, in contrast to the Republican "Daddy Party" of defense and crime. Kevin Phillips at one point explained the gender gap as rooted in women's sexual attraction to Clinton, the "Ozark Casanova," which caused men to flee to the Republican Party in resentment of the "slickster who gets the girl."[19] And Dole's suggestion that his 15 percent tax cut would permit working women to quit their jobs led one perplexed columnist to exclaim, "Buy that candidate a hand calculator!"

But even Naomi Wolfe's much-ridiculed memo, recommending that the Clinton campaign use the metaphor of the president as the Good Father, building and protecting the family home from the Republican bulldozers,[20] resulted in Clinton's using his veto pen to protect abortion, Medicare, Medicaid, education, and other safety-net programs. During the campaign, talk of "angry white males" faded as the term became linked with alleged Oklahoma City bomber Timothy McVeigh and as it became evident that this was a class, not a gender, cleavage that no party wished to address. Women voters were placed front and center, as Clinton pursued his winning strategy of M2E2 (Medicare, Medicaid, Education, and the Environment). Dole tried to firm up his natural constituency of women who are full-time homemakers, fundamentalist Christians, and social conservatives, while trying to convince other women that cutting taxes, government, and the deficit would ultimately help families. Republicans were correct in predicting the importance to women of family values and moral issues in the election, but these terms were redefined by women. Family values were equated with the economic security provided by health insurance, child care, and schools; poor health, crime, and holes in the safety net were seen as immoral.

Although Dole lost the soccer moms—the affluent suburban women who were undecided—he did best among college-educated women, married women, pro-life and anti-welfare voters, and those who have unfavorable views of Hillary Clinton.[21] The postelection period found the Republican Party regrouping in light of polls that indicated they had fared even worse among women than the exit polls had shown, perhaps losing 59 percent to 35 percent among women. A more compassionate tone and a focus on improving education, not abolishing the Department of Education, was one suggestion.[22]

WOMEN CANDIDATES

As women's rights groups and women's PACs entered the sequel to the "year of the woman," they seemed to be curiously preoccupied with the return to the polls of the 16 million women who had voted in 1992 but stayed home in 1994; this group was viewed as an especially Democratic-leaning voting bloc, heavily composed of non-college-educated women under 50. "Women Win When Women Vote" (EMILY's List) and "It's a Man's World Unless Women Vote" (NOW) became the rallying cries for the WOMEN VOTE! project of EMILY's List and over 110 other women's rights groups who formed "Women's Vote '96: The Deciding Vote." EMILY's List, in cooperation with the Democratic Party, planned to raise $10 million through the year 2000 for its WOMEN VOTE! project and targeted 10 to 15 states for special polling, focus groups, direct mail, and personal phone calls to targeted demographic groups of women. Caught up in the media attention to the gender gap, some women suggested that the GOP could win only through vote suppression, or by convincing women that there was no reason to vote.[23] Ironically, the concern over fe-

EMILY's List remained for the third election cycle the largest congressional PAC.

male "drop-off" voters in 1994 was misplaced; according to U.S. Census figures, 44.9 percent of all eligible female voters participated in the 1994 elections, compared with 44.4 percent of all eligible males (which translated into a 4.2 million vote-majority for women in that

Table 8.1

Women Candidates in 1996 for Federal and State Legislative Office

	State Legislature		U.S. Senate		U.S. House	
	#	% Who Won	#	% Who Won	#	% Who Won
Nominated	2,275	—	9	—	120	—
Elected	1,368	60%	2	22%	51	43%
Incumbent	1,032	94%	0	—	40	98%
Open Seat	271	53%	2	33%	5	36%
Challenger	65	10%	0	—	6	9%

Sources: Compiled from information provided by the Center for the American Woman and Politics, Eagleton Institute of Politics, Rutgers University. The percentages represent the rate of victory among those nominated and, among those elected, the rate of winning among different types of candidates (for example, 94% of those running as incumbents were elected to state legislatures).

election).[24] In 1996, women again constituted 52 percent of the electorate.

Once again, no woman ran for the presidential nomination of a major party; the one woman—former Labor Secretary Lynn Martin—who appeared on Gallup's list of possible Republican candidates in 1994 received less than 1 percent support, and 51 percent of those polled had never heard of her.[25] And by late March 1996, Governor Christine Todd Whitman of New Jersey had withdrawn her name from consideration as Dole's running mate; it had become clear that her pro-choice and other progressive social views made her unacceptable to the conservative wing of the party.

Even so, in 1996 there were 55 PACs and other donor networks that either give money primarily to women candidates or draw upon a predominately female donor base.[26] EMILY's List, with its 40,000 members, remained for the third election cycle the largest congressional PAC. In 1994 it contributed $8.2 million to pro-choice Democratic women candidates; by September 1996, contributions over a 12-month period had exceeded $7 million.

In November there were a record number of women nominees for the House of Representatives (120, or 14 more than in 1992), 9 ran for the Senate, 6 were nominated for governor, and almost 2,300 sought a state legislative seat. And there were a record number of winners as well (see Table 8.1); postelection stories accurately used terms such as "modest" and "moderate" to describe these gains. Women gained some 50 seats in state legislatures. The new

Congress will have 9 (6D/3R) female senators, 51 (35D/16R) female House members, and 1 female delegate from the District of Columbia, a net gain of 3. Of these, 2 (1D/1R) are new to the Senate and 11 (8D/3R) will be House freshmen.[27] As in 1992, most of these newly elected women came out of the political pipeline; of the 13 new members of Congress, 7 had served in their state legislatures, one had been a mayor, one had served in state executive office, and one was a congressional widow. Only three—Carolyn McCarthy, Ellen Tauscher, and Loretta Sanchez—could be termed genuine political outsiders.

But 1996 was not the same as 1992. There was no saturation coverage of women candidates, even though there were some interesting stories to be told (such as those of Charlotte Pritt, the coal miner's daughter, who had been favored to win her gubernatorial race in West Virginia, and Mary Landrieu, daughter of a legendary former mayor of New Orleans, who ran as a liberal in Louisiana). Only the story of Carolyn McCarthy, the Long Island housewife who changed her registration from Republican to Democratic to run against an incumbent who had voted to repeal the ban on assault weapons, captured the attention of the print and electronic media; McCarthy, the accidental activist, had been widowed in the shooting on the Long Island Railway that also critically wounded her only child. She became the "soccer mom" of female candidates.

Women candidates did well because there was a core of female incumbents despite seven retirements and the defeat of three in primaries or elections. Majorities of both men and women still agreed that the country would be governed better if more women were in political office, but Celinda Lake found in her polling in 1996 that women in Democratic primaries, who had in recent years started with a 10- to 20-point advantage when running against men, no longer had that edge.[28] Democratic candidates could run as agents of change, but the 1994 election of several very conservative Republican women to Congress showed that not all women were uniformly identified with compassionate government, inclusiveness, or, in the case of ex-member Enid Greene (R-UT), honesty.

One positive aspect of the election was that women were disproportionately successful in defeating House incumbents. Although women composed only 14 percent of all House candidates, they were almost a quarter of the challengers who defeated incumbents. Of the 22 losing incumbents, 6 were defeated by women. It should be noted that some of these incumbents were easily lampooned—such as Deborah Stabenow's opponent, who had defended the Michigan Militia in the wake of the Oklahoma City bombing; Darlene Hooley's opponent, who had left his wife and five children to marry his campaign manager and very well paid aide; and Ellen Tauscher's opponent, who once called welfare recipients "breeders" and introduced a group of high school students as "survivors of abortion."

The downside for women House candidates was that most ran as challengers, rather than for open seats. Although there were not as many open seats in 1996 (53) as there had been in 1992 (84), women were much less likely to be nominated for open seats in 1996 (14) than in 1992 (39). This is a problem that deserves more attention from women's groups active in recruiting and training women for congressional elections than the question of female voter turnout.

CONCLUSION

In retrospect, the return to a slow, incremental growth of women in public office may signal that women candidates have become institutionalized. As one communications scholar has written, "One of the most successful rhetorical

Women candidates may have become institutionalized.

strategies for silencing a voice is to celebrate that voice. . . . News stories [in 1992] often focused on women in public life as curiosities (calling attention to their unusual or unnatural presence in politics, as objects to be examined) rather than highlighting their concerns as important and worthy of serious coverage."[29] Annoying though those "soccer moms" became, the coverage of women voters in 1996 did address women's real concerns in a serious and empathetic manner.

ENDNOTES

1. Eleanor Smeal, *Why and How Women Will Elect the Next President* (New York: Harper and Row, 1984). See also Bella Abzug, *Gender Gap* (Boston: Houghton Mifflin, 1984).
2. Laura Blumenfeld, "And One of Them Shall Be First," *Washington Post National Weekly Edition,* April 8–14, 1996, pp. 6–7.
3. Anthony Mughan and Barry C. Burden, "The Candidates' Wives," in Herbert F. Weisberg, ed., *Democracy's Feast: Elections in America* (Chatham, NJ: Chatham House, 1995), pp. 136–152.
4. "The Campaign for First Lady," *National Journal,* July 13, 1996, p. 1550.
5. Richard Morin, "Clinton (as in Hillary) Rides High on the Leadership List," *Washington Post National Weekly Edition,* November 13–19, 1995, p. 38; *Gallup Poll Public Opinion 1993,* pp. 265–267.
6. Frank Newport, "First Lady a Growing Liability for Clinton," *Gallup Poll Monthly,* January 1996, pp. 2–5; Leslie McAneny, " 'First Lady' Contest: No News Is Good News for Elizabeth Dole," *Gallup Poll Monthly,* April 1996, pp. 16–18.
7. McAneny; "Tight Race For First Lady," *National Journal,* September 7, 1996, p. 1920.
8. "Seatmates," *National Journal,* October 19, 1996, p. 2250.
9. Tanya Melich, *The Republican War against Women* (New York: Bantam, 1996).
10. *Newsweek,* November 18, 1996, pp. 48, 74.
11. *The Gallup Poll Public Opinion 1995,* p. 213.
12. Alan I. Abramowitz, "It's Abortion Stupid: Policy Voting in the 1992 Presidential Election,"

Journal of Politics, 57 (1995), pp. 176–186; Mark J. Wattier, Byron W. Daynes, and Raymond Tatalovich, "Abortion Attitudes, Gender, and Candidate Choice in Presidential Elections: 1972 to 1992," *Women & Politics,* 17 (1997), pp. 55–72.

13. "The Abortion Plank," *National Journal,* August 10, 1996, p. 1731; James A. Barnes, "Will Dole Walk the Abortion Plank?" *National Journal,* March 30, 1996, p. 727; "G.O.P. Plays Down 'Ideas' Survey, Finding Some Are Divisive," *New York Times,* March 23, 1994, p. A22.

14. *Gallup Poll Monthly,* May 1996, p. 3.

15. Francis X. Clines, "A Return to a Familiar Debate as a Lawmaker Prepares to Exit," *New York Times,* March 28, 1996.

16. Carol M. Mueller, ed., *The Politics of the Gender Gap* (Newbury Park, CA: Sage, 1988); Center for the American Woman and Politics (CAWP), Eagleton Institute of Politics, Rutgers University, "Fact Sheet: The Gender Gap," July, 1996.

17. For an example of this, see Steven Stark, "Gap Politics," *Atlantic Monthly,* July 1996, p. 71.

18. Clarence Page, "Overrating the 'Gender Gap,'" *Chicago Tribune,* August 27, 1995, section 4, p. 3.

19. Kevin Phillips, "Election Offers a New 'Showdown at Gender Gap,'" *Los Angeles Times,* May 26, 1996, pp. M1, M6.

20. Al Kamen, "Is a Father Figure What America's Women Want?" *Washington Post National Weekly Edition,* January 19–February 4, 1996, p. 15.

21. Thomas B. Edsall and Richard Morin, "Winning Over the Women," *Washington Post National Weekly Edition,* November 11–17, 1996, p. 12.

22. "GOP Fared Worse with Women in Election than Polls Showed, Governors Told," *Milwaukee Journal Sentinel,* November 27, 1996, p. 4A.

23. Gloria Steinem, "Voting as Rebellion: There's a Conspiracy to Turn Women Voters Off," *Ms.,* September/October 1996, pp. 55–61.

24. "The Gender Gap in 1996: Setting the Context," *CAWP News & Notes,* 11 (Summer 1996) pp. 2–3.

25. *Gallup Poll Public Opinion 1994,* p. 61.

26. "Women's PACs and Donor Networks: A Contact List," *CAWP News & Notes,* 10 (Winter 1996), pp. 6–11.

27. Information on women candidates and winners is drawn from the Center for the American Woman and Politics (CAWP), National Information Bank on Women in Public Office, Eagleton Institute of Politics, Rutgers University.

28. *Gallup Poll Public Opinion 1995*; Adam Nagourney, "More Women, Fewer Causes," *New York Times,* April 28, 1996.

29. Suzanne M. Daughton, "Silencing Voices by Celebration: The Paradox of 'The Year of the Woman,'" *Iowa Journal of Communication,* 36 (1994), pp. 44, 45.

Chapter Nine

Women Voters and the Gender Gap

Debra L. Dodson

The 1996 election year may not go down in history as another "year of the woman," but it may well be remembered as the "year of women voters." With men dividing their votes evenly between Bob Dole and Bill Clinton (44 percent and 43 percent, respectively),[1] women voters' overwhelming support for Clinton (54 percent vs. 38 percent for Dole) turned what could have been an election "too close to call" into one where the outcome was never in serious doubt.

Yet women voters' significance went beyond the fact that their preferences determined the winner. Candidates, parties, PACs, and other political organizations, as well as the media, focused unprecedented attention on women voters. With non-college-educated working women who stayed home on election day 1994 first taking center stage through the efforts of labor unions and EMILY's List (a PAC that supports

pro-choice, Democratic women candidates), and later the "soccer moms" who typified the erosion of support within the GOP's ranks capturing the spotlight, Campaign 96's agenda seemed to connect private concerns of home and family to the political as never before, all in an effort to win women's votes.

In all fairness to the Dole campaign, it was neither the first, nor will it probably be the last, campaign that had to confront a gender gap.[2] Gender gaps of 6 to 9 points, with women more supportive than men of the Democratic candidate, occurred in presidential races in the 1980s (Table 9.1) and have frequently occurred in races for other offices.[3] Nevertheless, 1996's 11-point gender gap was the largest win in a presidential race. Compared with 1992, when Clinton seemed more concerned with attracting the votes of white men than of women,[4] the gender gap increased in 1996 among voters 30

Table 9.1

Gender Gap in Presidential Elections, 1980–1996

Year/Poll	% Supporting Democratic Presidential Candidate		Gender Gap
	Women	Men	
1996 Voter News Service	54%	43%	11 points
1992 Voter News Service	45%	41%	4 points
1988 CBS News/*New York Times*	49%	41%	8 points
1984 CBS News/*New York Times*	44%	37%	7 points
1980 CBS News/*New York Times*	45%	37%	8 points

Source: Center for the American Woman and Politics (CAWP), Eagleton Institute of Politics, Rutgers University, New Brunswick, NJ.

Table 9.2

Gender Gap among Selected Demographic Groups, 1992 vs. 1996

Demographic Groups	1992 Exit Polls Support for Democratic Presidential Candidate			1996 Exit Polls Support for Democratic Presidential Candidate			Change in Gap
	Men	Women	Gap	Men	Women	Gap	
All	41%	45%	4 pts.	43%	54%	11 pts.	+ 7
Whites	37%	41%	4 pts.	38%	48%	10 pts.	+ 6
African Americans	78%	87%	9 pts.	78%	89%	11 pts.	+ 2
18–29-year-olds	38%	48%	10 pts.	47%	58%	10 pts.	0
30–44-year-olds	39%	43%	4 pts.	41%	54%	13 pts.	+ 9
45–59-year-olds	40%	42%	2 pts.	44%	52%	8 pts.	+ 6
60+ -year-olds	49%	50%	1 pt.	43%	53%	10 pts.	+ 9
Married	38%	41%	3 pts.	40%	48%	8 pts.	+ 5
Unmarried	48%	53%	5 pts.	49%	62%	13 pts.	+ 8
Less than High School	48%	57%	9 pts.	56%	63%	7 pts.	− 2
High School Grad	43%	43%	0 pts.	46%	56%	10 pts.	+10
Some College	40%	42%	2 pts.	42%	53%	11 pts.	+ 9
College Graduate	40%	48%	8 pts.	41%	53%	12 pts.	+ 4

Source: Based on data from Voter News Service exit polls, compiled in "A Profile of the Electorate," *New York Times,* November 10, 1996, p. 28.

and older, white voters, married voters, and among high school graduates and those with some college (Table 9.2).[5]

Some would say winning women voters' support is critical in any year; they are a majority of the adult population, have outnumbered male voters in presidential elections since 1964, and have turned out at higher rates than male voters in those elections since 1980.[6] Women proved especially important in 1996. With a fairly strong economy and moderate image helping Bill Clinton remain competitive among men, Bob Dole needed to close the gender gap and win over enough female swing voters for victory. Yet doing so was going to be particularly difficult for two reasons: gender differences increased in response to the 104th Congress, and Bill Clinton evinced relatively greater success in shaping messages that resonated with women voters.

The Republican Party's Contract with America and the Gingrich-inspired revolution it fueled in the 104th Congress made closing the gender gap an uphill battle for Bob Dole. Women and men may be equally dissatisfied with the current state of government,[7] but they have diverged over what should be done about it. Men are more ready than women to see gov-

ernment as the problem, not the solution (54 percent vs. 44 percent, respectively), while women more often than men say that government can help solve our problems (50 percent vs. 36 percent, respectively).[8] Focus groups and public opinion polls showed that women, com-

Bill Clinton evinced greater success in shaping messages that resonated with women voters.

pared with men, are more supportive of the social safety net, less favorable toward cutting spending on social programs (60 percent among men vs. 47 percent among women),[9] less likely to prefer a smaller government with fewer services (74 percent of men vs. 52 percent of women),[10] and more concerned about the human impact of public policies and budget cuts, as well as being more tolerant of gay rights and more concerned about the environment.[11]

Women, consequently, were more likely than men to say that the budget cuts in the 104th Congress went too far (56 percent vs. 42 percent, respectively), and women were less likely to approve of the job Newt Gingrich was doing.[12] With men disproportionately in their ranks, those who approved of the 104th Congress went overwhelmingly for Bob Dole on election day, while the disproportionately female group that disapproved of the Congress voted overwhelmingly for Bill Clinton.

The 104th Congress may have made it more difficult for Bob Dole to bridge the gender gap, but the gender gap was almost certainly a response to campaign messages as well. Both Dole and Clinton wanted women's votes, yet their approaches were strikingly different in tone, substance, and ultimately in effectiveness. In part these differences reflected interparty ideological differences over the role of government. At the same time, these more traditional ideological differences that define the parties were overlaid by what some would describe as ideological differences rooted in cultural values—differences in perceptions of the connection between public and private, acceptance of the changing roles of women in the family and society, and comfort with acknowledging that gender might influence the way voters think about politics.

PLANNING FOR THE RACE

Strategists on the Dole team obviously recognized that they had a problem with women long before the general election campaign. Yet they did not have an effective plan to deal with it. Some saw Bob Dole's problem with women as primarily one of image. During the primary season, Kellyanne Fitzpatrick, a Republican pollster, attributed women's reluctance to support Dole to his tendency to surround himself with white men, while Clinton sent a more inclusive message, surrounding himself in pictures with more diverse groups of supporters.[13] Overcoming this image of exclusion (while also sending a message of moderation) was a major goal for the GOP national convention. Selecting Congresswoman Susan Molinari to be the keynote address speaker at the GOP convention and appointing Governor Christine Todd Whitman both to address and to cochair the convention

were pivotal to that strategy.[14] Giving Senator Kay Bailey Hutchison (who almost failed to get a delegate position due to opposition from the Religious Right) a high-profile speaking slot, not to mention featuring a major address by Elizabeth Dole, delivered Oprah-style, were also strategies geared toward winning back Republican-leaning moderate professional and suburban women by making the Republican Party seem more woman-friendly, moderate, and inclusive.[15] The convention did provide a sharp contrast with the less visible platform hearings, in which moderates lost repeatedly to the Christian Coalition and their allies. But

Clinton surrounded himself in pictures with more diverse groups of supporters.

these images from the convention inspired some discontent among those of the political right, and they were insufficient to keep the Republican-leaning swing voters in the Dole column.

While Bob Dole may have felt *comfortable* talking about women having a seat at the table, he often seemed *uncomfortable* acknowledging that gender might affect perspectives about policies.[16] A classic example of this problem was the controversy that erupted when Dole tried to portray the GOP Congress as "woman/family-friendly" by suggesting that welfare reform would help women because welfare contributed to domestic violence.[17] And this was not an isolated incident. In May, when asked how he was going to deal with the gender gap, Bob Dole simply went through the list of all the issues that he had already been talking about before—cutting spending, balancing the budget, and returning power to the states. Another time, he implied that he might try to reach women by having his wife, Elizabeth, debate Hillary Clinton.[18]

However, with the convention approaching and the battle between moderate Republican women and the GOP over the abortion plank threatening to capture center stage in the media and reinforce the image that Republicans had a problem with women, Bob Dole did attempt to confront the gender gap. Dole proposed that a "tolerance clause" (one that was nonnegotiable) be attached to the antiabortion plank; however, it then was negotiated away when Dole and platform committee chair Henry Hyde agreed on a separate tolerance plank that would explicitly note the diversity of opinion on abortion but leave the antiabortion plank intact. After the Christian Coalition and its allies defeated that proposal in the platform committee, Dole then managed to forge a compromise with cultural conservatives that allowed for a non-specific diversity plank, with pro-choice Republicans getting their failed amendments (along with failed substantive amendments on every other topic) included in an appendix attached to the platform.[19] While that compromise, along with the decidedly moderate cast of those in high-profile roles at the convention that followed, may well have avoided a rebellion by moderate GOP delegates over the platform, it apparently was not enough to bring back GOP-leaning suburban and professional women voters who were uneasy with the Republican Party and Bob Dole.

With a strong national economy and a move to the center helping Clinton run ahead of Dole among men during much of the fall campaign, the Dole campaign began to recognize that it had to find ways to reach more women if it were to achieve victory. Bob Dole abandoned his "gender-neutral" plea for support and adopted new ways of talking about his 15 percent tax cut, which, intentionally or unintentionally, were not incompatible with the values of cultural conservatives. Dole began to sell his 15 percent tax cut by showing how it could translate into the family budget—three or four months of mortgage payments or child care. At some points he seemed to wax nostalgic for the "good ol' days" when one wage earner could support the family, asserting that his tax cut would allow one parent to stay at home if desired. "It's your money! It's your money!" became a familiar refrain on the stump. Moreover, Elizabeth Dole took to the airwaves once again, this time in an advertisement aimed at convincing women that they could trust Bob Dole. And in a related vein, the Republican National Committee was almost certainly targeting women when its "Republican Plan Coupon" was inserted in Sunday newspapers in swing areas the weekend before the election. Complete with

coupons to be clipped (which expired, coincidentally, on election day), the insert promised that families could save $105 a month, or $24.25 per week, by voting Republican. And to drive home this message, the flip side of the insert showed Mary Smith's check for $1,261, originally written to the IRS, but altered to be made payable to "My Family."

While clearly targeted at women, these messages failed to close the gender gap. And there are several possible reasons for this. First, the Dole message of economic individualism, "It's your money! It's your money!" resonated less with women, who see a social safety net as important and whose own feelings of economic vulnerability make them more likely to envision themselves as having to rely on that safety net one day. Second, most Americans initially doubted that taxes could be cut *and* the budget balanced at the same time (50 percent doubted compared with 38 percent who thought it possible for both to be done simultaneously), but women were even more skeptical than men.[20] Third, Dole's messages relative to Clinton's seemed out of sync with the reality of women's lives in the 1990s, particularly the reality of the suburban and professional women swing voters whose support he needed. Bob Dole never really seemed to understand that women are less ambivalent than men about women's changing roles[21] and that many women want to find ways to combine family and paid employment. While President Clinton talked with pride about signing the Family and Medical Leave Act and pledged to try to expand it so that parents could take time from work for parent-teacher conferences, Senator Dole reiterated his staunch opposition to the Family and Medical Leave Act, arguing that it should be left to the employers and employees to work out. He thus nurtured his image of being out of touch with the lives of average people and failing to understand the problems of families today. This image probably contributed to his problem of reaching the moderate women voters whose support he needed to win.

REACHING OUT TO WOMEN

Bob Dole seemed like a fish out of water when he tried to reach women voters, but Bill Clinton fared swimmingly when faced with the task.[22]

Bill Clinton was far more willing to make "gendered" appeals. When Clinton targeted messages to women, he spent little time talking about hot-button feminist issues like abortion, affirmative action, or sex discrimination in the workplace—issues that might either have divided women or scared away male voters. Instead, Clinton wove together an eclectic mix of issues that, when taken as a whole, was a quintessential example of coalition building—but this time aimed at a group that is often talked about in monolithic terms—women. These issues included family leave, Social Security and Medicare, the ban on assault weapons, the minimum wage, the V-chip, tax credits for higher education, educational programming, student loans, child support enforcement, school uniforms, a new 911 number for domestic violence victims, underage smoking, the environment, and banning guns for those convicted of domestic violence.

Drawing on focus groups that showed women were more likely to value notions of community, to respond to messages that tapped their concern for their children and their children's futures, and to be aware of their economic vulnerability, the Clinton campaign reached out to women, speaking in their language about their issues in a way that no other presidential campaign has. The effort to reach women, "particularly mothers," was unmistakable in one Clinton commercial featuring a baby girl with a narrator saying, "Today you'll decide what she eats. You'll decide what she wears. On November 5, you'll decide what kind of America she'll grow up in."[23] This strategy was evident as well in Hillary Clinton's speech at the Democratic National Convention, when she attempted to show not only that she empathized with the challenges facing families today, but that the Clinton administration was working to provide families with the tools they need to help themselves. In short, her message that the personal is political drove home a feminist theme within a very traditional context; and, it presented a sharp contrast with the Dole campaign's refrain of economic individualism—"It's your money! It's your money!"—and his argument that the best way to help people was to get government out of the way.[24]

While these appeals to mothers and families were a dominant feature of the campaign, President Clinton reached out to other, narrower segments of women voters with differing concerns. He targeted low-wage working women through his efforts to force the GOP-controlled Congress to vote on a minimum-wage increase. With 60 percent of minimum-wage workers being women, Clinton's support of a minimum-wage increase was tangible evidence he was working to address their pressing concerns about economic security. Similarly, his attention to health care, retirement security, violence against women and children, and investing in children—particularly their safety and education—resonated with this group and other non-college-educated women. Focus groups conducted by Democratic consultants suggested that the message that Republicans wanted to cut

Clinton's support among older men was actually lower in 1996 than it had been in 1992.

funds for education, Social Security, and Medicare to provide tax breaks for the wealthy angered non-college-educated women. That anger may well account for the president's higher support among the women in this group, and it may well explain why his support increased substantially from 1992 among female high school graduates.

Yet the message that touched one group of women did not necessarily move others. Those same focus groups conducted early in the campaign by Democratic pollsters suggested that Clinton was reaching suburban and professional women through responses to somewhat different sets of concerns. Secular, pro-choice, uneasy with the Religious Right, but Republican-leaning on economic issues, professional and suburban women (who included the oft-discussed soccer moms) were attracted to Clinton because of concerns about social issues—abortion, the environment, and education.

Different messages resonated with seniors, but at the same time, the gender differences in economic vulnerability within this group became quite evident. Fears of the 104th

89

Congress and support for President Clinton's emphasis on protecting Medicare, Social Security, and pensions drove retired women and many non-college-educated women approaching retirement even more into the Democratic camp;[25] in contrast, Clinton's support among older men was actually lower in 1996 than it had been in 1992. With women living longer than men, and on less money, the Clinton message helped to create a gender gap larger than ever before among seniors, one that put the retirement havens of Florida and Arizona (which had gone for George Bush in 1992) into the Clinton column.

The result of the contrasting appeals of the two candidates was that Clinton and Dole supporters gave very different reasons for supporting their preferred candidates. Among the three things Clinton voters liked best about their presidential choice were, "He cares about people like me" (28 percent) and "He understands the problems of American families" (25 percent). Dole supporters rarely cited these reasons, focusing instead on honesty and integrity (34 percent) and leadership qualities (24 percent).[26] Some minimize the importance of Clinton's successful appeals to women, suggesting that the Democratic Party has become "feminized." But Clinton's campaign left his voters more likely than Dole voters to say that they voted for their candidate because they liked him and his policies (70 percent vs. 61 percent).[27]

Looking Ahead

The focus on women voters in the 1996 campaign is remarkable, coming a mere two years after the election dubbed "the year of the angry white male." Some leading Republicans are now arguing that the GOP must do more to address the concerns of women, and leaders of the women's movement are pressing Clinton to demonstrate that he values women as a critical constituency by appointing more women to high positions in his administration. But will the gender gap and women's contribution to the reelection of Bill Clinton have any effect on policy? Is it any more likely that government will provide families with the tools to help them help themselves, as Clinton urged throughout the campaign? Will appointments to the second

Clinton administration give women more voice than they had during the first adminstration? Will more of the policy goals of the women's movement be realized in the 105th Congress than were in the 104th?

The Clinton adminstration will face virtually the same Congress in the 105th as it did in the 104th. Granted that Democrats did pick up a few seats in the 1996 election, and that women were substantially more likely than men to vote Democratic in the House races (55 percent vs. 47 percent),[28] the fact remains that the leaders of the Republican Revolution in the 104th Congress will be back in power for the 105th. Moreover, even if some Republicans took the gender gap in the presidential race as a warning, there will be many obstacles to changing that party's course. The Religious Right is powerful within the GOP, and its opposition to policies that ease the burdens on families coping with social change (to say nothing of policies that promote gender equity) will make it difficult for the Republican Party to co-opt many of the policies that the president advocated on the campaign trail. Furthermore, the fact that the GOP retained control of the House *despite* a gender gap nationally in House voting may make efforts to accommodate women's concerns less urgent to its members.

Yet Congress may not be the only obstacle that women's organizations face if they hope to reap the rewards from women's election of this president. The Washington-based women's movement showed remarkable pragmatism, de-emphasized traditional feminist appeals. Instead, the movement incorporated a mixture of appeals that resonated with feminists as well as with women who might not consider themselves feminists, but whose political perspectives were shaped by their economic autonomy from men, their greater economic vulnerability, and their responsibilities for family. Yet where does this eclectic agenda—V-chips, family leave for teacher conferences, tax credits for college tuition, the Internet in every classroom, stopping underage smoking, school uniforms, and 911 numbers for domestic violence victims—actually take the policy agenda of the women's movement? This question is particularly relevant, since this was the same year in which politicians retreated from affirmative action, presidential candidates seldom mentioned

> *The policy agenda of the women's movement was difficult to find in the rhetoric of the 1996 campaign.*

abortion, and welfare mothers became symbols of what was wrong with this nation.

In many respects, the policy agenda of the women's movement was difficult to find in the rhetoric of the 1996 campaign, as the Clinton campaign selected limited, often small-scale, issues to try to reach women without dealing with the fundamental causes of the problems that concerned them. Certainly there is every reason to believe that the Clinton administration will continue to use the veto pen to stop at least some legislation that women's organizations staunchly oppose and that it will probably attempt to pass legislation that was part of its eclectic women's agenda. Accordingly, the women's movement policy agenda will fare better than it would have had Bob Dole been elected. However, as women's organizations fight in the short term to advance policies they see as helping women, their long-term prospects for political gain may depend not only on their continued clout from a gender gap that determines who wins, but also on what they do to reach out to still more women. The next time politicians run for office, they may listen to women's voices and be compelled to offer more comprehensive solutions to the problems that face women and their families.

ENDNOTES

1. "Portrait of the Electorate," *New York Times,* November 10, 1996, p. 28.
2. In this chapter, the gender gap is the difference between the proportion of women and the proportion of men supporting the Democratic candidate.
3. Center for the American Woman and Politics, Gender Gap Fact Sheet, July 1996.
4. Thomas B. Edsall and Richard Morin, "Clinton Benefited from Huge Gender Gap," *Washington Post,* November 6, 1996, p. B7.
5. Married whites showed no evidence of a gender gap in 1992, when Bush outpolled Clinton 45 percent to 31 percent among married white women and 43 percent to 30 percent among their male counterparts. But the story changed in this group in preelection polls, when Clinton carried the women, 49 percent to 39 percent for Dole, but lost the men to Dole, 33 percent to 49 percent (Elaine Sciolino, "Political Battle of the Sexes is Tougher than Ever," *New York Times,* September 6, 1996, p. A1). And the differences apparently remained on election day when middle-class suburban women, a.k.a. "soccer moms," went for Clinton over Dole, 49 percent to 41 percent, while their male counterparts went for Dole, 56 percent to 34 percent (Associated Press, "Clinton Scores Goal with 'Soccer Moms,'" *USA Today,* November 6, 1996 [database online]).
6. Center for the American Woman and Politics, "Sex Differences in Voter Turnout," July 1995.
7. Sixty-one percent of both women and men agreed that government does little to help middle-class families (Celinda Lake, "The Gender Gap: The Democratic Puzzle," *Campaigns and Elections,* October/November 1995 [database online]). And this is nothing new. In the 1994 National Election Study, for example, 76 percent of both women and men said that government was run by a few big interests, and 72 percent of men along with 69 percent of women said that government wastes a lot ("People, Opinions, and Polls," *Public Perspective,* August/September 1996, p. 11).
8. Celinda Lake, "The Gender Gap: The Democratic Puzzle," *Campaigns and Elections,* October/November 1995 [database online].
9. Gary Langer, "The Gender Gap: A Pocketbook Issue," *ABC News August 13, 1996* in *Politics Now,* August 14, 1996 [database online].
10. Ibid.
11. Mike Meyers and Carol Byrne, "Women and the GOP," *Star Tribune,* Metro Edition, April 1, 1996, p. 1A.
12. Gingrich's job approval rating near the midpoint of the 104th Congress was 54 percent among white men, but only 37 percent among white women (Celinda Lake, "The Gender Gap: The Democratic Puzzle," *Campaigns and Elections,* October/November 1995 [database online]). Sixty-six percent of men, but only 50 percent of women said government was doing too much (CNN/*USAToday*/ Gallup poll reported in *AllPolitics,* June 12, 1996 [database online]).
13. *Associated Press,* "Dole Has Gender Gap to Close," May 13, 1996 [database online]; also see Susan Page, "Clinton Camp Mobilizing to Keep Women's Vote," *USA Today,* June 10, 1996, pp. 1–2.
14. And certainly it is little surprise that Christie Whitman, the temporary cochair of the convention, got far more air time than the permanent chair of the convention, Newt Gingrich.

15. The Dole campaign was not alone in its efforts to attract women. The National Federation of Republican Women's "Get Out the Vote Campaign" was aimed at bringing some 1.5 million more female voters into the GOP, and the GOP's regional briefing program for women called "A Seat at the Table" were both efforts to narrow the gender gap (*AllPolitics,* "Wanted: About 1.5 Million Women," June 26, 1996 [database online]).

16. On the surface at least, it often seemed that his reluctance was because he just did not understand. Others, however, argue that it was more than that. The Dole campaign's adoption of a previously successful strategy that gave top priority to gaining the support of the Religious Right, at the expense of women, then made it impossible for him to moderate his positions when it became clear that he actually needed women's support. (Remarks by Tanya Melich, National Council for Research on Women, November 20, 1996; also see Tanya Melich, *The Republican War against Women: An Insiders' Report from behind the Lines,* New York: Bantam Books, 1995.)

17. Laura Ingraham, "Convention Preview: How the 'Gender Gap' Is Driving Dole Girl Crazy," *Washington Post,* August 4, 1996, p. C1.

18. Katharine Q. Seeyle, "Dole Says He Has Plan to Win Votes of Women," *New York Times,* May 8, 1996, p. A1.

19. Brian Hartman, "Moderates Swallow Abortion Compromise, Declare Party Unity," *PoliticsNow,* August 7, 1996 [database online].

20. *PoliticsNow,* "Interview with Pollsters Ed Goeas and Celinda Lake," Inter-Action/Direct Access, August 13, 1996 [database online].

21. Arlene Hoschild, *The Second Shift* (New York: Viking Press, 1989); Roberta Sigel, *Ambition and Accommodation: How Women View Gender Relations* (Chicago: University of Chicago Press, 1996).

22. Both campaigns used formal structures aimed at directly reaching women voters about the administration's policy accomplishments. Clinton's Office of Women's Initiatives and Outreach helped keep the White House focused on how issues affect women (Alison Mitchell, "A Calculation in Tears," *New York Times,* April 12, 1996, p. A1). He also organized presidential appointees across the country to host a series of round tables called "At the Table," which aimed to inform women about the Clinton administration's accomplishments and to give women an opportunity to voice their concerns regarding the way their government could serve them. The Clinton campaign set up a women's "kitchen cabinet" of advisers and held weekly strategy sessions with women in the administration. A group called the Interagency Committee focused on the concerns of women business owners—probably the group of women the Republicans feel the most affinity with. And the Democratic National Committee and EMILY's List jointly ran projects to turn out blue-collar women who did not vote in 1994 (Susan Page, "Clinton Camp Mobilizing to Keep Women's Vote," *USA Today,* June 10, 1996, pp. 1–2).

23. Alison Mitchell, "Clinton Campaign Puts an Emphasis on Female Voters," *New York Times,* October 28, 1996, p. A1.

24. Even when it came to the V-chip, Dole's limited government principles came through. Rather than involving a government solution, he believed it was ultimately up to parents to "just turn the trash off" (Barbara Vobejda, "Nurturing Issues That Hit Home with Voters," *Washington Post,* October 30, 1996, p. A19).

25. EMILY's List Women's Monitor, April 1996.

26. Both Clinton and Dole supporters frequently mentioned "experience" (28 percent for Clinton and 33 percent for Dole) (*Los Angeles Times* Exit Poll, November 1996 [database online]).

27. Ibid.

28. Mario Brosserd, "A Closer Look at the Voters," *Washington Post National Weekly Edition,* November 11–17, 1996, p. 11.

Chapter Ten

Black Politics, the 1996 Elections, and the End of the Second Reconstruction

Dean E. Robinson

In reviewing the 1996 election, we should not be surprised that Bill Clinton received 83 percent of the black vote, and that Bob Dole, who received 12 percent of his votes from blacks, did not manage to secure more. Indeed, blacks of all age groups and regions of the country voted solidly for Clinton, though there was a gender gap (89 percent of black women to 78 percent of men). Despite the fact that the GOP enjoyed 18 percent of the black vote in House elections, the same pattern held: blacks remain solidly Democratic.[1]

What might be surprising is that despite these statistics, it is unlikely that this "race gap" will mean that American government will be more responsive to the issues that concern black voters. What issues? In a general sense, black interests are the same as everyone else's: employment, education, housing, health care, and so on. However, because of their historical and current experiences as a racial minority, their more particular concerns as a group involve ensuring that discrimination does not limit their access to employment, housing, and education, and that the government maintains its commitment to substantive equality. Despite the fact that black Americans are not monolithic—they work in different occupations, live in different parts of the country, have different ideas about religion, and so on—certain objective circumstances and subjective orientations separate them from white Americans.[2]

Consider objective measures. The relative economic position of most black families with respect to whites has deteriorated in recent times, especially during the decade of the 1980s. By 1989 the median white family had 20 times the wealth of the median nonwhite family.[3] This is not helped by a black male unemployment rate of 11.5 percent, compared to 5.3 for white males. Further, despite an expanded middle class, one-third of all blacks remain impoverished and nearly half of black children under the age of six live in poverty.[4] These statistics result from the fact that discrimination, inferior education, inadequate health care, and crippling unemployment are still the rule for black communities across the country. Perhaps not so surprisingly, blacks are considerably more supportive of government efforts to help the disadvantaged in general and Afro-Americans in particular. Blacks and whites differ sharply over this issue. Blacks overwhelmingly think the government can do things to help. They also overwhelmingly (76 to 36 percent for whites) favor affirmative action for racial minorities.[5]

Despite these trends, and despite black voter loyalty, it is unlikely that President Clinton and the Democratic Party will respond to these sorts of concerns. Clinton's strategy has been to pursue centrist goals, divorced from any strong commitment to policies targeted toward racial minorities and the poor. Centrist goals have meant less rhetorical and substantive support for the programs and policies that seek to address some of the problems mentioned above.

Black voters are "stuck" in ways reminiscent of a century ago. Then and now, politics

> *Blacks in the first South Carolina legislature outnumbered whites 87 to 40.*

has swung to the right. At the end of the nineteenth century, the party backing civil rights retreated in the face of white opposition, and the Supreme Court undercut civil rights legislation. Then, as now, black voters voted solidly for one particular party, only to be sacrificed in the game of national politics. And liberals abandoned racial equality on the grounds of political pragmatism. Finally, in the face of a rightward turn, many blacks themselves adopted conservative (accommodationist) stands.

THE FIRST RECONSTRUCTION

One hundred years ago, black people threw their weight to the Republican Party—when they could. Because, of course, by then the political ground was crumbling beneath them. Well before the *Plessy v. Ferguson* (1896) decision sanctioned Jim Crow in national law, whites had begun to purge blacks from the mainstream. The mainstream was, in fact, where blacks had been—in the middle of political action. Throughout the Reconstruction South, blacks voted and held political office at local, state, and national levels. They had the greatest influence in South Carolina, where, in the first state legislature, they outnumbered whites 87 to 40. The first legislature in Mississippi had 40 blacks, some of whom had been slaves. And Louisiana, as a final example, had 133 black legislators between 1868 and 1896.[6] The first black representatives to Congress came from the states with high black populations. Between 1869 and 1901, 20 blacks served in the House of Representatives and 2 in the Senate.[7] The two senators, Hiram R. Revels and

Blanche K. Bruce, both represented Mississippi.[8]

This political success—limited from our contemporary vantage point—was the direct result of Republican Party support. The party of Lincoln was determined to strengthen its position following the war, and they did so with the help of the freedmen. Republicans established the Freedmen's Bureau in 1865 in order to distribute clothing, food, and fuel to destitute freedmen and oversee all policies related to their condition.[9] The Bureau also fostered political activity. Many Freedmen's Bureau officials were interested as much in expanding the Republican Party as they were in the welfare of ex-slaves. Another benevolent group, the Union League of America, also encouraged political activity among blacks in chapters throughout the South. And other organizations like the Lincoln Brotherhood and the Red Strings "delivered the black vote to the Republican party in national as well as state and local elections."[10]

These political efforts, in turn, had been facilitated by three amendments to the Constitution and an array of legislation. The Thirteenth Amendment abolished slavery. The Fourteenth Amendment made Americans citizens of *both* the United States and the states in which they resided. And the Fifteenth Amendment gave black men the right to vote. The 1866 Civil Rights Act "gave all U.S. citizens equal rights to inherit, purchase, lease, hold, or convey real or personal property."[11] The Reconstruction Act of 1867 disenfranchised vast numbers of white southerners, allowing whites and blacks who had been loyal to the Union access to the ballot. It also divided the Confederate states, except Tennessee, into five military districts under commanders authorized to protect the peace.[12] The Civil Rights Act of 1875 prohibited racial discrimination in public accommodations.

CONSERVATIVE BACKLASH

The momentum of integration had already started to wane well before the Compromise of 1877 effectively ended Reconstruction. From the beginning, Republicans had confronted the open hostility many white northerners felt toward the granting of rights to black Americans.

Most white Americans, northerners as well as southerners, thought blacks unfit for political life, and support for black suffrage depended upon the support of the small radical block of the Republican Party. As the leadership of the party changed, and as political elites, North and South, worked to buttress economic links between regions, southern whites pushed blacks to the political, economic, and social margins.

As early as 1870, the border states began to go Democratic. "The issue of white supremacy, low taxes, and control of the black labor force dominated the Democratic campaigns of the mid-1870s," and to great effect.[13] "Redeemers" took control in North Carolina and Virginia and, in 1871, Georgia gave way to Democratic control. In 1874 and 1875 Texas, Arkansas, and Alabama did the same.[14] This reflected the fact that many white southerners resisted efforts to transform the South's system of racial castes. Such stalling foreshadowed a similar resistance to federally imposed civil rights policy in the 1960s.

Southern "Redeemers" benefited from a number of Supreme Court rulings that effectively undercut civil rights enforcement. In the *Slaughter-House Cases* (1873), the Supreme Court ruled that the Fourteenth Amendment "protected only those rights that owed their existence to the federal government."[15] In *U.S. v. Cruikshank* (1876), the Supreme Court overturned the convictions obtained under the Enforcement Act of 1870. Remarkably, the Court argued that the postwar amendments could only prohibit the violation of black rights by states. When individual whites violated black rights, they were subject to state, not federal, laws. This ruling effectively ended federal protection against acts of terror from blacks in the South.

Jim Crow was aided by Supreme Court rulings. In the *Civil Rights Cases* (1883), the Court took the position that the Reconstruction Amendments did not apply to private accommodations and that the federal government could not interfere with "social rights." And, of course, *Plessy* (1896) established the "separate but equal" doctrine. The Court argued, "If one race be inferior to the other socially, the Constitution of the United States cannot put them on the same plane."[16]

LIBERAL CAPITULATION AND BLACK POLITICS: PHASE I

As blacks' gains were rolled back, the "liberals" in the North increasingly offered opinions regarding racial policies that mirrored the South's. First, with sights set on economic development, commentators in journals like *Harper's* and the *Atlantic Monthly* argued that black rights had to be subordinated on the grounds of the South's need for "home rule"—a first step toward regional prosperity. In the 1880s and 1890s it was common in journals like the *Nation* and *Harper's* to hear accounts of black people's innate inferiority and inability to meet the requirements of citizenship. These attitudes were helped along by Social Darwinian studies like Frederick L. Hoffman's influential *Race Traits and Tendencies of the American Negro* (1896). Hoffman argued, among other things, that black poverty "was not the result of white discrimination or lack of opportunity but stemmed directly from an innate tendency toward 'crime and immorality.' "[17]

> *Blacks played an increasingly marginal role in politics after the Compromise of 1877.*

Blacks played an increasingly marginal role in politics after the Compromise of 1877 because of procedural barriers like "literacy" and "grandfather" clauses, as well as intimidation and violence. By the last decade of the nineteenth century, black politics had accommodated to white supremacy and Jim Crow. Indeed, Booker T. Washington seized the mantle of Afro-American leadership in 1895 by promising that black people would not agitate for civil rights or make demands on the federal government; rather, black people would be self-reliant, patient, disciplined, and morally upright citizens. Washington's vision of industrialization and accommodation to Jim Crow placed him squarely within "mainstream" racial policy. This was clear when he remarked a year before *Plessy*:

The wisest among my race understand that the agitation of questions of social equality is the extremest folly.... It is important and right that the privileges of the law be ours, but it is vastly more important that we be prepared for the exercises of these privileges.[18]

THE SECOND (DE)CONSTRUCTION

Developments in national politics suggest that we may be witnessing the end of the second reconstruction. The second reconstruction began with the Civil Rights Act of 1964 and the Voting Rights Act of 1965—the culmination of more than a decade of struggle by blacks and their allies for civil rights. The Civil Rights Act forbade discrimination in most public places. It increased the power of the attorney general to protect citizens against segregation and discrimination in voting, education, and public facilities. It established a federal Community Relations Service and the more significant Equal Employment Opportunity Commission (EEOC). And, among its more controversial provisions, the Civil Rights Act required the elimination of discrimination in federally assisted programs. The Voting Rights Act of 1965 gave teeth to the Fifteenth Amendment. This act

---

Studies demonstrate that companies subject to EEOC requirements have higher levels of black employment.

---

stationed federal examiners in those individual southern counties with the worst histories of abuse. The act also required states with a history of low black participation to submit all proposed changes in election procedure to the U.S. Department of Justice for "preclearance." The Voting Rights Act had a profound impact on black voter participation. In three decades—1940–1970—black registration in southern states increased from 3.1 to 66.9 percent. Over roughly the same period of time, the number of black elected officials—city, state, and national—increased from 33 to 1,469.[19]

The late 1960s and early 1970s were periods of federal activism geared toward expanding opportunity for black Americans specifically and poor Americans generally. President Lyndon B. Johnson's Great Society began with the Economic Opportunity Act of 1964. This act created the Office of Economic Opportunity (OEO), which oversaw the establishment of new programs geared toward community development. The Economic Opportunity Act also provided day care in conjunction with other programs. Operation Head Start, for instance, had its origins in the community action programs administered by the OEO.

Affirmative action evolved through a series of executive orders, administrative policies, and court decisions. As opposed to "non-discrimination" policies that "merely enjoined employers from practicing discrimination," "affirmative action committed employers to go a step beyond non-discrimination and to *actively* seek out protected groups in employment." Historically, "good-faith efforts to increase minority representation were generally ineffective until they were backed up by specific 'goals and timetables' that, in effect, gave preference to minority applicants who met basic qualifications."[20] AT&T and the former Bell System offer a good example of the ways in which companies enacted affirmative action policies. In 1973, AT&T employed 351,000 persons nationwide in low-paying operator or clerical classifications, 95 percent of whom were women. The overwhelming majority of higher-paid craft workers (95 percent) were male, and only 6 percent of these were black. Few women or blacks were in management positions. Only after the federal government investigated the Bell System's employment practices did the company agree to raise salaries for women and blacks and to meet employment targets for these groups.

Affirmative action propelled millions of Afro-Americans into all levels of the labor force. Studies demonstrate that companies subject to EEOC requirements have higher levels of black employment than do companies not under scrutiny. Furthermore, the occupational spheres where blacks are now best represented—"in government service, major blue-collar occupations, corporate management, and the professions—are all areas where vigorous affirmative action programs have been in place over the past two decades."[21]

In a reversal of political momentum similar in some ways to that of the late part of last century, the Supreme Court under Chief Justice William Rehnquist began to pull the teeth out of laws designed to achieve racial equality. The Court first narrowed the terms under which affirmative action programs could legitimately exist. The *Bakke* (1978) decision outlawed the use of quotas. And in *Richmond v. Croson* (1989), the Court found that a set-aside program was deficient on the grounds that (1) there was no direct evidence that the city's contractors had discriminated against minority-owned subcontractors; and (2) it was inappropriate to use national statistics of racial discrimination in the construction industry as a basis for establishing the set-aside program.

The Court has also made it more difficult for blacks to elect representatives by challenging the constitutionality of black or minority-majority districts designed to promote minority representation in Congress. *Shaw v. Reno* (1993) was perhaps the most significant decision regarding black-majority districts. Writing for the majority, Justice Sandra Day O'Connor argued that appellants had stated a claim under the Equal Protection clause by alleging that the North Carolina General Assembly adopted a reapportionment scheme so irrational on its face that it could be understood only as an effort to segregate voters into separate voting districts because of their race.[22] The majority rejected the idea that "race" can be an appropriate criterion in a context of historical inequity.

Regarding employment discrimination, the Court has also shifted to the right. In *Wards Cove Packing Company, Inc. v. Frank Antonio* (1989), the Court rejected statistics used by minority employees that hiring and promotion practices had accounted for their disparate positions in relation to white employees. The Court also argued that the burden of proof should not shift to the employer but should remain with the plaintiff.

In these decisions, the Rehnquist Court has chipped away at the concrete methods that minority-majority districting and affirmative action laws used to achieve representation and parity. And, in so doing, the Court has responded to broader trends in national politics, particularly the civil rights orientation of the Bush and Reagan administrations.

Indeed, Ronald Reagan did not wish simply to ignore civil rights programs; he sought to *reduce* government's role in the enforcement and administration of them. For instance, "almost immediately upon assuming office in January 1981, Reagan suspended Carter's affirmative action guidelines and reduced their enforcement."[23] That same year, Reagan also decreased the number of contractors that were required to have affirmative action plans. Small firms, Reagan argued, did not need to comply. Reagan's Omnibus Budget Reconciliation Act removed 400,000 individuals from the food stamp program. It reduced or eliminated welfare and Medicaid benefits for the working poor. It also eliminated the entire "public service jobs program, and the minimum benefit for low-income Social Security recipients, ended the modest death benefit, and phased out benefits for older children of deceased workers."[24]

Between 1981 and 1992 the federal budget dropped steeply in almost all issue areas: 40 percent for community development, 63 percent for job training, and 82 percent for subsidized housing.[25] The cuts disproportionately affected black Americans.

A RACIAL REALIGNMENT

This reversal toward conservatism was fueled by a "conversion" of some traditional supporters of the Democratic Party based on a backlash against programs of Johnson's Great Society and more race-specific efforts like affirmative action and busing. Democrats had long understood the potential costs of supporting civil rights. In fact, the New Deal's origins had depended upon a number of agreements that would not upset the racial caste system of the South.[26] President Franklin D. Roosevelt needed southern congressmen to move his programs through key House and Senate committees. Southern congressmen, however, opposed *any* program "that would grant cash directly to black workers, because direct cash could undermine the entire foundation of the plantation economy." Hence the core programs of the Social Security Act left out agricultural workers and domestic servants, the occupational spheres where most black men and women worked.[27]

The Civil Rights and Voting Rights Acts and Johnson's War on Poverty were, in effect,

Table 10.1

Democratic Percentage of White Vote in the Presidential Election by Ethnicity and Region, 1972–1996

	1972	1976	1980	1984	1988	1992	1996
All Whites	31%	47%	36%	35%	40%	39%	43%
Protestants	22	41	31	27	33	33	36
Catholics	44	54	42	45	47	44	53
Jews	64	64	45	67	64	80	78
From the East	34	49	38	42	45	36	51
From the Midwest	32	46	37	35	42	40	45
From the South	23	47	35	28	32	34	36
From the West	36	44	32	33	41	39	43

Table 10.2

Republican Percentage of White Vote in the Presidential Election by Ethnicity and Region, 1972–1996

	1972	1976	1980	1984	1988	1992	1996
All Whites	67%	52%	56%	64%	59%	40%	46%
Protestants	76	58	63	72	66	47	53
Catholics	54	44	50	54	52	35	37
Jews	34	34	39	31	35	11	16
From the East	65	50	52	57	54	36	37
From the Midwest	65	52	55	64	57	39	43
From the South	76	52	61	71	67	49	56
From the West	60	54	55	66	58	37	44

Source: "Portrait of the Electorate," *New York Times,* November 10, 1996.

the Freedmen's Bureaus of the 1960s. And, where "the New Deal had excluded African Americans, the War on Poverty would favor them." The War on Poverty sought to integrate blacks into local politics, local job markets, and local housing markets.[28] Under the OEO, Community Action Agencies channeled resources into civil rights organizations, job and educational programs, and similar efforts. By so doing, the War on Poverty bypassed the traditional political elites that had effectively locked blacks out.

Hence, the Johnson administration's support of the civil rights cause in 1964 and the Republicans' support of "home rule" started the process in which white southern Democrats turned Republican, and the Republican Party essentially abandoned liberalism. By 1972, with George McGovern's nomination, the process of racial realignment was complete. Table 10.1 shows the percentage of whites who have supported Democratic presidential candidates from 1972 to 1996. During this same period, whites have consistently thrown their weight to Republican candidates, as shown in Table 10.2.

And, of course, over the same period of time, blacks have represented the most solidly Democratic constituency.

LIBERAL CAPITULATION AND BLACK POLITICS: PHASE II

The defeat in 1984 and 1988 of the Democratic Party's nominees for president, Walter Mondale and Michael Dukakis, led many analysts and Democratic Party strategists to the conclusion that the party's "liberalism" and association with "special interest groups"—blacks in particular—was no longer good strategy. A study conducted by Stanley Greenberg in 1985 concluded that the party's identification with blacks was a problem:

> These white Democratic defectors express a profound distaste for blacks, a sentiment that pervades almost everything they think about government and politics. . . . Blacks constitute the explanation for their [white defectors'] vulnerability for almost everything that has gone wrong in their lives; not being black is what constitutes being middle class; not living with blacks is what makes a neighborhood a decent place to live. . . . Ronald Reagan's image [was] formed against this backdrop. . . . Reagan represented a determined consistency and an aspiration to unity and pride.[29]

Subsequent analyses built upon this idea to reach one conclusion: the Democratic Party needed to distance itself from blacks and their interests and recast itself as the party of the white middle class. A 1989 study by the Progressive Policy Institute, the research arm of the Democratic Leadership Council, also argued that the party needed to reconnect with the middle class.[30]

President Clinton has relied on this strategy. Clinton's domestic policy agenda has not, and probably will not, tackle issues of pressing concern to the black poor. As a "New Democrat," Clinton has distanced himself from the tradition of New Deal liberalism, declaring that the "era of big government is over." In his first term, Clinton managed to combine this neoliberal posture with appeals to egalitarian commitments. But he is clearly a centrist. His health care reform proposal, support for NAFTA and GATT, his anticrime and antiterrorism legislation, and his signing of the welfare bill solidified his centrist credentials.

Furthermore, black Americans may interpret several of Clinton's gestures as racially coded. He "got tough on crime" in 1992 when he oversaw the execution of the black, mentally impaired convict Ricky Ray Rector. And he signed the welfare reform bill while being flanked by two black women. This act can be seen as drawing on a racist stereotype—that black women make up the majority of welfare recipients. In the 1996 election, Clinton gave tepid support to affirmative action through his pledge to "mend it, not end it." Ironically, it took GOP vice presidential candidate Jack Kemp to bring racial policies to the fore, spe-

The Million Man March was noteworthy because of its liberal/conservative view of black problems.

cifically affirmative action and "empowerment zones" for inner cities.

Robert Smith notes that in post–civil rights opinion poll data, the majority of whites consistently, and wrongly, view blacks as more prone to crime and violence than whites, more lazy, more sexually promiscuous, and lacking in family values.[31] This is a picture of black America that the Right has painted in literally thousands of forms—from *Wall Street Journal* editorials to the columns of George Will and the speeches of Rush Limbaugh.[32]

There is, in fact, a liberal tradition arguing that aberrant black behavior is an independent cause of black poverty. The most significant formulation of this sort appeared in Daniel Patrick Moynihan's controversial "The Negro Family: The Case for National Action" (1965). This report offered mountains of evidence showing high rates of divorce, illegitimacy, and female-headed households. More importantly, Moynihan suggested that this "pathology" had a dynamic all its own—based on "the disintegration of the Negro family"—independent of joblessness and poverty. The implication of Moynihan's study was the view of "inner-city poverty as driven by behavior defects and social pathology among the poor themselves, and explicitly in ways linked to black women's reproductive activity."[33] Even before Moynihan's report, he and Nathan Glazer had reached similar conclusions about black Americans' lack of comparative success. "It was the heritage of two hundred years of slavery" that deformed family and community life, making it more difficult for blacks to "make use of a free educational system to advance into higher occupations."[34] In a more recent article, Glazer remarked that policy cannot solve "the social and personal problems of people who . . . are engaged in self-destructive behavior—resisting schools, [and] taking to drugs and crime."[35]

99

The same focus has cohered around analyses of the so-called "underclass" that began during the Reagan era. The underclass is said to comprise between 10 and 20 percent of the poor. Furthermore, according to liberal analysts like Isabel Sawhill and former Clinton appointee David Ellwood, this group suffers in part because their values differ from those of the mainstream.[36] Joe Klein offered the latest spin on the underclass in an October issue of the *New Republic*. Here Klein criticized liberals like William Julius Wilson for denying the fact that poor black people's bad behavior and attitudes, not lack of jobs, are the real cause of inner-city poverty. Klein argued, "They are isolated from us; they have different values. And it seems very clear that their problems were neither entirely caused by the loss of work, nor will they be entirely solved by government action." He notes at another point that, in inner cities across America, "the rudiments of civilization have vanished like cellophane on fire."[37] Such theories have deep roots in American policy discourse. A similar focus on "deviance" and family "disorganization" can be seen in sociological studies beginning in the early decades of this century.

Ironically, the only recent and significant stirring in black politics—the October 1995 Million Man March—was most noteworthy because of the liberal/conservative view of black problems and their solutions that it apparently adopted. The Million Man March may explain the upsurge in black male voting from 1992 (roughly 3 million to 4.8 million) as well as relatively high-level support for the GOP in House races.[38]

Indeed, Louis Farrakhan's rise to power follows the latter-day version of the deconstruction of Reconstruction. As conservatives have undermined black political gains of the 1960s, and as conditions have worsened for large portions of the Afro-American population, Farrakhan has risen as the lone "radical" voice, champion of the oppressed and marginalized. Yet, as many have noted, Farrakhan's ascension is also connected to his social vision—his political and economic agenda blends smoothly into contemporary conservative political thought. When black men pledged to take greater responsibility for their lives, the words echoed the accommodationism of Booker T. Washington and his supporters 100 years ago.

Like Washington, Farrakhan is not bothered by racial segregation. Instead, he invites political acquiescence while promoting moral rehabilitation and strict discipline. His anti-Semitism and his unorthodox version of Islam are perhaps the obstacles that prevent Farrakhan from becoming a Booker T. Washington–like power broker.

CONCLUSION: LESSONS PAST AND PRESENT

Historically, the only times that national parties have confronted the legacy of racism have come in the aftermath of enormous social upheavals: the Civil War and the civil rights movement. During the first Reconstruction, Republicans realized that they needed the political participation of the freedmen to maintain their hegemony. After 1877, however, the Republican Party adopted schemes that would attract southern white men to Republicanism.[39] This, Republicans knew, was the only way they could hope to win power over Democrats.

The civil rights movement triggered the second reconstruction in the 1960s, and for both Presidents Kennedy and Johnson the Afro-American vote was key. But at least since the New Deal, Democratic calculations have been not unlike those of Republicans at the end of the last century. The argument runs like this: Since America is too racist to support programs targeted specifically for blacks, highlighting racial issues drives whites out of the Democratic Party. From the New Deal forward, Democrats seem to have defended their wavering commitments to racial equality on these grounds.

Black voters may feel they have too few choices now, but that need not remain true. They could consider a third-party alternative—such as the Labor Party, the New Party, or an independent black party—that would work toward policies that address their concerns. Easier registration and campaign finance reform could also further their cause.

ENDNOTES

1. "Portrait of the Electorate," *New York Times,* November 10, 1996.
2. Carol M. Swain, *Black Faces, Black Interests: The Representation of African Americans in*

Congress (Cambridge, MA: Harvard University Press, 1993), p. 7.

3. Edward N. Wolff, *Top Heavy: The Increasing Inequality of Wealth in America and What Can Be Done about It* (New York: New Press, 1996), pp. 1–3.

4. Figures come from the Bureau of Labor Statistics and are cited in Holly Sklar, *Chaos or Community? Seeking Solutions, Not Scapegoats for Bad Economics* (Boston: South End Press, 1995), p. 62.

5. See "Race in the United States: It's Not a Matter of Black and White," *The Public Perspective,* Volume 7, Number 2, February/March 1996, pp. 26–27.

6. John Hope Franklin and Alfred A. Moss Jr., *From Slavery to Freedom: A History of African Americans,* 7th ed. (New York: McGraw-Hill, 1994), p. 239.

7. Swain, *Black Faces, Black Interests,* pp. 21–23.

8. Franklin and Moss, *From Slavery to Freedom,* p. 242. In 1874 Bruce was elected to a full term. It wasn't until the election of Edward Brooke in 1966 that another black would be elected again.

9. Eric Foner, *A Short History of Reconstruction: 1863–1877* (New York: Harper & Row, 1990), p. 31.

10. Franklin and Moss, *From Slavery to Freedom,* p. 249.

11. Steven A. Shull, *A Kinder Gentler Racism? The Reagan-Bush Civil Rights Legacy* (Armonk, NY: M. E. Sharpe, 1993), pp. 32–33.

12. Foner, *A Short History of Reconstruction,* p. 122.

13. Foner, *A Short History of Reconstruction,* p. 251.

14. Franklin and Moss, *From Slavery to Freedom,* p. 251.

15. Foner, *A Short History of Reconstruction,* p. 224.

16. Taken from Sheldon Goldman, *Constitutional Law: Cases and Essays* (New York: Harper & Row, 1987), p. 794.

17. George M. Fredrickson, *The Black Image in the White Mind: The Debate on Afro-American Character and Destiny, 1817–1914* (Middletown, CT: Wesleyan University Press, 1971), p. 251.

18. Booker T. Washington, *Up from Slavery* (New York: Oxford University Press, 1995), p. 131.

19. *A Common Destiny: Blacks and American Society* (Washington, DC: National Academy Press, 1989), pp. 225–238.

20. Stephen Steinberg, *Turning Back: The Retreat from Racial Justice in American Thought and Policy* (Boston: Beacon Press, 1995), p. 165.

21. Steinberg, *Turning Back,* p. 167.

22. Quoted in Michael W. Combs, "The Supreme Court, African Americans, and Public Policy: Changes and Transformations," in Huey L. Perry and Wayne Parent (eds.), *Blacks and the American Political System* (Miami, FL: University Press of Florida, 1995), p. 193.

23. Shull, *A Kinder Gentler Racism,* p. 183.

24. Jill Quadagno, *The Color of Welfare: How Racism Undermined the War on Poverty* (New York: Oxford University Press, 1994), p. 162.

25. Shull, *A Kinder Gentler Racism,* p. 191.

26. Charles Hamilton, "Minority Politics and 'Political Realities' in American Politics," in *The Democrats Must Lead* (San Francisco: Westview Press, 1992), p. 149.

27. Quadagno, *The Color of Welfare,* p. 21.

28. Quadagno, *The Color of Welfare,* p. 31.

29. Quoted in Thomas Byrne Edsall and Mary D. Edsall, *Chain Reaction: The Impact of Race, Rights, and Taxes on American Politics* (New York: W. W. Norton, 1991), p. 182.

30. Robert C. Smith, *We Have No Leaders: African Americans in the Post–Civil Rights Era* (Albany, NY: State University of Albany Press, 1996), p. 256.

31. Smith, *We Have No Leaders,* p. 264.

32. Lewis Lapham, "Reactionary Chic: How the Nineties Right Recycles the Bombast of the Sixties Left," *Harper's Magazine,* March 1995, pp. 39–42.

33. Adolph Reed Jr., "Dissing the Underclass," *The Progressive,* December 1996, p. 21.

34. Quoted in Steinberg, *Turning Back,* p. 105.

35. Quoted in Steinberg, *Turning Back,* p. 239.

36. Adolph Reed Jr., "The Underclass as Myth and Symbol: The Poverty of Discourse about Poverty," in *Radical America,* vol. 24, January 1992.

37. Joe Klein, "The True Disadvantage," *The New Republic,* October 28, 1996, p. 33.

38. David A. Bositis, "Blacks and the 1996 Elections: A Preliminary Analysis," November 13, 1996.

39. Stanley P. Hirshon, *Farewell to the Bloody Shirt: Northern Republicans and the Southern Negro, 1877–1893* (Bloomington, IN: Indiana University Press, 1962), p. 253.

Chapter Eleven

The Politics of Inclusion: Ethnics in the 1996 Election

John A. Kromkowski

Like Jimmy Carter before him, Bill Clinton became president without winning the majority of the "white" vote. In order to achieve a national victory, both men needed more than 80 percent of the 16 percent of the electorate that the exit polls designate as "racial/ethnic" voters. Polls, the media, and the prevailing conventions of political science have framed the racial/ethnic vote as those in the following categories: black, Hispanic, Asian, and Jewish. Table 11.1 arrays data by the percentage of ethnic/religious populations that voted for the winning party from 1972 to 1996.

White Protestants have consistently supported the Republican Party for the last quarter century, and Catholic, Jewish, black, and Hispanic voters have supported the Democratic Party, except for a dip in Catholic support to 44 percent in 1992. These findings indicate an embedded, structural affinity within the electorate that should not be undervalued as a dimension of American politics. The U.S. Census generally uses categories found in Table 11.2.

Table 11.3 provides additional measures of voters by region and ethnic/religious categories. These data indicate declining participation among whites and white Protestants; increases in Catholic, Hispanic, Asian, and black voters, except for 1992; declines in the East and Midwest, and increases in the West and South. Census data and the categories used in the exit polls about voters, their levels of support for candidates and the winning party, their regional distributions, and their respective magnitudes in the actual vote are the broad strokes that shape much of our political discourse. Such data prompt commentators to leap to the conclusion that the presidential election of 1996 was

Table 11.1

Percentage of Vote for Winning Party and Ethnic/Religious Populations

Year	1996	1992	1988	1984	1980	1976	1972
Party	D	D	R	R	R	D	R
White Protestant	36	33	66	72	63	41	76
Catholic	53	44	52	54	50	54	54
Jewish	78	80	35	31	39	64	34
Born-Again	XX	23	81	80	63	XX	XX
White	43	39	59	64	56	47	67
Black	84	83	12	9	11	83	18
Hispanic	72	61	30	37	33	76	35
Asian	43	31	XX	XX	XX	XX	XX

Source: NCUEA Exit Poll Data File.

Table 11.2

Exit Poll Data by Traditional Census Bureau Categories

Year	Candidate	Ethnic/Racial Categories				
		Black	Hispanic	Asian	White	Other
1996	Clinton/Gore	84	72	42	44	64
	Dole/Kemp	12	21	49	45	23
	Perot/Choate	9	5	8	9	9
1992	Clinton/Gore	83	61	NA	39	NA
	Bush/Quayle	10	25	NA	40	NA
	Perot/Stockdale	7	14	NA	20	NA
1988	Dukakis/Bentsen	89	70	NA	40	NA
	Bush/Quayle	11	30	NA	60	NA
1984	Mondale/Ferraro	91	66	NA	34	NA
	Reagan/Bush	9	34	NA	66	NA
1980	Carter/Mondale	83	56	NA	36	NA
	Reagan/Bush	14	37	NA	56	NA
	Anderson/Lucey	3	7	NA	8	NA
1976	Carter/Mondale	83	82	NA	48	NA
	Ford/Dole	17	18	NA	52	NA

Source: NCUEA Exit Poll Data File.

decided by the minority and the ethnic vote. But this judgment blurs the fact that most of the states with the highest proportion of African Americans (Alabama, Mississippi, Georgia, North Carolina, South Carolina, and Virginia) voted for Bob Dole, as well as the fact that there has been no meaningful change in the African American or Jewish voting patterns since 1972.

Table 11.4 presents a new, quantitative foundation for fuller ethnic disaggregation and a contrasting view of American ethnicities. The new politics of pluralism and the uses of such data require a fresh explanatory model for the interaction of ethnicities and elections.

The collection of ancestry data in Table 11.5 from the U.S. Census for 1990 provides an important set of basic information about the American polity. Such measures of the electorate continue because ethnicity is an important dimension of personal and group identity. But

Race is a too-broad category that does not explain political phenomena well.

constructing a model of the interaction of ethnicity and politics is not simple. The competing models of "race" and the more fluid ethnicity begin with contrasting views: the former is dichotomous, while the latter is pluralistic.

Moreover, if the old concept of race or majority/minority can only reveal that African Americans tend to vote Democratic, this model has little to say about the elections of the last five presidents. Race is a too-broad category that does not explain political phenomena well, and it is time to reconsider race and ethnicity as descriptive terms.

Table 11.3

**Exit Poll Population: Race/Ethnic/
Religious Profile of the Percentage
of Total Vote**

Race/Ethnic	'96	'92	'88	'84
White	83	87	85	86
Black	10	08	10	10
Hispanic	05	03	03	03
Asian	01	01	XX	XX
White Protestant	46	49	48	51
Catholic	29	27	28	26
Jewish	03	04	04	03
Born-Again	NA	17	09	15
Region				
East	23	24	25	24
Midwest	26	27	28	28
South	30	30	28	29
West	20	20	19	18
Whites in East	20	21	21	22
Blacks in East	02	02	02	02
Whites in Midwest	24	25	25	25
Blacks in Midwest	02	02	02	03
Whites in South	23	24	23	25
Blacks in South	05	04	04	04
Whites in West	16	16	15	15
Blacks in West	01	01	02	XX

Source: NCUEA Exit Poll Data File.

The extent of regional variation in ethnicity and its potential impact on the nation's political culture, electoral strategies, and campaign tactics are considerable. One can discern possible patterns of ethnic group politics—a group voting bloc, the prospect of group-specific issues, combinations of conflict and convergence among groups.

Presidential elections are decided by a winner-take-all system for each state. But the patterns of ethnicities in each congressional district provide a meaningful method of viewing how support for each candidate coalesces. So widespread is the presence of ethnic groups that only one congressional district, KY 5, does not have a meaningful concentration of any of the ten groups listed in Table 11.5.

The study of ethnicity in American politics requires some understanding of variation. For example, suppose you take 50 marbles from a batch of 4,000 marbles that is known to be a mixture of 20 percent red and 80 percent white. Your sample is highly unlikely to consist of 10 red marbles and 40 white ones. Instead, you can only predict that the percentage of red marbles in your sample will fall within certain control limits, probably 1 and 19. Applying this methodology to the U.S. Census data regarding ethnicity in congressional districts, we find that American ethnic demography is remarkably unmixed. Two political strategies can be expected to emerge: division/wedge-driving or inclusion/addition.

THE POLITICS OF ADDITION

In 1992, Clinton and vice-presidential candidate Al Gore initiated the politics of inclusion and the celebration of diversity, campaign tactics that enabled the Democrats to regain the presidency. The politics of inclusion was a strategy that overcame the divisions and fragmentation that had plagued the Democratic Party and made it vulnerable to the Republican tactic of using wedge issues to change the southern states into Republicans strongholds. In 1992 Clinton and Gore reclaimed the border states from which they hailed. Their tactics of outreach to ethnic concentrations that had previously been neglected by national Democrats enabled them to fashion a coalition that was committed to the new politics of inclusion. This campaign doctrine strengthened the relationships of voters of Eastern and Southern European descent to congressional Democrats. Moreover, the politics of inclusion played well in California, owing to its amenability to niche media campaigning and its ethnically pluralistic composition. Other western states with Democratic affinities also responded to the rhetoric of diversity. And, extensive attention to Cuban Americans in 1996 increased their votes for Clinton by 13 percent, which helped achieve the victory in Florida.

Clinton's doctrine of inclusivity enabled him as no other Democratic candidate for the presidency since Jimmy Carter to hold the crucial center of electoral support among northern Catholic urban ethnics. As practiced by Clinton and Gore, the politics of inclusion is pragmatic. Combining one designation of the racial/ethnic electorate—blacks, Hispanics, Jews, and Asians—

Table 11.4

Measurement of Ethnicity in America, U.S. Census 1990, 1980, 1970

Group	1990	1980	1970
English	32,652,000	49,598,035	2,465,050
German	57,947,000	49,224,146	3,622,035
Irish	38,736,000	40,165,702	1,450,220
French	10,321,000	12,892,246	343,367
Italian	14,665,000	12,183,246	4,240,779
Scottish	5,943,000	10,048,816	NA
Polish	9,366,000	8,228,037	2,374,244
Mexican	11,586,000	7,692,619	NA
Native American	7,227,000	6,715,819	763,594
Dutch	6,227,000	6,304,499	NA
Swedish	4,681,000	4,345,392	806,138
Norwegian	3,869,000	3,453,839	614,649
Czech	1,296,000	1,892,456	759,527
Hungarian	1,582,000	1,776,902	603,668
Welsh	2,033,000	1,664,598	NA
Portuguese	1,153,000	1,024,351	NA
Greek	1,110,000	959,856	434,571
French-Canadian	2,167,000	780,488	NA
Slovak	1,883,000	776,806	NA
Lithuanian	812,000	742,776	330,977
Ukrainian	741,000	730,056	NA
Finnish	659,000	615,872	NA
Canadian	550,000	456,212	3,034,556
Yugoslavian	260,000	360,174	447,271
Croatian	544,000	252,970	NA
Armenian	308,000	212,621	NA
Slovene	124,000	126,463	NA
Serbian	117,000	100,941	NA
Asian	7,226,000	3,726,440	NA
Black	29,930,000	26,482,349	NA
White	199,827,000	189,035,349	NA
Hispanic	21,900,000	NA	NA

Source: U.S. Census Bureau Ancestry Data File.

with other ethnic populations that are designated as white can mobilize an electoral majority in the northeastern and midwestern states.

ETHNICITY REMAINS FLUID

Ethnicity has been used to describe varied, ill-defined, and sometimes contradictory sets of experiences and identities. Along with black, Hispanic, and Asian populations, American eth-nicities include African Americans, Mexican Americans, Cuban Americans, Japanese Americans, Arab Americans, Italian Americans, Polish Americans, Irish Americans, German Americans, Greek Americans, and many other groups that are woven into the patchwork of citizenship from which the American polity draws its spirit and purposes.

The confusion arises because ethnicity is contextual: Its meaning changes for each group with time and circumstances. In the United States,

Table 11.5

Ancestry Data for 1990

Group	National Percentage	Number of Congressional Districts with Meaningfully High Percentage
African American	9.6	141
American Indian	3.5	14
Asian American	2.9	105
English American	13.1	226
French American	4.1	48
German American	23.3	186
Hispanic American	8.8	127
Irish American	15.6	225
Italian American	5.9	135
Polish American	3.8	131

Source: NCUEA U.S. Census Data File.

ethnicity is one of the modern identities developed by the former peasants, slaves, indentured workers, and migrants who have poured into the United States during the last three centuries. Although the nation has not had an established religion since the end of colonial times, its population was once largely Protestant. Buddhist, Hindu, and Islamic immigrants have now joined the Catholics, other Christians, and Jews who constitute the overwhelming majority of the American population. This nation of immigrants can be fashioned into various majority and minority configurations. For most immigrants, their ethnicity replaced loyalty to village or region as the reference point around which they organized their lives and located their families in their new communities in America. The intersection of ethnic communities with the American polity in the electoral process includes the historical development of political

parties, but it also points to the wider range of ethnic articulations: ethnicity in the electorate, ethnicity in government, and ethnic representatives within political parties and presidential campaigns.

Analyses of recent campaigns have often marginalized ethnicity to accounts of ethnic faux pas.

When ethnic groups and ethnic leaders attempt to influence politics and policy, they behave as interest groups and issue constituencies. They use various approaches and forms of participation: they raise big money for candidates and political parties; provide parties with blocs of voters; and move specific foreign and/or domestic policy issues into the agenda-setting process by framing them as national needs, goals, or threats.

IS THERE AN AVERAGE AMERICAN?

The following data compiled by the National Opinion Research Center were commissioned by the National Italian American Foundation (NIAF). NIAF, along with the National Center for Urban Ethnic Affairs (NCUEA), has sponsored forums designed to seek issues common to various ethnic groups and to promote the concept of pluralism. Although ethnicity has no legal or constitutional status, it is a crucial social and cultural factor.[1]

The data found in Tables 11.6 and 11.7 indicate voter views and opinions that are not typically disaggregated by ancestral group. Thus, they provide a sense of how ethnic tendencies may have electoral relevance. These tables report findings regarding such 1996 issues as medical costs, welfare, and taxation, along with such political affinities as party identification, ideology, confidence in government, and election participation. In effect, these tables offer a peek behind the curtain of voters' ap-

Table 11.6

Support for Government Programs and Taxation by Ethnic Groups (1988–1994)

A. Government Should Help Pay Medical Costs (% Agreeing)		C. Government Should Reduce Income Differences (% Agreeing)	
Black	70.4	Black	34.7
Jewish	62.5	Other	31.3
Native American	57.6	Native American	28.9
Eastern European	57.5	Hispanic	28.6
Italian	57.4	Other White	21.3
Hispanic	56.4	Italian	20.9
Asian	56.1	French	20.5
Scandinavian	55.0	Asian	19.8
Other	52.9	Irish	18.5
French	52.5	Eastern European	18.1
Polish	51.9	Scandinavian	17.5
German	47.5	Polish	15.9
Other White	47.0	German	15.7
British	44.8	British	14.1
		Jewish	13.3
Average	51.8		
		Average	20.6

B. Government Should Help the Poor (% Agreeing)		D. Federal Income Taxes Are Too High (% Agreeing)	
Black	51.9		
Hispanic	39.9	Polish	71.3
Other	39.1	Black	67.9
Asian	38.5	Italian	67.4
Native American	32.0	Native American	65.8
Scandinavian	31.8	Other	65.2
Italian	31.7	Jewish	65.0
Jewish	30.1	Hispanic	63.5
Other White	28.9	French	62.1
French	27.8	Other White	58.9
Polish	25.8	German	58.8
Irish	25.5	Asian	57.9
Eastern European	24.9	Irish	57.7
German	24.7	British	57.0
British	23.7	Eastern European	56.0
		Scandinavian	54.2
Average	30.0		
		Average	60.6

Source: NAIF, 1996, compiled from National Opinion Research Center survey results.

parent homogeneity, and they may reacquaint political science with the rich texture of electoral demography. That ethnic factors may be more systematically reviewed than in the past is due partly to the availability of such data and more importantly to the persistence of ethnicity in the electorate. The reemergence of ethnicity as a feature of niche-focused campaigning argues for the practice of the politics of inclusion and for a new politics of pluralism.

ETHNIC POLITICS: CONNECTING WITH VOTERS AS PEOPLE

Presidential campaigns dread the ethnic gaffe that will appear on the nightly news or the blunder that arouses scorn among opinion leaders and voters who are influential in ethnic groups. When energized and impassioned, such voting blocs can determine the outcome in close elec-

(Continued on p. 109)

Table 11.7

Politics by Ethnic Groups (1988 –1994)

A. Party Identification (% Republican)

British	43.0
German	39.5
Italian	36.9
Scandinavian	34.5
Irish	32.6
Other White	32.3
Eastern European	31.8
French	29.6
Polish	25.6
Native American	21.2
Asian	20.3
Hispanic	19.7
Other	18.1
Jewish	15.6
Black	06.6
Average	30.6

B1. Vote for President in 1988 Elections (% Bush)

German	71.7
British	70.9
Other White	68.4
Eastern European	66.8
French	65.9
Irish	64.4
Italian	63.2
Polish	62.0
Scandinavian	54.9
Other	53.1
Native American	50.7
Hispanic	49.5
Asian	47.9
Jewish	29.0
Black	19.2
Average	61.2

B2. Vote for President in 1992 Election
(% Voting for Candidates)

	Bush	Clinton	Perot
French	52.8	33.9	13.2
British	49.8	32.5	17.3
Asian	49.2	36.8	14.0
German	45.0	33.2	21.4
Italian	44.1	37.8	18.2
Irish	39.7	41.2	18.1
Other White	38.4	38.1	22.7
Polish	33.8	39.0	26.4
Native American	29.1	48.8	21.5
Hispanic	27.8	57.7	11.9
Scandinavian	31.6	42.9	24.5
Eastern European	26.6	49.0	24.4
Jewish	21.2	73.0	05.8
Other	18.6	66.4	14.9
Black	05.3	91.8	02.7
Average	36.8	44.8	14.9

C. Political Ideology (% Conservative)

British	43.6
Scandinavian	40.8
Eastern European	39.7
German	39.6
French	37.4
Other White	36.4
Italian	34.4
Native American	34.1
Asian	33.9
Irish	32.4
Polish	29.5
Other	28.1
Hispanic	25.8
Black	25.6
Jewish	18.6
Average	35.5

D. Confidence in the Executive Branch of the Government (% Great Deal)

Asian	29.9
Hispanic	27.4
Eastern European	24.3
Polish	22.3
Jewish	19.6
Irish	17.9
British	17.9
Italian	17.6
Other White	17.2
German	17.2
Black	16.1
Scandinavian	15.5
French	14.1
Native American	13.6
Other	13.5
Average	17.7

E. Confidence in Congress (% Great Deal)

Hispanic	23.6
Asian	21.1
Other	20.6
Italian	18.4
Eastern European	17.7
Jewish	16.5
Black	15.9
French	12.9
Scandinavian	12.3
Irish	12.3
Other White	11.7
German	11.2
British	10.5
Native American	10.5
Polish	09.7
Average	13.0

F. Government Officials Don't Care about the
Average Person (% Agreeing)

Native American	80.6
Other	80.0
Black	76.3
French	72.8
Italian	71.9
Hispanic	71.6
Eastern European	70.4
Other White	70.2
German	67.9
Polish	67.8
British	67.1
Asian	66.2
Scandinavian	65.4
Jewish	64.3
Average	70.9

G1. Voted in 1988 Presidential Election (% Yes)

Jewish	82.1
Eastern European	79.2
British	74.8
Irish	70.7
Scandinavian	69.9
German	68.4
Polish	67.0
French	66.8
Other White	60.1
Italian	59.2
Black	59.0
Native American	53.5
Hispanic	37.4
Other	32.2
Asian	17.0
Average	63.9

G2. Vote in 1992 Presidential Election (% Yes)

Jewish	84.9
Polish	81.6
British	77.4
Scandinavian	76.8
Irish	75.4
German	70.5
Italian	66.6
Black	65.8
Other White	65.4
French	64.9
Native American	56.8
Asian	47.0
Hispanic	45.2
Other	33.8
Average	68.5

H. Membership in Political Organizations
(% Yes, Member)

Polish	5.8
British	5.7
Jewish	5.2
Eastern European	4.4
French	4.0
Irish	3.9
Other White	3.8
German	3.7
Scandinavian	3.5
Hispanic	3.3
Black	3.0
Native American	2.6
Other	1.5
Italian	1.1
Asian	0.8
Average	3.9

Source: NAIF, 1996, compiled from National Opinion Research Center survey results.

tions. Analyses of recent presidential campaigns have often marginalized ethnicity to accounts of ethnic faux pas—Jimmy Carter saying "I"-talians in his acceptance speech; Jerry Ford eating the husk of a tamale at a Mexican American campaign rally; George McGovern asking for milk with his kosher hot dog in Queens; Jesse Jackson referring to New York as Hymietown; George Bush enraging Ukrainian Americans by urging Ukraine to stick with Gorbachev and the "new world order." The rise of ethnic consciousness and the phrase "political correctness" prompt some to wonder whether Tip O'Neill erred when he claimed "All politics is local"; perhaps he should have said "All politics is ethnic."

Bill Clinton's 1992 chastisement of Sister Souljay at the Rainbow Coalition Convention enraged some, as did Bob Dole's refusal to attend the NAACP Convention in 1996. In the 1992 encounter, Sister Souljay's fundamentalist race consciousness and critique of authority were attacked. Not only did Dole fail to attend the NAACP Annual Meeting but he attended a Slovak American commemoration of Slovakia's independence rather than speaking at the U.S. Conference of Mayors/League of Cities annual meeting. Both meetings were held during the same week in Cleveland. Dole's attention to Slovak Americans in Ohio may have been good retail politics for his campaign in that state, which almost always votes for the winning candidate in presidential elections. But the impact of his efforts to capture this bellwether state reinforced the domestic policy gap and to some extent the ethnic gap in Ohio. The implication was to diminish the significance of urban voters.

Dole voters ranked issues in the following order: taxes—75 percent, foreign policy—60 percent, the deficit—53 percent, and crime and drugs—48 percent. Clinton voters generally had other issues that mattered most to them: education—79 percent, Medicare and Social Security—69 percent, economy/jobs—60 percent, and crime and drugs—42 percent. That is, except for crime and drugs, the issue matrices of the two candidates were mirror opposites of each other—the lowest priorities for Clinton voters were the highest priorities for Dole voters.

The Republican Convention attempted to announce its affinity with ethnic groups. The selection of the Hon. Susan Molinari as keynote speaker had particular meaning for ethnic groups, as well as for women. Molinari's first political work was for the Republican National Committee in the 1980s, when she was in charge of ethnic outreach and successfully recruited many Reagan Democrats to play active roles in the party. Colin Powell's convention speech played a similar role. Following the convention, the Dole campaign activated a Coalitions Division composed of four sectors, each of which focused on issues of ethnic concern. The following groups and related issues were featured as talking points for volunteers and in newsletters:

- Hispanic Americans: immigration policy/anti-immigrant sentiment, welfare reform, education, and the illegal-alien policy.
- Asian Americans: immigration, education, affirmative action, racial issues, crime and drugs, small business policy, and welfare.
- Eastern European Americans: crime, education, tax cuts, supporting NATO entrance for Poland, the Czech Republic, and Hungary, and the continuation of foreign aid to emerging democracies.
- African Americans: 15 percent tax cut, school vouchers, $500-per-child tax credit, education, small business initiatives, and inner-city crime.[2]

In addition to campaign outreach to ethnic groups, organizations representing these constituencies spoke out. Ethnic leaders used a variety of means to announce their interests and to shape the positions of candidates on these concerns.

The American Jewish Committee Election Guide 1996 posed several questions to the candidates. The following samples illustrate the issues that the AJC wished to clarify in responses from Clinton, Dole, and Perot, which were published in their guide for voters:

> What in your view would be the most effective ways for the United States to advance the cause of peace in the Middle East? Please offer your assessment of Israel's security concerns and views about a satisfactory, achievable settlement to the Arab-Israeli conflict.
>
> What priority would you assign to the need for U.S. leadership in confronting international terrorism and state sponsors of terrorism, including Iran? What is your view with respect to continued economic and military assistance to Israel, and how do you assess the utility of foreign aid in general as an instrument of foreign policy?[3]

A new magazine, *Hispanic,* published a voters' guide titled, "Presidential Platforms: Clinton and Dole Tell *Hispanic* Their Positions on Issues Affecting Latinos." Responses to the editors' questions followed this introduction:

> It's personal. That is what U.S. Department of Housing and Urban Development Henry Cisneros called the impact of the upcoming presidential election on the Latino community during the National Council of La Raza conference in July. For millions of Latinos, the 104th Congress, led by a Republican majority, appears to have staged a personal attack on the Latino community. However, less-than-aggressive efforts by President Clinton to defend Hispanics against Republican attacks may offset this negative perception.[4]

Joseph Barrett and Robert Tobin, in an advocacy research paper sponsored by the Ancient Order of Hibernians and titled "Patterns of Change in the U.S. Catholic Vote," devoted much attention to moral issues that are important to Irish Americans. They argue that Irish voters are openly hostile to the prevailing orthodoxy in the Republican Party:

> On social issues such as abortion and homosexuality, . . . Irish traditional Democrats still feel no natural affinity for the GOP. . . . There is a lingering aversion to what is seen as a WASP private political society with no feeling

for grassroots ethnic politics of the organized concerns for working people.... Catholics felt, with some justification, that they were not welcome in the GOP.[5]

In 1992 and 1996 the Clinton-Gore campaign team demonstrated its mastery of the politics of inclusion. The group devoted much effective attention to campaigning among and for ethnic Americans. For example, early in the campaign at a conference titled "Italian Americans: A Political Force for the 21st Century,"

> *On social issues, Irish traditional Democrats still feel no natural affinity for the GOP.*

an official of the Clinton campaign delivered a polished and rousing ethnic and issue testament to the conference. She was followed by the chairman of the Democratic National Committee, who made it clear that the Democratic Party was inclusive. The National Democratic Ethnic Coordinating Committee includes a roster of names with the following ethnic affiliations: Arab American, Swedish American, Armenian American, Italian American, Czech and Slovak Americans, Lithuanian American, German American, Serbian American, Irish American, Ukrainian American, Hungarian American, Greek American, and Polish American.

By contrast, candidate Bob Dole, fresh from his resignation from the Senate, sent a surrogate to the conference. His representative's message was diffuse, generically Republican, and clearly lacking in attention to the issues of ethnic politics. An Irish American and a former Reagan appointee, the surrogate presented a view of American politics and government that was unrelated to the findings about ethnic politics that the National Italian American Federation had commissioned. His failure to symbolically invoke ethnic foods, festivals, and famous Italian American Republicans underscored the mismatch.

The message of the Clinton team was riveting, and it continued for the next four months. John Pikarski, a Chicago Democrat and chair

of Polish Americans for Clinton, reported in an interview that the DNC targeted states that had large Polish American concentrations.

> Polish Americans felt they were genuinely invited to rejoin the Democratic Party. Someone was listening to their concerns, and they were actively being included in the political life of our nation. Because of White House briefings on crime, health care reform, welfare reform, and immigration issues with senior administration officials and leaders, the community perceived that the president shared their domestic policy concerns. Additionally, President Clinton was directly addressing their interests in Poland's well-being and entry into NATO. President Clinton visited Poland once, Vice President Gore twice, and the First Lady once during the past four years. Polish Americans were invited to White House briefings, roundtable discussions, and various events in record numbers. The Office of Public Liaison provided unprecedented access to the president, vice president, and senior administration policy makers.[6]

A Specific Democratic Strategy

In 1996 the Democratic National Committee targeted 15 states with significant ethnic communities (25 to 56 percent of the total population). These states were New Jersey, Pennsylvania, Ohio, Illinois, Michigan, New York, California, Massachusetts, Florida, Minnesota, Connecticut, Wisconsin, Iowa, and Delaware, which together had a total of 277 electoral votes.

States with the highest concentrations of Hispanic/Latino Americans overwhelmingly voted for Clinton/Gore: New Mexico, California, Arizona, Florida, Nevada, New York, New Jersey, and Illinois. Dole/Kemp won only Texas and Colorado.

Of states with the highest concentration of Asian Americans, Clinton/Gore won Hawaii, California, Washington, Nevada, New York, New Jersey, Maryland, Oregon, Illinois, and Massachusetts. Dole/Kemp won only Alabama and Virginia.

Of the states with the highest concentrations of African Americans, Dole/Kemp won Mississippi, South Carolina, Georgia, Alabama, North Carolina, Virginia, and Texas. Clinton/Gore won Louisiana, Maryland, Delaware, New York, Tennessee, Arkansas, Illinois, Michigan, Florida, and New Jersey. Of the states that are home to more than 500,000 Italian Americans, Clinton/Gore won Massachusetts, Con-

111

necticut, New York, New Jersey, Pennsylvania, Ohio, Michigan, Illinois, California, and Florida. Dole/Kemp won only Texas.

Of the states with more than 100,000 but less than 500,000 Italian Americans, Dole/Kemp won Colorado, Indiana, Georgia, North Carolina, and Virginia; Clinton/Gore won Washington, Arizona, Louisiana, Missouri, Wisconsin, Maryland, and Delaware.

Clinton/Gore won all states with Polish American populations of over 500,000: Illinois, Michigan, Wisconsin, New York, New Jersey, and Pennsylvania. Of states with more than 200,000, they won Connecticut, Ohio, Minnesota, California, and Florida.

But Is Adding Up All There Is?

The story of 1996 may be that Bill Clinton knows how to get elected. But have we learned how to fashion the politics of pluralism as an ongoing doctrine for an ethnically diverse citizenry? Or does the future hold more political divisiveness in race and ethnicity? The 1996 election may be viewed as a contest for strategically important portions of the mosaic that is the 50 states and 435 congressional districts. Each is composed of ethnic clusters that define the specific approaches to voters and the specific concerns of interests and groups that seek some accommodation from the government they will elect. The efficacy of any electoral effort, then, can be measured by its multicultural competence and interethnic coalitions. Thus politicians in multiethnic contexts are learning and teaching a new rhetoric of fairness and inclusion. The politics of pluralism are likely to be a persistent feature of elections and policy and political science in America.

Endnotes

1. See thematic essays in Stephen Thernstrom, ed., *The Harvard Encyclopedia of Ethnic Groups in America* (Cambridge, MA: Belknap Press of Harvard University Press, 1980), especially Philip Gleason, "American Identity and Americanization."
2. Internal document of the Dole for President Coalitions Division, September 19, 1996. NCUEA 1996 Election Data File.
3. AJC Voter Guide, NCUEA, Data File #17.
4. *Hispanic,* October 1996.
5. Joseph A. Barrett and Robert W. Tobin Jr., "Patterns of Change in the U.S. Catholic Vote," *Ancient Order of Hibernians in America*, February 23, 1995.
6. Interview with John Pikarski, NCUEA Data File #16, 1996.

Chapter Twelve

Money in the 1996 Elections

Candice J. Nelson

That money was to be a key factor in the 1996 presidential and congressional elections was obvious right from the start of the election cycle. The conventional wisdom was that presidential candidates would need to raise $20 million by January 1, 1996, to be competitive in the primaries; some candidates aggressively raised money in 1995 to try to reach this goal, while other potential candidates felt they'd be unable to raise that kind of money and thus decided not to run. On the congressional side, freshman Republicans, enjoying the fruits of a Republican majority in the House of Representatives for the first time in 40 years, raised money in record amounts during the first six months of 1995. The AFL-CIO, reacting to the Republican agenda in the 104th Congress, announced that it would spend $35 million on an issue advocacy campaign targeted at freshman Republicans in the House.

This chapter chronicles the money raised and spent by presidential and congressional candidates, political parties, and interest groups in the 1996 elections. Each of these actors in the electoral process raised and spent more money than in any previous election cycle. When the final figures are in, they will likely show that over a billion dollars was spent to elect one president, 435 House members, and 34 senators.

THE PRESIDENTIAL PRIMARIES

Under federal law, candidates for president of the United States are eligible for federal matching funds during the prenomination phase of the election if they raise $5,000 in 20 states in amounts of $250 or less. Once a candidate qualifies for matching funds, for each contribution of $250 or less from an individual to the candidate's campaign, the campaign receives an equal amount of money from the federal treasury (contributions from political action committees are not matched). In return for the federal matching funds, a candidate must agree to abide by the spending limit set for the primary campaigns, which in 1996 was $37.1 million. In 1996, 11 presidential candidates received federal matching funds in the primaries.

Each of these actors in the process raised and spent more money than in any previous election cycle.

What made the 1996 primary season unique, and what drove spending in the early months of 1996, was the candidacy of Steve Forbes. Forbes, a wealthy businessman and publisher of *Forbes* magazine, chose to seek the Republican nomination, but chose not to accept partial public funding of his campaign. Because he was not accepting any public funds, Forbes was not bound by the spending limits that constrained the other candidates. Between October 1 and December 31, 1995, Forbes spent $14 million, compared to $8.4 million spent by Bob Dole, $5.4 million spent by Phil Gramm, $3.5 million spent by Lamar Alexander, and $3.2 million spent by Pat Buchanan.[1] By the end of

113

January 1996, all presidential candidates had spent a total of more than $138 million. At the same time in 1992, when, unlike 1996, both the Democratic and Republican Parties had contested primaries, total spending for all candidates was $23.3 million, less than a fifth of what was spent in 1995 and early 1996.[2]

As the caucuses and primaries began, Forbes continued to spend lavishly. Estimates are that he spent $4 million on advertising prior to the Iowa caucus, or approximately $400 per vote he received.[3] In all, Forbes spent over $41 million in his unsuccessful effort to win the Republican nomination.[4]

Forbes's early and aggressive spending, coupled with the early schedule of the primaries and caucuses,[5] forced Senator Dole to spend his own campaign resources early in the prenomination phase. Dole became the presumptive nominee of his party before the end of March, but found himself with very little money to spend between April 1st and the Republican convention in August. By the end of April, the Dole campaign had less than $200,000 to spend before exceeding the prenomination spending limit.[6] During the late spring and early summer months, Dole's campaign spending became an issue in the election and led to the first of what were to become a series of allegations of illegal spending in the 1996 elections. In mid-June the Democratic National Committee filed a complaint with the Federal Election Commission alleging that the Dole campaign had exceeded the prenomination spending limit by at least $344,000, and perhaps by as much as three-quarters of a million dollars.[7]

Regardless of the legality of Dole's spending in the months preceding the convention, the amount of money he was forced to spend to secure the nomination left him unable to compete with the Clinton campaign's spending during the late spring and summer. In the absence of a Democratic challenger, President Clinton was able to spend relatively little money during the primary season, leaving him with money to spend in the months leading up to the convention. In mid-June the Clinton campaign reported having $18.1 million left to spend prior to the Democratic convention in August.[8] In July alone, the Clinton campaign spent $6.5 million, of which $4 million was spent on television.[9] The consequences of Steve Forbes's presence in the Republican primaries

came back to haunt the Dole campaign in the summer of 1996, long after the primaries had ended.

THE PRESIDENTIAL ELECTION

Once they became the nominees of their respective parties, Bob Dole and Bill Clinton each received $61.8 million from the federal treasury. In exchange for accepting public funds, each candidate agreed to accept no private contributions during the general election campaign. The following Associated Press wire story, published in the *New York Times*, illustrates how anxious the Dole campaign was to get its $61.8 million:

> At 9:08 Wednesday night [August 14th], the nomination was officially his, and Mr. Dole was eligible for the money—and free to start spending. At 9:30 a young Dole aide had boarded a red-eye flight back to Washington to pick up the check. . . . The aide carried a signed letter from Mr. Dole and his running mate, Jack Kemp, agreeing to follow Federal Election Commission rules in spending the money. She was met at Baltimore-Washington International airport just after dawn. There, the letter was handed off to another member of Dole's accounting staff, who drove the letter to the commission offices in downtown Washington, arriving about 9:15 A.M., just after the doors opened. Federal Election officials, who had been put on standby alert, walked the letter around their office for formal approval by the five funding commissioners. Then it was back in the car—an F.E.C. auditor in tow— and out to the Treasury Department's payout station in Hyattsville, MD, where the final wire transfer was arranged out of the department's Philadelphia office. By the close of business [on August 15th]—fully five hours before Mr. Dole was set to begin his acceptance speech—$61,820,000 was sitting in his bank account.[10]

Ross Perot, because he had received 19 percent of the popular vote in 1992, was eligible to receive $29.2 million in federal funds. In 1996, unlike 1992, Perot accepted federal funds, and in doing so agreed to limit spending of his personal funds to $50,000,[11] in marked contrast to the $60 million he reportedly spent in the prior election.

The biggest money story of the 1996 presidential election, however, had little to do with the federal funds that Clinton, Dole, and

Perot received. Indeed, for President Clinton and Senator Dole, the $62 million that each spent was but the tip of the proverbial iceberg that was campaign spending in the fall of 1996.

While the Federal Election Campaign Act limits the amount of money an individual can contribute to the political parties to $20,000 per year, there is no limit on the amount of money individuals can contribute to the parties for so-called "party-building" activities, such as voter registration and get-out-the-vote drives. These unrestricted contributions are called soft money, and it was soft money contributions that became the biggest money story of Campaign '96.

Soft money became a part of the campaign finance landscape in 1979, when the Federal Election Campaign Act was amended. While soft money contributions did not play much of a role in the 1980 and 1984 presidential elections, by 1988 both the Democratic and Republican Parties were raising soft money in earnest. The Democratic Party raised $23 million in soft money in 1988, and the Republican Party raised $22 million.[12] In 1992 Democrats increased their soft money receipts by 50 percent, raising $37 million, and Republicans almost doubled their soft money receipts, raising $52 million.[13]

However, the increase in soft money receipts by the political parties between 1988 and 1992 paled in comparison to the increase in soft money receipts between 1992 and 1996. During the first 18 months of the 1996 election cycle, soft money contributions to the Democratic Party increased 382 percent over receipts in the same period in 1992, and soft money contributions to the Republican Party increased 142 percent.[14] By late November, the Republican Party had raised $141 million in soft money, and the Democratic Party had raised $122 million.[15]

One purpose of the Federal Election Campaign Act (FECA) of 1974 was to remove large, unlimited contributions by wealthy individuals, corporations, trade associations, and labor unions from campaigns for federal office. By 1996, that aspect of the FECA had been completely undermined. Soft money contributions in the hundreds of thousands of dollars were rampant in both the Republican and Democratic Parties. Wealthy contributors were squarely back in the campaign fund-raising process.

Individuals who make large soft money contributions receive special recognition by both the Republican and Democratic Parties. In 1988 the Republicans established "Team 100" to recognize individuals who contributed $100,000 or more to the party, and in 1992 Democrats followed suit by recognizing "trustees," who give $100,000 or more to the party, and "managing trustees," individuals who give $200,000 or more.[16] However, in 1996 a contribution of $100,000 or more to the Republican Party was no longer seen as top dollar; Republicans created a special class of contributors, "season ticket holders," to recognize individuals who contributed $250,000 or more.[17]

The sources of some contributions became a story that dogged the Clinton campaign.

Corporations, trade associations, and labor unions were just as generous as individuals in making soft money contributions.[18] Through just the first half of 1996, the Association of Trial Lawyers contributed $100,000 to the Democratic Party, the Laborers' International Union gave $230,000, the American Federation of Teachers contributed $100,000, and the Revlon Group gave $340,250. On the Republican side, Philip Morris contributed $479,000 to the party, R. J. Reynolds Tobacco contributed $252,000, and Amway Corporation, Tele-Communications Inc., and the Atchison, Topeka and Santa Fe Railroad each gave $250,000. In some cases, corporations contributed to both parties: Anheuser-Busch and Joseph E. Seagram and Sons each gave $100,000 to both the Republican and Democratic committees, and MCI gave $140,000 to the Republican Party and $100,000 to the Democratic Party.[19]

While the sheer amount of soft money raised by the political parties was in and of itself an important story in 1996, the sources of some of these contributions, particularly to the Democratic Party, became a story that dogged the Clinton campaign in the closing weeks before the election and into the president's second term.[20]

In early October the press began to uncover questionable fund-raising practices by John Huang, who had joined the Democratic National Committee (DNC) in an influential financial role in January 1996. From 1985 until mid-1994 Huang, a naturalized U.S. citizen, had been head of U.S. operations for the Lippo Group, an Indonesian banking and real estate conglomerate. He subsequently raised $2.5 million from the Asian American community for the DNC, and some of those donations either were illegal or raised suspicions of illegality.[21] For example, the DNC returned a $250,000 contribution solicited by Huang when the committee discovered that the contribution was from a South Korean company, not its U.S. subsidiary. A second questionable contribution was a $425,000 donation from an Indonesian couple, Arief and Soraya Wiriadinata, who had no previous history of giving to political parties, and by October were no longer residing in the United States.[22] Huang also organized a fundraiser in a California Buddhist temple in April of 1996, which Vice President Al Gore attended. A woman visiting the temple at the time of the event claimed she was approached by a "Democratic activist," given $5,000 in small bills, and asked to write a check for $5,000 made out to the Democratic National Committee.[23] By late October the financial activities of the DNC and Mr. Huang were the subject of press accounts nearly every day. In early November the Justice Department established a task force within the Public Integrity Section of its Criminal Division to look into the DNC's fund-raising practices.[24]

By late November the Democratic National Committee had returned $1.27 million in questionable campaign contributions, almost one-half the total amount of money raised by Mr. Huang, including the $425,000 contribution from the Wiriadinatas. The committee began an internal investigation of its fund-raising, and announced new procedures for scrutinizing contributions.[25] Senator John McCain asked the Justice Department to appoint an independent prosecutor, a request that Attorney General Janet Reno denied.[26] In early December the FBI assigned a number of its agents to work with the Public Integrity Section task force investigating the DNC's fund-raising practices.

Whatever the outcomes of investigations into fund-raising practices in the 1996 elections,

it is clear that the drive to raise ever-larger sums of money dominated the activities of the party committees. Precautions that had been taken in previous election cycles were apparently abandoned. Funds from foreign interests found their way into the U.S. political system, if only for a brief time.

Money dominated the 1996 presidential election, from the early months of 1995 until long after the final ballots had been counted. Recognizing that the ability to raise large amounts of money would be the key to success, some potential candidates—notably former secretary of defense Dick Cheney, former secretary of housing and urban development Jack Kemp, and former vice president Dan Quayle—chose not to run. Those Republican candidates who contested the nomination found themselves struggling to keep up with Steve Forbes's massive spending on media advertising. Following the primaries, money continued to dominate the campaign, as an election intended to be free of such influences became consumed not only by private contributions in the form of soft money but also by potentially illegal contributions from foreign contributors and companies.

THE CONGRESSIONAL ELECTIONS

Money was no less a dominant force in the congressional elections of 1996. It became clear almost from the moment the 1994 elections ended that a great deal of money would be raised and spent in the subsequent cycle. Republicans wasted no time in capitalizing on their new majority-party status. During the first half of 1995, two-thirds of all political action committee (PAC) contributions went to Republicans; in 1993 two-thirds of all PAC money had gone to Democrats.[27] By the end of 1995, PAC contributions to Republican candidates were double what they had been two years earlier—$42 million compared to $20 million.[28]

Contributions to congressional candidates continued to break records, ensuring that the 1996 elections would be the costliest ever. Between January 1, 1995, and November 25, 1996, House and Senate candidates raised $659.6 million, 8 percent more money than during the same period in the 1993–1994 election cycle, and spent $626.4 million, a 6 percent increase over 1993–1994. The increase was a result of increased spending by House candidates, who spent $405 million in 1996, 24 percent more than in the 1993–1994 election cycle. Republican candidates raised 67 percent more money than they did during the 1993–1994 cycle, while Democrats raised only slightly more money than they had in the previous election cycle. And, Republicans' early pattern of successful PAC fund-raising continued into 1996. Between January 1, 1995, and November 25, 1996, PACs contributed $102 million to Republican candidates and $89.3 million to Democratic candidates. In the previous election cycle, when Democrats were in the majority and Republicans in the minority, PACs contributed just $61.9 million to Republican candidates and $107 million to Democrats.[29]

With Democratic campaign receipts keeping apace of previous years and Republican receipts increasing substantially, there was more money in the congressional elections, just as there was more money in the presidential election, than ever before. But in 1996 there was a new twist in the congressional spending landscape—issue advocacy campaigns by interest groups.

In early 1996, the AFL-CIO pledged that it would spend $35 million in 75 Republican, primarily freshman, congressional districts to fight the "GOP legislative agenda in the House and Senate."[30] During the first phase of the campaign, the union ran "issue ads" criticizing Republican candidates for their positions on issues such as Medicare, pensions, and the minimum wage.[31] Later the AFL-CIO changed its advertising approach and began running "voter guides" in targeted Republican districts, making explicit comparisons between Democratic and Republican candidates.[32]

The National Republican Congressional Committee (NRCC) filed repeated complaints with the Federal Election Commission and petitioned television station managers not to run the ads. The NRCC chairman, Congressman Bill Paxon, charged that the "exclusive purpose of these partisan ads is to unlawfully influence the elections in November. . . . It is unquestionably illegal for unions to spend general treasury funds in this fashion, and it is irresponsible for broadcasters to aid and abet the AFL-CIO's flagrant abuse of federal election laws."[33]

Under Federal Election Commission regulations, interest groups can produce and dis-

tribute voter guides and other advocacy communications, which may be paid for with union or corporate treasury funds, and which are not subject to campaign finance expenditure limits. In 1996 the FEC filed suit against the Christian Coalition for producing voter guides that were "thinly veiled partisan attacks."[34] The NRCC accused the AFL-CIO of similar partisan attacks, and some political observers agreed. Professor Darrell West, a media specialist at Brown University, testified, "These ads are really testing the frontier in terms of what you can say about candidates without it being considered a campaign ad. . . . These are really campaign ads but they're not . . . subject to any of the campaign finance regulations."[35]

Other interest groups also used issue advocacy advertisements. The business commu-

Issue advocacy advertising meant that yet another piece of the campaign finance puzzle was beyond the reach of federal law.

nity, led by the U.S. Chamber of Commerce, formed The Coalition, a group of 35 business groups, to try to counter the AFL-CIO's campaign.[36] The League of Conservation Voters planned to spend $1.5 million and the Sierra Club $7.5 million on the election, most of it on advertising against candidates with poor records on the environment.[37]

Such issue advocacy advertising meant that yet another piece of the campaign finance puzzle was beyond the reach of federal law. The Supreme Court has ruled that campaigns of this type are not subject to expenditure limits unless they "expressly advocate" for or against a candidate by using such words as "defeat," "vote against," "vote for," or "elect." Labor and business interests continued to make PAC contributions to congressional candidates, while issue campaigns enabled them to spend unlimited amounts of money to influence congressional races. For example, the Sierra Club planned to make about $750,000 in PAC contributions to congressional candidates, but to spend 10 times that amount, $7.5 million, on issue advocacy advertisements.[38]

CAMPAIGN FINANCE REFORM

Following the 1996 elections, promises to work toward a bipartisan campaign finance reform proposal were made on both sides of the legislative aisle and at both ends of Pennsylvania Avenue. A week after the election, House Speaker Newt Gingrich and House minority leader Richard Gephardt agreed to try to produce a reform bill, and President Clinton announced in his first postelection news conference that he wanted to "enact bipartisan campaign finance reform" as soon as possible.[39]

However, despite these intentions, achieving reform in the 105th Congress will likely be as difficult, and as elusive, as it has been in the past. On top of the usual partisan disagreements over spending limits, public funding, and the role of PACs, new partisan disagreements arose during the 1996 elections. For example, Republicans dismayed over the AFL-CIO's attacks on them wanted to find a way to limit the use of union treasury funds for such advocacy campaigns. Republican leaders claimed that all union members' dues were being used to support candidates that some members did not support.[40] Democrats, some of whom can at least partially credit their election to union political activity, may find it difficult to find common ground with Republicans on this issue.

But there are some areas on which common ground may easily be found. Both parties will likely support restrictions on contributions to federal campaigns by non–U.S. citizens, arguing that anyone who isn't eligible to vote in a federal election ought not to be able to try to influence the outcome of that election. Both parties seem willing to support a ban on soft money, yet reaching agreement on changes in the amount of "hard money" political parties can raise and spend may be difficult, given partisan differences in fund-raising success.

An additional difficulty are the complications arising out of Supreme Court decisions in the area of campaign finance. As I mentioned earlier, the Court has not restricted advocacy campaigns. Should the Federal Election Commission and the Court decide that 1996 issue campaigns were within the law, legislators could find it hard to limit the spending of candidates and political parties in the face of unlimited spending by interest groups.

Similarly, limiting party spending was made more complicated by the June 1996 decision in which the Court ruled that political parties may spend unlimited amounts of money in congressional elections, as long as the expenditures are "independent" of the candidates. While such spending played only a limited role in the 1996 elections, it is likely to be much more visible in the future.

As the year came to an end, then, the promised spirit of cooperation was tempered with the realization that a truly bipartisan reform effort would be difficult.

CONCLUSIONS

Understanding the role of money was key to understanding the outcome of the 1996 elections. Early on, money winnowed the field of Republican candidates. Bob Dole won the Republican nomination, but Steve Forbes's spending forced Dole to spend his limited prenomination funds in the early primaries and caucuses, leaving him little money to spend during the late spring and summer, when President Clinton was on television and radio promoting the accomplishments of his administration. By fall, the entire campaign finance system had collapsed, as soft money dominated hard money, issue advocacy spending outpaced political action committee contributions for some groups, and both real and alleged incidents of illegal contributions surfaced.

A campaign finance system put in place to restrict special interest money in elections and remove large contributions by wealthy individuals from the funding process had disappeared by 1996. Wealthy contributors returned as major players in federal elections, and all interests, both domestic and foreign, seemed to have a role in financing campaigns. A retiring member of the House described 1996 fund-raising as "a literal cascade of money."[41] What to do about the cascade was the question that faced the president, members of Congress, interest groups, and the public in 1997.

I would like to thank my research assistant, Douglas Weber, for his help.

ENDNOTES

1. Ruth Marcus and Walter Pincus, "Forbes Spent $18 Million on Race Last Year," *Washington Post*, February 2, 1996, p. A1.

2. Ruth Marcus and Walter Pincus, "It's Taking a Lot More Money for '96 Race," *Washington Post*, February 29, 1996, p. A1.

3. Elizabeth Kolbert, "Forbes Ads Credited for Role in Outcome but Not for Helping Him," *New York Times*, February 14, 1996, p. B8.

4. Federal Election Commission, Http://www.fec.gov/pres96/presmstr.htm.

5. In 1996 a number of states, including the two largest, California and New York, moved their primaries closer to the beginning of the season. California moved its primary from early June to late March, and New York moved its primary up a month, from early April to early March. As a result, over one-half the delegates to the national conventions were chosen in the six-week period between February 1 and March 15.

6. Ruth Marcus, "Dole Spending Report Rekindles Charges," *Washington Post*, June 21, 1996, p. A8.

7. Marcus, "DNC Accuses Dole Campaign of Overspending," *Washington Post*, June 12, 1996, p. A14.

8. Ruth Marcus, "DNC Spending Report Rekindles Charges."

9. Ruth Marcus and Ira Chinoy, "Lack of Primary Season Foe Leaves Clinton In the Money," *Washington Post*, August 24, 1996, p. A1.

10. "Dole Relay Team Loses No Time Making a $62.8 Million Deposit," *New York Times*, August 16, 1996, p. A25.

11. Under the Federal Election Campaign Act Perot was also eligible to accept contributions in amounts up to $1,000 from individuals, up to a limit of $32 million, in order to allow him to match the spending of the major party candidates. Donald P. Baker and David S. Broder, "Perot to Accept Federal Funds in White House Bid," *Washington Post*, August 19, 1996, p. A8.

12. Herbert E. Alexander, *Financing Politics: Money, Elections and Political Reform*, 4th ed. (Washington, D.C.: Congressional Quarterly Press, 1992), p. 115.

13. Federal Election Commission, "Democrats Narrow Financial Gap in 1991–92," March 11, 1993.

14. Federal Election Commission, "FEC Releases 18-Month Report on Political Party Finances," August 7, 1996.

15. Federal Election Commission, "Political Parties' Fundraising Hits $881 Million," January 10, 1997.

16. Peter Stone, "Return of the Fat Cats," *National Journal*, October 17, 1992, p. 2351.

17. According to Haley Barbour, Chair of the Republican National Committee during the 1996 presidential cycle, the idea came from those contributors who asked to be solicited only once. In Barbour's words, "They asked, 'Won't you please let me have a season ticket and leave me alone?' " Charles R. Babcock and Ruth Marcus, "A Hard-Charging Flood of 'Soft Money,' " *Washington Post*, October 24, 1996, p. A1.

18. While corporations and trade associations are prohibited under federal law from using corporate or treasury funds to make contributions to candidates for federal office, state restrictions on contributions vary. In states that do not restrict corporate and labor contributions, contributions may be made from corporate and labor union treasuries to state political parties, which in turn can support "party-building" activities using these corporate and union funds.

19. Ruth Marcus and Charles R. Babcock, "Parties' National Committees Set Records for 'Soft Money,' " *Washington Post*, July 18, 1996, p. A8.

20. While much of the attention of the press and the public was focused on possible illegal fundraising practices by the Democratic National Committee, the Republican Party was not free from scandal. In late October a former vice chair of Senator Dole's campaign finance committee was fined $1 million and sentenced to six months of house arrest after pleading guilty to making $120,000 in illegal contributions to the Dole campaign, the 1992 Bush-Quayle campaign, and the Republican National Committee. His company was fined $5 million, making the total penalty the largest fine for a political contribution. Associated Press, "Ex-Dole Finance Official Is Fined for Illegal Gifts," *Washington Post*, October 24, 1996, p. A16.

21. Serge F. Kovaleski, "Democrats Open Investigation into Questionable Donations," *Washington Post*, November 27, 1996, p. A6.

22. Ruth Marcus and Ira Chinoy, "A Fund-Raising Mistake," *Washington Post*, October 17, 1996, p. A16.

23. Ruth Marcus and R. H. Melton, "DNC Donor Controversy Widens as Republicans Step Up Criticism," *Washington Post*, October 18, 1996, p. A37. The woman later changed her story, saying she had used her own money to make the contribution. Serge Kovaleski, "Buddhist Nun Changes Story on DNC Donation," *Washington Post*, December 6, 1996, p. A33.

24. Letter to Ann McBride, president, Common Cause, from Mark M. Richard, acting assistant attorney general, November 8, 1996.

25. Kovaleski, "Democrats Open Investigation into Questionable Donations."

26. Pierre Thomas, "Reno Rejects Call for Special Counsel," *Washington Post*, November 30, 1996, p. A1.

27. Larry Makinson, "Republicans Rake In the PAC Dollars in Early '95," *The Capital Eye*, Center for Responsive Politics, November 1, 1995, p. 1.

28. Tim Curran, "Final Tally Shows Record Year of Giving by PACs," *Roll Call*, April 8, 1996, p. A1.

29. Federal Election Commission, "1996 Congressional Financial Activity Continues Climb," December 31, 1996, and Federal Election Commission, "1994 Congressional Spending Sets Record," December 22, 1994.

30. Tim Curran, "The Two Parties Clash over Labor's Stepped-Up Politics," *Roll Call*, March 25, 1996, p. 11.

31. Benjamin Sheffner, "AFL-CIO Escalates Campaign Effort," *Roll Call*, September 30, 1996, p.18.

32. Ruth Marcus, "Taking 'Voter Guides' to the TV Audience," *Washington Post*, October 17, 1996, p. 16.

33. Sheffner, "AFL-CIO Escalates Campaign Effort."

34. Ibid.

35. Marcus, "Taking 'Voter Guides' to the TV Audience."

36. Robin Toner, "Battered by Labor's Ads, Republicans Strike Back," *New York Times*, July, 15, 1996, p. A8.

37. Gary Lee, "Environmental Groups Target Candidates," *Washington Post*, October 29, 1996, p.

A10, and John H. Cushman Jr., "Environmentalists Ante Up to Sway a Number of Races," *New York Times*, October 23, 1996, p. A21.

38. Cushman, "Environmentalists Ante Up To Sway a Number of Races."

39. John E. Yang, "House Leaders Pledge Bipartisan Finance Reform," *Washington Post*, November 15, 1996, p. A8, and "Excerpts from President Clinton's News Conference," *Washington Post*, November 9, 1996, p. A16.

40. By the AFL-CIO's own admission, 35 percent of members voted for Republican congressional candidates. However, AFL-CIO President John Sweeney claimed that only 15 percent opposed the union's political activities. Steven Greenhouse, "Despite Setbacks, Labor Chief Is Upbeat over Election Role," *New York Times*, November 15, 1996, p. A20.

41. Francis X. Clines, "Goodbye, and Mostly Good Riddance," *New York Times*, November 15, 1996, p. A28.

Chapter Thirteen

The Ethics of the 1996 Campaign: Money, Strategies, and Scandals

John S. Shockley

Another American national election is over, and once again citizens and scholars are asking themselves if there is a better way to conduct elections. Is there a way that campaigns can appeal to our better instincts instead of our worst? Is there a way to change the nature of incentives for candidates, so that they will act and speak more substantively and with fewer gimmicks? What can we do about the unprecedented amount of money that was funneled into so many races? Is that money corrupting the process? Also, is there a better way to assess the merits of all the charges of ethical violations and "scandals"? And why, some ask, was the presidential campaign so "boring"?

The record low turnout for the 1996 elections adds more weight to these concerns about the health of our electoral process. This chapter will try to address all of these questions, and explore the ways in which they are related.

As many have noted, 1996 saw a record-breaking amount of money spent in the presidential and congressional races (see Chapter 11, "Money in the 1996 Elections"), even as turnout declined. A combination of Supreme Court decisions restricting the regulation of money in campaigns and ingenious operators willing to take advantage of loopholes brought the total spent during the 1995–1996 election cycle to over $1.7 billion.[1] Since fewer than 100 million Americans voted, which was less than half the total eligible voters, that means roughly $20 was

spent per voter to influence his or her behavior, and this total does not include money for state and local races. Almost 90 percent of this $1.7 billion came from private rather than public sources. Only the matching funds in the presidential primaries and grants for the general election presidential campaigns and the national nominating conventions came from public funding. What did those people want in return for their one and one-half billion dollars?

Roughly $20 was spent per voter to influence his or her behavior in 1996 national elections.

Most of this money was no doubt given by those who agreed with the policies of those to whom they contributed. But much of it came from interests with very specific requests in mind, such as the tobacco industry fearing regulation, or the trial lawyers fearing tort reform. Successful candidates are placed in a "conflict of interest" situation when they vote for measures that would obviously benefit their major contributors, because these candidates are also personally benefiting.

121

THE EFFECTS OF THE MONEY

Career politicians like Bob Dole and Bill Clinton have developed long-term relationships with many special interests. We already know, for example, that Bob Dole has pushed for tax breaks for ethanol (and helped block products competitive with ethanol), which is just what Dwayne Andreas and his agribusiness, Archer Daniels Midland, wanted from him with their contributions. We already know that Bob Dole has pushed the American government to pressure the European community to allow Chiquita bananas from Central America into the European market, which is just what Carl Lindner and Chiquita Bananas wanted. We already know that Bob Dole has sponsored tax breaks for the Gallo wine family, which is just what the Gallo family wanted from their contributions to Dole. We also know that Bill Clinton has accepted money and favors from many during his political career: Tyson Foods in Arkansas (the nation's largest poultry producer); Goldman Sachs, the Wall Street investment banking firm, and its chairman, Robert Rubin;[2] and the trial lawyers of America. Tyson Foods and Goldman Sachs wanted policies that would clearly benefit these businesses. Trial lawyers wanted to stop business-oriented tort reform, which would limit damages to consumers (and their lawyers). All these relationships, as long as they were not direct exchanges of money for favors (which would be either bribery or extortion, depending upon who initiated the deal) are perfectly legal in our campaign finance system. All of them, however, give most Americans the uncomfortable "feeling that politicians listen more to financial contributors than to ordinary people."[3] Not all contributors get what they want, of course, and not all donors are as self-interested as these examples. Observers agree, however, that large contributions bring "access" at the very least, and with it the chance to plead their cases in a way that ordinary people cannot.

As with effects on policy, money's effect on candidates' campaigns is almost always beneficial, but it likewise does not guarantee success. Money is a necessary but not sufficient condition for election to major office in America. It does not guarantee victory (ask Steve Forbes, Ross Perot, or failed Senate candidates Michael Huffington and Oliver North). Without it, however, one cannot run a credible campaign

for office. Candidates are therefore constantly aware of the need for money and cannot help but think of the consequences of their actions and their votes within the context of their constant need for money. The partial public funding of presidential elections was designed to reduce this dependence upon private contributions, but as we have seen, it no longer makes much difference in lessening the need for money.

Congressional races were never part of the public funding system, and thus the money chase for these contests has been even more obvious as the costs of campaigning have increased. This need for large amounts of money unquestionably reduces the pool of qualified candidates able to run for office, as people who otherwise would be excellent public servants cannot (or do not wish to) raise the necessary funds. The need also can place pressures on the candidates before and after the election, as they are forced to balance their electoral constituency with their financial constituency. These two groups may not have the same needs and interests.

Of course, the need for money would not be so important in our system if wealth and income were not as unequally distributed as they are, and if the very wealthy were more representative of the views of ordinary Americans. The figures tell the tale. The top 1 percent of Americans earn about two and a half times as much as the bottom 20 percent. Wealth is even more skewed, since it is the accumulated earnings and inheritance of families. The top one-half of 1 percent of American households holds more than one-quarter of all net family worth, which is far more than the total family wealth held by all those in the bottom half. The top 10 percent of American families control more than two-thirds of all family wealth.[4]

There is evidence that the money chase undermines citizen confidence in the electoral process and in government and may reduce voter turnout. Although it is hard to get directly at this question, and question wording can make a difference in citizen responses, an autumn 1996 CNN/*USA Today* poll found that 65 percent of voters thought a public financing system—with private donations banned—would be a good idea. That total was up from 56 percent supporting such a system in June 1996.[5]

PUSH POLLING

For 1996, money was not the only ethical issue of prominence: a number of campaign strategies also raised ethical questions. Steve Forbes was the first to raise questions about his rivals' (including Dole's) use of "push polling" to turn prospective voters against Forbes. By going public with his charges, Forbes drew attention to the common practice of using "push polls" to gain an advantage on an opponent. Material from these polls is commonly used to determine what will push a voter over the line into withdrawing support from his or her first choice. ("If you knew that so-and-so were a liberal/conservative/extremist/Jew/homosexual/in favor of releasing known child molesters/voting to cut Medicare/against the death penalty . . . , would you still support him?") That knowledge is then used in attacking opponents, and it is a new technology being employed more frequently, even in lower-profile state legislative races.[6] In Forbes's case, his supporters began receiving phone calls about his less-than-hard-line stances against abortion and gay rights.

Obviously, some questions to prospective voters are less ethical than others, but push polling also raises the question of whether it is proper for candidates' surveys to masquerade as public opinion polls conducted by disinterested professionals. Both the American Association for Public Opinion Research and the National Council on Public Polls have condemned "push polls" that claim to be surveys when they are really mechanisms to transmit negative information about opponents, do not identify their sponsors, or present false or misleading information. Nevertheless, the temptation to use them will remain.

ATTACK ADS

Again in 1996 there were a number of attack ads on both sides and from various quarters, and again scholars criticized a number of these ads for being biased or deceptive. Republicans criticized Democratic claims that Republicans wanted to "cut Medicare." Republicans said that they merely wanted to cut the *growth* of Medicare (which, given demographic changes among the elderly, would likely mean cuts in individual benefits), and noted that Clinton

himself had already agreed to cutting the growth. Democrats criticized some Republican ads, including those featuring the face of a Democratic candidate who opposed the death penalty that morphed into the face of the killer of 12-year-old Polly Klaas. Some ads criticized individual congressmen for supporting bills that many others in both parties had also voted for. In one example, the National Republican Senatorial Committee, chaired by Senator Alfonse D'Amato of New York, produced an ad attacking Democratic Senator Paul Wellstone's votes on crime issues. The ad juxtaposed Wellstone's picture against images of a gang member and a stabbing victim and also suggested that his voting record on crime was unusually liberal. But his positions on the votes cited in the ad were similar to those of Senator D'Amato himself.[7]

All sides are tempted to engage in misleading ads if they think they can get away with it.

One Dole ad charged that the Clinton administration had had more people investigated, prosecuted, and convicted than any administration in over two decades. It ended with the plea, "Does the truth matter? Does it matter to you?" Ironically, this ad was pulled after it was pointed out that more people in both the Reagan and Nixon administrations had been indicted and convicted.[8] The broader point, however, is that all sides are tempted to engage in distortion and in misleading (or even untruthful) ads if they think they can get away with it. Policing of ads remains in the hands of opposing candidates and the media, with very uneven effectiveness. While "Ad Watches" have been instituted by some of the media, this move toward accountability can backfire if the Ad Watches ultimately spread the falsehoods and distortions still further.[9]

An innovation in the Republican presidential primary debate in South Carolina in February was the requirement that candidates defend in front of the other candidates their negative ads. If all candidates knew they would have to defend their own negative ads in this very public way, they might be less likely to engage in distortion or unfair attacks.

POWER PHRASES

Modern technology has also created the "power phrase," words that allow politicians to "resonate" with different segments of the population. Through focus groups or through sampling, a campaign can ask voters to rate the speeches of candidates, getting prospective voter response second-by-second to words the candidates are saying. Those that the voters like are known as power phrases because of their ability to win over audiences. Those that the voters don't like are assigned to the junk heap of history, avoided because of their negative connotations or unpersuasive rhetoric.

A common criticism of the presidential and many other campaigns this year was that the candidates were speaking in "sound bites"—saying very little of substance about important problems. The need for entitlement reform, specifics on how to balance the budget, health care problems, causes and cures for crime and poverty, and foreign policy were all areas where the next president and the next Congress would need to devote attention and resources. Yet complaints were made about brief and superficial answers to these problems. Power phrases help politicians avoid serious answers to complex questions. The two presidential and one vice-presidential debates should have been the best time for voters to hear and compare what the opposing candidates had to say, since the debaters had to answer questions and could not control the format as they could in stump speeches or ads. But the techniques of modern marketing, which have already dominated so many other aspects of the political campaigns, made their presence obvious even in these forums. Debates are supposed to be the last preserve of spontaneous argument, but the current style has now become what one commentator called "focus grouping the mother tongue into a sweet porridge of centrist gruel."[10] A number of commentators have charged that voters are treated as if they were stupid and childlike. The repetition of poll-tested slogans and the avoidance of addressing more difficult, complex issues in ways other than the superficial are what lead many to conclude that campaigns are "boring."

Once again, however, technology and marketing techniques are available, and it is hard for politicians to refuse their advantages. The incentive structure for winning will have to be changed—with both voters and the media demanding more—before candidates' behavior will change. Hoping for the right image for himself and hoping to damage his opponent at the same time, Clinton used words like "opportunity, responsibility, and community" endlessly in the debate and on the campaign trail, and the phrase "risky scheme" to describe Dole's 15 percent tax cut. Dole often used "character" and "trust," apparently but cryptically referring to his opponent. Symbols and labeling, however, are very different from substantive argument, which requires listening carefully, developing a case, and responding to critiques of one's points. What gets lost in the politics of symbols and labeling is genuine discussion and dialogue.

THE CAMPAIGN STRATEGISTS THEMSELVES

Because campaigns are competitive (and indeed should be if democracy is to work and citizens are to have choices), there is often a sense that they are sports or games. Sometimes the analogy seems healthy, as when opposing teams shake hands afterwards rather than imprison or kill each other. George Bush, for example, escorted Bill Clinton to his inauguration. The defeated recognized the legitimacy of the victor, and this is our normal practice. But the sports analogy can also trivialize politics, turning citizens into nothing but spectators, with no sense that anything more is at stake than which team wins or loses.

In campaigns, as in sports, there are "coaches," and "rules of the game." Where winning is the only objective, the temptation is to break the rules, especially if one does not get caught or the penalties are not severe. Many of the tactics of strategists have already been mentioned (such as push polling and deceptive advertising), because they raise ethical questions about the conduct of campaigns. But the behavior of elite campaign strategists merits more attention, because their behavior can undermine citizen confidence in the fairness of the game, leading voters to believe either that the "umpires" have been bought or that there are no umpires.

Since strategists do not run for office themselves, they are not generally known to the public until something dramatic erupts. The most dramatic eruption in 1996 involved Dick Morris. A sometime adviser to Clinton over the years, Morris had also worked for Senate Majority Leader Trent Lott and a number of other Republicans. Morris's behavior reinforced the stereotype that these elite operators lack humility and ethical standards. Indeed, they seem too often to be arrogant manipulators of candidate images and symbols. Morris claimed credit for "guiding" Clinton to recovery from his 1994 election debacle. A promoter of "family values" issues for the president, Morris was forced to resign when it was revealed that he had been having a long-term affair with a Washington prostitute. Morris not only discussed sensitive campaign issues and polling results with the $200-an-hour call girl, but also apparently allowed her to listen in during some of his conversations with the president.[11] Seemingly without shame, Morris posed with his wife for a *Time* magazine cover after the story broke, and then revealed that, unbeknownst to the president, he had earlier signed a multimillion dollar contract for a book on his work with Clinton.

While Morris was the best-known example of unethical behavior by individuals running a major campaign, the memoirs of Republican strategist Ed Rollins, *Bare Knuckles and Back Rooms*, published in 1996, did little to inspire more respect for strategists or those they work for. While fascinating, his work seemed cynical and unscrupulous. Rollins became famous when he claimed credit for Christine Todd Whitman's upset victory as governor of New Jersey, saying he had paid black ministers to curtail the black voter turnout. Since his remarks were caught on tape, he could not deny having made them. Instead, he later responded that his own statement was probably untrue. Commented one reviewer of the book, "If even half of the author's stories are true, voters are worse off than they already think."[12]

Arthur Finkelstein, a Republican strategist who played an important role in Senate races in 1996, has worked for a number of conservative Republicans. Many of these, such as North Carolina Senator Jesse Helms, have been labeled "gay-bashers" for their harsh condemnation of homosexual behavior. Yet Finkelstein is himself gay. What does this say about his

If voters are really turned off by negative campaigns, why do such practices so often work?

ethics, and the ethics of those who employ him? Finkelstein has said his own philosophy of campaigns is that "aggressively negative campaigns always had worked and always" would. Voters "barely pay attention to politics," so candidates should "stick to one or two basic themes and repeat them constantly, like a mantra, avoiding the temptation to talk in specifics or offer detailed plans."[13]

In truth, the personal contradictions and unethical behavior of strategists like these lead us to more interesting and difficult questions: Why are these people hired, and why do their strategies so often work? In other words, what does their success say about the American public and about the people who run for office? If Finkelstein is right, does that mean that voters allow or encourage strategists to convince politicians to avoid specifics and detailed plans? If voters are really turned off by negative and shallow campaigns, why do such practices so often work? Or perhaps people are turned off, or confused, by campaigns, so that fewer vote. Simultaneously, ever-more-sophisticated techniques in the hands of operators like Morris, Finkelstein, and Rollins may allow them to anticipate our reactions more accurately and manipulate us more effectively.

What are some of the best suggestions for ways of changing these patterns? (1) Ban paid political commercials on television and radio, and allot longer segments of free time to candidates and political parties (as nearly all other democracies do). This would deprive the negative artists of their main forum, eliminating the typical attack ad. Longer ads may force candidates and parties to be more substantive, although there is no guarantee of this. This proposal, however, is opposed by the broadcast media, who stand to lose money unless the government compensates them for their lost ad revenues. (2) Require candidates to appear in their own ads, personally vouching for the accuracy of their ads. This might bring greater accountability to campaign rhetoric. Most negative ads involve unidentified and unseen voices making the charges.[14]

Journalists are essential for monitoring and "umpiring" various campaign charges. Whenever candidates claim credit for something, the plausibility of the claims needs to be examined. Voters need to be able to consider whether all charges, even if true, are basically deceptive. Do broader facts about the matter destroy the power of an accusation? Are the charges true but trivial? Voters cannot easily determine these points on their own. They need the help of competent journalists. Many examples of the true but deceptive or trivial charge exist. To cite just two: a Democratic candidate for governor of New Jersey accused his Republican opponent of keeping toxic waste in his backyard. In fact, several drums of unused heating oil were left on some property the candidate co-owned with his brother. Not to be outdone, the Republican accused the Democrat of taking campaign money from a corrupt union linked to organized crime. Again, the charge was true, but the money was contributed before the union was under investigation, and the incumbent Republican governor had also taken funds from the union. In both these instances, the candidates would have been less likely to engage in such true but deceptive attacks if they had known that journalists would expose and publicize the broader contexts of the charges or their trivial nature.

Finally, as the role of strategists becomes more important in campaigns, journalists need to hold these people accountable for their past practices and questionable ethics. If practitioners know that their pasts cannot escape them, they may be more reluctant to engage in questionable practices.[15] But a broader point needs to be remembered: As long as voters are perceived as paying little attention to politics, the temptation and pressure to behave as many now do will always be there.

SCANDALS AND SCANDAL MONGERING

Related to the question of what campaigns and campaign coverage tend to avoid is what they cover instead. If foreign and economic policy appears complex, and voters aren't sure what a capital gains tax is, they can understand adultery. Any candidate who puts forth a detailed and effective proposal to balance the federal budget runs the risk of having it picked apart by scores of interest groups. Hence, the temptation is strong to engage instead in the politics of "moral annihilation."[16] Politicians are often advised to avoid the voters' main concerns because "important issues can be of limited value."[17] The focus on scandal in many instances is actually a substitute for discussion of more important issues, and many voters sense this. GOPAC, Newt Gingrich's PAC designed to train Republican candidates, has had as one of its main tacticians Joseph Gaylord, who wrote a how-to textbook that Gingrich called "absolutely brilliant." In the book, Gaylord urges challengers to "go negative" early and "never back off." The book suggests looking for a minor detail to use against any opponent and cautions candidates not to make positive proposals if doing so might harm money-raising efforts.[18] In such a cynical environment, all candidates committed to more ethical behavior must know that they may face these tactics and that they may not have alert journalists or an aroused public to help them withstand the assaults.

Knowing that top strategists are counseling candidates to avoid important issues and opt instead for scandals, we must address what constitutes a scandal. How and when should peccadilloes be reported, and how much should we make of them? That question seemed more relevant than ever as scandal overload characterized the 1996 elections. Were any of the Clinton scandals serious enough to be considered comparable to Watergate or Iran-Contra? If they were not, were they still important enough to override voters' policy preferences on abortion issues, the environment, and other domestic and foreign concerns? To most voters, the answer was no. Toward the end of the campaign, the *New York Times* compiled a list of eight areas of "scandals" involving the administration.[19] These included independent counsel investigations of Clinton and three present or former cabinet members; the Whitewater matter itself and whether Clinton might later pardon some of those convicted; Hillary Clinton's billing records from the Rose law firm in the 1980s, and whether she had hidden those records in the White House; the firing of several members of

Time *and the* Post *decided not to release the story of Dole's extramarital affair before the election.*

the White House travel office in 1993; the general charge that the Clinton administration had withheld important documents from a Republican Congress and special prosecutors who wanted to examine these matters; and two more charges coming out during the campaign itself—the improper access to FBI files by two aides in the White House, and fund-raising by the Democratic National Committee.

It was not easy for citizens to assess the seriousness of these charges. While all the allegations caused some damage, they failed to do serious harm, in part because some were complex, stemmed from events long ago, and seemed to come from Republicans such as Alfonse D'Amato, who had a long-time reputation as a fierce partisan with ethics problems of his own. Most voters seemed inclined to wait until more information was available, or to wonder whether the Republican Party or a Dole administration would be much of an improvement in these regards.

To many in our entertainment-oriented culture, scandal implies unethical sexual behavior. What should the media report, and how should citizens assess alleged sexual scandals? This issue was faced more than once in the last four years.

In January 1992, Gennifer Flowers was paid by a tabloid newspaper, *The Star*, to say at a press conference that she had had a 12-year affair with Bill Clinton. Because Clinton denied the charges, some of the mainstream media at first refused to report the story. While she had tapes to document her claims, and she clearly

knew Clinton, the tapes also showed evidence of having been tampered with. When some of the news media aired the story, however, the rest were under severe pressure also to report the story, and they did. The press faced a similar dilemma later in Clinton's first term when a conservative, anti-Clinton organization called a press conference to showcase Paula Jones, who accused the president of sexually harassing her while he was governor of Arkansas.[20]

In the summer of 1996, a woman contacted the *Washington Post* and *Time* magazine to say that she had had an affair with Bob Dole toward the end of his first marriage, which continued for several years. These two major news organizations were then faced with the dilemma of what to do with this report. The woman had not been paid by a tabloid to make the charges, nor was she seeking publicity. (She is currently an editor for a Washington, D.C.–area trade association.) "Trust" and "character" were main themes in the Dole attack on Clinton, and Dole had even said in 1994 that "the personal lives of politicians—including marital infidelity—are 'fair game.'"[21] The *Washington Post* decided to contact Dole before running the story. Dole did not deny or confirm the affair, saying, "If this comes out it will be my word against hers." He told aides that the relationship had not been "that intense." The Dole campaign prepared for the bombshell, and agreed that they would not deny the charges, but would attack the *Post* for engaging in trash journalism. But what did *Time* and the *Post* do? They decided not to release the story before the election. A majority of the *Post* editors felt that there was a "distinction between public trust and private actions." They did not want to get into the business of investigating the dalliances of presidential candidates. Dole was able to make character and trust the central claims of the last three weeks of the campaign, with *Newsweek* and *Time* mentioning the story only after the election was over.

Was this the correct decision? In this case the mainstream media made the decision for the voters. They protected Dole, and perhaps they also hoped that refusing to run the story might elevate the presidential campaign to more important issues. But how should American voters sift through the heap of charges against politicians of sexual peccadilloes? At least seven criteria seem important: (1) the credibility of the person making the charge; (2) the nature of the accusations, such as whether or not the behavior was consensual; (3) whether the behavior was purely personal or involved violations of the public trust—for example, was taxpayer money used; (4) how recently the alleged indiscretions took place; (5) whether the charges appear to be part of a pattern or an isolated incident; (6) whether the accused candidate makes similar charges against an opponent; and (7) whether the behavior seems to indicate a reckless disregard for the accused's own security, thus putting him or her at risk of blackmail, or for national security.[22] In Dole's case, even though the charges were credible, only one of the other six criteria—that he appeared to be making similar charges against an opponent—seemed to be met.

This is the third straight presidential campaign is which the press has had to grapple with questions of marital infidelity, and it will likely not be the last. Yet the rules of "relevancy" are still being contested, and there is no easy answer to the question of whether or how much attention to give to such charges.

CONCLUSION

Candidates will always be fallible human beings. But there are structural flaws in the American electoral process where change is possible. These flaws—the unethical behavior encouraged by the constant need for money and the pressure to "go negative" and ignore the voters' main concerns—are subject to regulation and new incentives. Public financing, replacing paid political ads on television and radio with free time, a press more vigilant in examining candidate claims and criticisms—all these might alter candidate behavior and make a difference.

The current practices have real consequences. Campaigns, after all, do matter. Not only do they select our leaders and provide some guidance on policies, but they also turn off some people to the whole process, giving those who remain additional clout. Politicians understand the risks of engaging in responsible policy proposals on complex issues. They can be attacked with 30-second ads, sound bites, or power phrases. The fate of Clinton's comprehensive and complex health care proposal stands as a striking example. Far safer is "three strikes and you're out," a slogan that became a

substitute for serious discussion of crime. Similarly, polls showed that nearly everyone favored "welfare reform," so that to be against the specifics of any bill so labeled became risky.

The pervasiveness of television also plays an important role in the conduct of our campaigns. As the primary source of information on campaigns for most people, television encourages simplistic responses to serious problems because it is entertainment, a "feeling" rather than a "thinking" medium. This is why more careful regulation of television in our campaign processes is important. Our campaign environment matters in many ways, and it makes sense for us to be concerned about the larger consequences of the multiple pressures on candidates to engage in unethical behavior.

Yet these criticisms of American campaigns and elections need to be put in perspective. If our process is compared to that operating in Mexico—where in the most recent presidential election the leading candidate was assassinated (with evidence pointing to a conspiracy within his own party), and where massive vote fraud occurred in the previous election—our own problems seem less serious. If our process is compared to the Russian election of 1996 won by Boris Yeltsin, their process seems fragile and full of irregularities. But if we compare the American process with those of other developed countries, such as Canada, Germany, or the Scandinavian nations, we find elsewhere far higher turnout, much less money grubbing, and much more responsible use of television.[23] These comparisons remind us that we do not *have* to remain stuck with our current system, and that it is not hopeless idealism to expect campaigns to be run more ethically. Change toward a better system will not be easy. Most pressures—from ever-more money to ever-more-sophisticated campaign strategies—seem to be pushing us in the opposite direction. But change toward a more responsible democratic system is not impossible, and the ideas for that change lie waiting to be implemented.

ENDNOTES

1. Public Citizen news release, November 6, 1996. Their preliminary analysis of the totals spent on the presidential campaigns, congressional campaigns, funds to party committees, party conven-

tions, and interest group independent expenditures came to $1,762,290,000.

2. Most of these people and companies are mentioned in Charles Lewis, *The Buying of the President* (New York: Avon Books, 1996). For more on Dole, see Charles Babcock and Ruth Marcus, "The Rise of Dole, Inc.," *Washington Post National Weekly Edition*, August 26–September 1, 1996, p. 9. Babcock and Marcus say the Dole money machine has raised $100 million since coming to Washington in 1961, with three-fourths of that amount raised since Dole became majority leader of the Senate in 1985. Carl Lindner and Chiquita Bananas are discussed in John Greenwald, "Banana Republican," *Time*, January 22, 1996, pp. 54–55.

3. Polling data is consistent and disturbing on this subject. National Election Studies and Gallup poll data show sharp decreases in the number of Americans who trust the government and the political process. Those who said that "government is pretty much run by a few 'big interests' looking out for themselves" rather than "for the benefit of all the people" jumped from 29% in 1964 to 63% by 1988. Those who answered "always" or "most of the time" to the question, "How much of the time do you think you can trust government in Washington to do what is right?" slipped from 75% in 1964 to only 26% in May of 1996. (The first finding is discussed in Michael Gant and Norman Luttbeg, *American Electorate Behavior* [Itasca, IL: Peacock, 1991], pp. 128–129, and the second in *The Gallup Poll Monthly*, May 1996, p. 45.)

4. See, for example, Kevin Phillips, *The Politics of Rich and Poor* (New York: Random House, 1990), p. 13, and Appendix B (charting data furnished by the Federal Reserve Board and the Census Bureau).

5. "Democratic, GOP Chiefs Say Campaign Finance Needs Fixing," [Minneapolis] *Star Tribune,* November 8, 1996, p. A16.

6. Richard Morin, "When Push Comes to Shove," *Washington Post National Weekly Edition*, February 19–25, 1996, p. 37. On state legislative examples, see Jim Parsons, "DFLers Find Some Questions in GOP Survey a Bit Upsetting," [Minneapolis] *Star Tribune*, November 1, 1996, p. B7. Perhaps the original push polling was done in Richard Nixon's first campaign (1946). Using a five-second script, anonymous callers said, "This is a friend of yours, but I can't tell you who I am. Did you know that Jerry Voorhis [Nixon's opponent] is a communist?"

7. Patricia L. Baden and Tom Hamburger, "Boschwitz Hires Hardball Campaign Consultant," [Minneapolis] *Star Tribune*, August 20, 1996, p. 1ff.

8. See Molly Ivins, "Giving the Voters Little to Admire," [Minneapolis] *Star Tribune*, October 24, 1996, p. A25.

9. It is too early to know if attack ads were more common in 1996 races. A preliminary study by the Annenburg Public Policy Center of the University of Pennsylvania found that only 7 percent of Clinton's and Dole's speeches were devoted to attacks, but that 41% of the news coverage of the speeches focused on that 7%. See Eric Black, "Coverage Leaves Room for Even More Improvement Next Time," [Minneapolis] *Star Tribune*, November 6, 1996, p. A10.

10. The quotation is from Francis Cline, quoted in Eric Black and Tom Hamburger, "Turning a Well-Tested Phrase," [Minneapolis] *Star Tribune*, October 18, 1996, p. A18.

11. See, for example, the *Time* cover story of September 9, 1996. On page 29, the woman, who was paid about $50,000 for her story, says: "He told me Prez's deepest secrets as we lay in bed together. He even let me listen in on Bill's hush-hush phone calls."

12. *Bare Knuckles and Back Rooms* (New York: Bantam, 1996). The reviewer is Mathew Dallek, "The Political Pugilist Strikes Back," *Washington Post National Weekly Edition*, September 30–October 6, 1996, p. 35. Dallek also says that part of the blame for the behavior of the likes of Rollins lies with voters: "Don't we often vote for the candidates with the most money, the harshest attacks, and the most cutting remarks?"

13. David Rosenbaum, "GOP's Senate Hopes Riding On an Enigma," *New York Times*, October 27, 1996, p. 26.

14. For more on the practices of other democracies, see, for example, Arthur Gunlicks, ed., *Campaign and Party Finance in North America and Western Europe* (Boulder, CO: Westview Press, 1993). Paul Taylor, "Standards So Low That Even Joe Isuzu Would Blush," *Washington Post National Weekly Edition*, April 2–8, 1990, proposes requiring candidates to appear on screen to vouch for the veracity of their ads.

15. The New Jersey examples are discussed in Michael Kinsley, "Electioneering Etiquette," *The New Republic*, November 13, 1989, p. 4. David Broder discusses accountability and other issues in his "How to Stop a Political Mudbath in Five Easy Steps," *Washington Post National Weekly Edition*, January 22–28, 1990, p. 23.

16. The phrase is from E. J. Dionne, *They Only Look Dead* (New York: Simon & Schuster, 1996), chapter 1.

17. Dionne, ibid, p. 22, quoting Joseph Gaylord, a close aide to Newt Gingrich and one of the architects of the 1994 Republican victory.

18. Phil Kuntz, "Joseph Gaylord, Newt Gingrich's 'Eyes and Ears,' Is Expected to Play a Major Role in Washington," *Wall Street Journal*, December 8, 1994, p. A20.

19. "Ethical Issues Facing the White House," November 3, 1996, p. 20.

20. For more on Paula Jones, see E. J. Dionne, *They Only Look Dead*, and Larry Sabato and Robert

Lichter, *When Should the Watchdogs Bark?* (Washington, DC: University Press of America, 1994).

21. "Clinton II: The Inside Story of His Big Victory," *Newsweek*, November 18, 1996, pp. 109–110. The matter is also covered (after the election) in some detail by Howard Kurtz, "The Dole Affair," *Washington Post National Weekly Edition*, November 25–December 1, 1996, p. 10.

22. Sabato and Lichter, *When Should the Watchdogs Bark?* especially pp. 62–63, also develop criteria for when to report on private sexual behavior.

23. See Gunlicks, *Campaign and Party Finance in North America and Western Europe*, mentioned earlier, and Martin Linton, *Money and Votes* (London: Institute for Public Policy Research, 1994), comparing Britain to Germany and Canada.

Chapter Fourteen

The Collapse of the Old Order

John Kenneth White

Nearly 200 years ago, Thomas Jefferson wrote: "The election of a president some years hence will be much more interesting to certain nations of Europe than the election of a King of Poland ever was."[1] The reelection of Jefferson's namesake, William Jefferson Clinton, puts the Founding Father's observation to a stringent test. To be sure, Polish citizens freed from the shackles of communism took some notice of the desultory contest. Their interest was aroused when Clinton promised to "complete the unfinished business of the cold war" by admitting the once-captive nations to the North Atlantic Treaty Organization (NATO).[2] Clinton's pledge also may have caught the attention of those of Polish ancestry who had fled com-

---

To call the Clinton-Dole match-up a "race" seems generous.

---

munism and were now living in this country. But most Americans seemed determined to add a corollary to Jefferson's contention by their casual attention to the Clinton-Dole contest. A *Los Angeles Times* survey found 54 percent saying that whoever won would have "no major impact on my life."[3] Even to call the Clinton-Dole matchup a "race" seems generous. From Labor Day to Election Day, more than 300 polls were taken, and Republican Bob Dole was

ahead in none. Moreover, turnout for the so-called "contest" was a mere 48.8 percent—a trough unequaled since the forgettable Calvin Coolidge–John W. Davis rout of 1924. Jefferson would have been disappointed. So, too, would have been his erstwhile political rival, Alexander Hamilton. Hamilton once wrote: "Every vital question of state will be merged in the question, 'Who will be the next president?' "[4] Many Americans 200 years later would have answered Hamilton by saying, "Who cares?"

Of course, Bill Clinton would instinctively resist being paired with Republican Coolidge—preferring to be linked instead with Democrats of more recent (and honorable) vintage: Franklin D. Roosevelt and especially John F. Kennedy. Kennedy admirers have often sought to connect Clinton with their assassinated hero. Addressing the Democratic National Convention in August 1996, Massachusetts senator Edward Kennedy pointed to a famous photograph of his brother shaking hands with 17-year-old Bill Clinton. Kennedy said, "Thirty-three years ago this summer, a young man from Boys Nation stood in the Rose Garden and shook the hand of a young president. That day, Bill Clinton took my brother's hand, and now he is the young president who has taken up the fallen standard: the belief that America can do better. And we will do better, with President William Jefferson Clinton leading us into the next American century."[5]

What is long forgotten about that Kennedy-Clinton handshake is what Kennedy told his Boys Nation audience—that the United States was standing guard in the battle with

131

communism "all the way from Berlin to Saigon."[6] Indeed, from Adolf Hitler's demise in 1945 until Mikhail Gorbachev's resignation in 1991, the United States was locked in a titanic struggle with communism. The cold war touched everyone—especially baby boomers. In his campaign tract entitled *Between Hope and History*, Clinton described how the cold war had influenced his childhood:

> I was born half a century ago, as the Second World War ended and the cold war began. It was a time of great hope, as people rebuilt their lives here at home and as our nation committed itself to rebuilding the war-ravaged economies of Europe and Asia—a commitment that made close friends out of former enemies. But by the time I was in school, it had become a time of looming nuclear peril, an era of "duck and cover" exercises in class and fallout shelters at home. We had a new and singular challenge: an expansionist and hostile Soviet Union that vowed to bury us. And we had a single-minded defense objective: containing that enemy.[7]

The cold war affected nearly every aspect of American life—from spawning the spy novel to creating an economy built on a permanent warlike footing. Along with civil rights, it gave birth to a new party system—one that ultimately helped to elect Republican presidents.[8] Of the 10 presidential elections held from 1952 to 1988, Republicans won 7. The winners—Dwight Eisenhower, Richard Nixon, Ronald Reagan, and George Bush—promised to make America "number one" militarily, often contrasting their bellicose rhetoric with their Democratic counterparts' allegedly "soft" stances on communism. One of the few Democratic victors in this period, Lyndon B. Johnson, was so wary of the Republicans' repeated assaults on his party's motives that he told Assistant Secretary of State George Ball not to worry about Vietnam War protesters: "I don't give a damn about those little pinkos on the campuses. The great black beast for us is the right wing. If we don't get this war over soon, they'll put enormous heat on us to turn it into an Armageddon and wreck all our other programs."[9] Johnson repeatedly told intimates that, by God, he was not going to be the president who first lost Vietnam, then Congress, and ultimately the White House.

Republicans have not always cast such a frightful image. In fact, before the cold war began, they were a demoralized bunch. In the election 60 years ago, Franklin D. Roosevelt carried every state except Maine and Vermont—both won by Clinton in 1996. Congressional Democrats fared nearly as well, winning 333 seats in the House and 75 in the Senate. These majorities were so huge that some Democrats had to sit with the Republicans because there wasn't enough room for them on their side of the aisle! But the Democratic triumph was more than a partisan victory—it was a triumph of ideology. Political columnist Heywood Broun wrote in the *Nation* that he could "see no interpretation of the returns which does not suggest that the people of America want the president to proceed along progressive or liberal lines."[10] Republicans were less enthusiastic. The *Phoenix Republic* warned that Roosevelt's "present position is comparable only with that of Joseph Stalin."[11]

But Roosevelt did not have to resort to dictatorial methods to obtain a public consensus about what needed to be done. Asked by George Gallup in 1936, "Which theory of government do you favor: concentration of power in the federal government or concentration of power in state government?" 56 percent of respondents wanted the federal government to take the lead.[12] Republicans sputtered that, like Stalin, Roosevelt had encroached on some precious liberties: "America is in peril. The welfare of the American men and women and the future of our youth are at stake. We dedicate ourselves to the preservation of their political liberty, their individual opportunity, and their character as free citizens, which today for the first time are threatened by government itself."[13] Such fulminations meant little to most voters. In battling the Great Depression with an array of New Deal–inspired agencies, one thing was clear: Big government helped the "common man." Although some Republicans tried to equate the New Deal with communism, the tactic backfired. Addressing the Democratic State Convention in Syracuse, New York, Roosevelt declared that it was the *Republicans* who had been the unwitting dupes of the U.S. Communist Party during the ruinous Hoover years: "In their speeches, they deplored [communism], but by their actions they encouraged it. The injustices, the inequalities, the downright suffering out of which revolutions come—what did they do about these things? Lacking courage, they evaded. Being selfish, they neglected. Being short-sighted, they ignored. When the crisis came—as these wrongs made it sure to come—America was unprepared."[14]

The cold war took the sting out of Roosevelt's attack. For 50 years, Republicans had charged that Democrats were "soft on communism," and in making their accusations they were aided by a pro-peace faction within the Democratic Party, first led by Henry Wallace and later by George McGovern. Appealing for understanding of the Soviet Union's place in world geography (surrounded as it was by an array of hostile neighbors such as Turkey and Iran) was noble, and several Democrats made the gesture, but it was no way to win presidential contests. In the emerging cold war party system, Republicans won the presidency by pursuing hard-fought arms agreements with the Soviets while assuring voters that they were hard-headed negotiators. "Peace through strength" became a Republican mantra, and would-be GOP presidents chanted it over and over again. Democrats protested that they were not muddle-headed pantywaists when it came to dealing with the Soviet Communist Party. John Kennedy, for instance, out-hawked Richard Nixon in their famous 1960 encounter. Lyndon Johnson's 1964 appeal to "reason together" provided a stark contrast to Barry Goldwater's view that the cold war must be won, even if that meant "lobbing one [an A-bomb] into the men's room of the Kremlin."[15] But, more often than not, the Democratic responses were ineffectual. In 1988, Michael Dukakis climbed aboard a tank to show that he, too, could be tough on communism. After Dukakis lost to Bush, some Democrats wondered whether their party would ever win the presidency again.

When he denounced the Soviet Union as the "evil empire" in 1983, Ronald Reagan told the National Association of Evangelicals, "I believe that communism is another sad, bizarre chapter in human history whose last pages even now are being written."[16] Many in Reagan's born-again audience were skeptical. Miraculously, however, the cold war ended with the tumbling of the Berlin Wall in 1989 and the implosion of the Soviet Union two years later. With Clinton's election in 1992, some Democrats thought the Almighty was smiling on them once more. Joe Lyons, a Democratic precinct campaign in Chicago, enthused: "There is a God: A Democrat can be president again."[17]

At first, Republicans were disbelieving—they refused to accept Clinton's election as legitimate. After all, Clinton had won with only 43 percent of the vote, as they liked to remind everyone who would listen. The GOP faithful also blamed Ross Perot for their party's poor presidential showing. But Perot's absence in 1992 would have changed the outcome in just one state: Ohio. Instead, something even more significant than a Democratic win was underfoot—namely, the collapse of the Republican order established by the cold war. Throughout the long struggle with the Soviet enemy, Re-

Throughout the long struggle with the Soviet enemy, presidents prepared for every contingency except one: victory.

publican presidents (and the occasional Democratic chief executive) prepared for every contingency except one: victory. But with the cold war won, Republicans sought to make the most of it. Bush told the GOP delegates in 1992: "This convention is the first at which an American president can say the cold war is over, and freedom finished first."[18] Ronald Reagan remembered that he had seen the "evil empire" and declared that he, not the Democrats, deserved credit for its demise: "I heard those speakers at the other convention saying 'we won the cold war'—and I couldn't help wondering, just who exactly do they mean by 'we'?"[19] But the Eisenhower-Nixon-Reagan formula of a strong defense, tough foreign policy, and plugging the economy into the cold war machine did not work. George Bush in 1992 had lost 16 percentage points from his 1988 scores. Not since 1968, when Democrat Hubert H. Humphrey saw his party's support plummet by 18 points from the previous election, had such a free-fall occurred. Among some demographic groups, the Bush losses from 1988 were staggering: white Protestants showed a 20-point decline; college graduates, 21 points; those with some college credits, 20 points; men, 19 points; westerners, 18 points; independents, 23 points; and Republicans, 18 points. Recriminations were widespread. Looking back, Dan Quayle recalled: "This was the most poorly planned and executed incumbent presidential campaign in this century."[20] Bush himself called 1992 "the most unpleasant year of my life."[21] In 1996, Bob Dole could have said much the same.

THE LAST WARRIOR AND THE COLD WAR

During his long, unsuccessful march toward the presidency, Bob Dole trotted out what had worked for Republicans for so long: anti-communism. Following in the footsteps of his mentor, Richard Nixon, Dole accused Clinton of "coddling communists" in North Korea after that country refused to let inspectors visit areas where nuclear weapons–producing facilities were suspected. The entrance of Jimmy Carter as a negotiator with North Korea's communist dictator, Kim Il Sung, reinforced Dole's battle cry. If elected, Dole promised to keep North Korea isolated until there had been a full accounting of the POWs and MIAs from the Korean War. Still keeping his eye on Asia, Dole trained his sights on Vietnam. Addressing the Republican Convention, he startled the delegates with a critique of the Johnson administration's handling of the Vietnam War: "For those who might be sharply taken aback in thinking of Vietnam, think again, for in Vietnam the long gray line did not fail us, we failed it in Vietnam. The American soldier was not made for the casual and arrogant treatment that he suffered there, where he was committed without clear purpose or resolve, bound by rules that prevented victory, and kept waiting in the valley of the shadow of death for 10 years while the nation debated the undebatable question of his honor."[22] Finally, Dole took aim at a target closer to home—chiding Fidel Castro for shooting down a private U.S. airplane in international waters, and promising never to waver in his determination to restore democracy to that imprisoned island.

As these examples illustrate, Dole was still a cold war captive. Speaking to a convention of automobile dealers, the Republican candidate momentarily forgot that the hammer and sickle had been ripped from the Kremlin towers: "What would you want the president to do if he were informed in the middle of the night or the middle of the day . . . that there was an incoming missile, maybe from the Soviet Union? You may say, 'Shoot it down.' But we can't shoot it down."[23] Dole's solution—the Defend America Act of 1996, which would require a national defense system for all 50 states by 2003. Dole's immersion in the politics of the cold war even affected his view of Clinton. In retrospect, it seems clear that Dole believed that his opponent was not Clinton but the candidate whose Texas campaign Clinton had managed in 1972, George McGovern. For Dole, Clinton was the spoiled child of the 1960s "who never grew up, never did anything real, never sacrificed, never suffered, and never learned."[24] Using rhetoric reminiscent of his days as Richard Nixon's Republican national chairman, Dole maintained that Clinton clung to all the misconceptions about national defense once held by McGovern and his ilk: "We are the party whose resolve did not flag as the cold war dragged on, we did not tremble before a Soviet giant that was just about to fall, and we did not have to be begged to take up arms against Saddam Hussein"—implying that it was the Democrats, as usual, who were "soft" on all counts.[25] Dole thought Clinton especially derelict regarding his Pentagon budgets which, he observed, cut the armed forces from 18 divisions to 10, trimmed fighter wings from 25 to 13, and mothballed 200 naval ships.[26] The 1996 Republican platform was even more dramatic: "In a peaceful world, such limitations would be impudent. In today's world, they are immoral. The danger of a missile attack with nuclear, chemical, or biological weapons is the most serious threat to our national security. Communist China has mocked our vulnerability by threatening to attack Los Angeles if we stand by our historic commitment to the Republic of China on Taiwan."[27]

Republicans believed the lessons of the cold war still applied: "Because this is a difficult and dangerous world, we believe that peace can be assured only through strength, that a strong national defense is necessary to protect America at home and secure its interests abroad, and that we must restore leadership and character to the presidency as the best way to restore America's leadership and credibility throughout the world."[28] Reacting to the Republican invocation of "peace through strength," Democrats dryly observed that Dole was "locked in a cold war mentality" without a "coherent strategy to nurture and strengthen the global progress toward peace and democracy."[29] But Republicans clung to their old anticommunist script. The GOP-controlled 104th Congress, for example, proposed building a privately funded international memorial dedicated to those who once lived in the former captive nations, who constituted the "100-million victims of communism."[30] In the absence of tangible monuments, other Republicans relied on their words to summon the ghosts of the cold war past. Vice presidential candidate Jack Kemp, for instance, paid homage to Reagan: "Make no mistake about it. Communism came down not because it fell but because he pushed it."[31] At campaign's end, Dole traveled with Gerald Ford and George Bush—three of the last World War II soldiers to either serve or seek the presidency. Accompanying them was Arizona senator John McCain, himself a Vietnam War hero, who dubbed Dole "the last warrior." But the Dole caravan only emphasized their man as a candidate of the past. As Simon Rosenberg of the centrist New Democrat Network observed: "For a newer, younger America, Bob Dole was always a black and white movie in a color age."[32]

Indeed, the Dole campaign had the ambiance of an old movie. Unlike the 1950s, few Americans were worried about a Chinese attack on Los Angeles. For much of 1996, it seemed as though Dole and his advisers were rummaging around the Republican attic looking for old kinescopes of their "greatest hits." But a score of headlines underlined the fact that the cold war was finally over. In September, Spiro Agnew, Richard Nixon's disgraced vice president—whose colorful alliterative descriptions of Vietnam War protesters included such hits as "nattering nabobs of negativism," "pusillanimous pussy-footers," and "vicars of vacillation"—died.[33] Ten days after Clinton was reelected, Alger Hiss, aged 92, also died. The day after Hiss's death the Emergency Broadcast System, established by President Kennedy in 1963, announced that it was curtailing the long shrill tone used in television warnings about a potential nuclear attack, followed by the disclaimer: "This is a test of the Emergency Broadcast System—this is *only* a test." Instead of the long whine, which scared many children and annoyed most adults, a few short buzzes would be substituted.[34] But while Republicans could not leave the cold war alone, Clinton harkened to an even earlier era: that of Franklin D. Roosevelt and the New Deal.

CLINTON REDUX: BACK TO THE FUTURE

Some years ago, journalist Samuel Lubell wrote: "More than any other single factor, voting is dominated by continuity with the past, being truly like a river that rises in the past and empties into the future."[35] Throughout the long campaign, Bill Clinton never tired of talking about the future—implying that the 73-year-old Dole was a man of the past. Clinton constructed a powerful metaphor to make his case that he was best able to lead, stating that he would "build a bridge to the twenty-first century." During his acceptance speech, Clinton repeated his "bridge" metaphor 15 times. But Clinton's bridge seemed more like that engineered by Franklin D. Roosevelt than one designed to move the nation (and the Democratic Party) into the next century. For 60 years, Democrats had told voters that they would protect the New Deal, Fair Deal, New Frontier, and Great Society programs from Republican-inspired efforts to dismantle them. Back in 1936, Democratic platform writers boasted: "We have built foundations for the security of those who are faced with the hazards of unemployment and old age; for the orphaned, the crippled, and the blind. On the foundation of the Social Security Act, we are determined to erect a structure of economic security for all our people, making sure that this benefit shall keep step with the ever-increasing capacity of America to provide a high standard of living for all its citizens."[36]

Although Clinton's reelection bid was nearly as far removed in time from Roosevelt's bid for a second term as the New Deal was from the Civil War, the Democratic repertoire often began with a hymn of praise to FDR followed by a reprise for those who had yet to benefit from his programs. In 1964, Lyndon Johnson promised a Great Society that included Medicare for the elderly, Medicaid for the poor, food stamps for the hungry, legal assistance for the indigent, economic revitalization plans for distressed areas, and more money for research and treatment of heart disease and cancer. Thus it was that Johnson engineered congressional passage of the Civil Rights Act of 1964, the Voting Rights Act of 1965, a highway beautification program, the Corporation for Public

---

One of the holdouts who opposed Medicare to the end was Kansas congressman Bob Dole.

Broadcasting, a food stamp program, and a Model Cities program. Of these, Medicare stood out as a singular achievement. Johnson had told the large crowds that came to greet him on the campaign trail in 1964 that Medicare would be "at the top of my list" of proposals to be submitted to the new Congress.[37] The Johnson landslide allowed him to keep his promise by bringing 71 new Democrats into the House. But one of the 12 holdouts who truculently opposed Medicare to the end was three-term Kansas congressman Bob Dole. Thirty years later, Dole proudly recounted his opposition to the Republican faithful: "I was right then; I knew it wouldn't work."[38] But Dole's recalcitrance was not enough to overcome the groundswell for Medicare, and when Johnson scrawled his signature on the new law, the only New Deal objective left unfilled was universal health care—a goal that also eluded Bill Clinton.

The success of Clinton's foes in blocking his health care proposal nearly doomed his presidency and contributed mightily to the Republican victory in 1994, but it cemented the Democratic reputation as the party that "cares more about people like you." Ever since the Great Depression, Democrats have been viewed as more compassionate, while Republicans have been depicted as cruel, heartless louts. Back in 1932, former President Calvin Coolidge intoned, "The charge is made that the Republican Party does not show solicitude for the common run of people but is interested only in promoting the interests of a few favored individuals

and corporations. . . . All this is a question of method. . . . We have advocated strengthening the position of the employer that he might pay better wages to his employees."[39] But it was the "common run of people" who greeted Roosevelt along the campaign trail in 1936 with cries of, "He saved my job! He saved my home!"[40]

Roosevelt's portrayal of caring Democrats and cold-hearted Republicans persisted throughout the cold war—and thereafter. Republicans protested with cries of "bleeding-heart liberal!" but their attempt to equate liberalism with do-gooders did not erase their unsympathetic image, to which Democrats referred whenever they were in trouble. In 1968, for example, Hubert Humphrey recalled how his party had stood by Roosevelt's common man: "Our Republican friends have fought every piece of social legislation that has benefitted this country. They have fought against Social Security, they have been against all forms of federal aid to education, they have been against Medicare for our senior citizens. They have been against minimum wages. . . . Why you just name it, and I'll guarantee you that you will have found a majority of them in Congress against it."[41]

Humphrey's description matched that held by most voters—even as they elected Republican presidents to cope with the Soviet menace. A 1951 Gallup poll found that most respondents would tell a new voter that the Democratic Party stood for "the working man" and that the Republican Party promoted the "privileged few."[42] The Roosevelt portrayal was still intact 45 years later: 65 percent said that it was the Republicans who were "concerned with the needs of business and powerful groups"; just 19 percent thought that the Democrats were worried about these forces.[43] After Republicans seized Congress in 1994, Clinton issued a warning: "We must not go back to an era of 'every man for himself.' "[44]

But it was Newt Gingrich and his followers who took up Republican Alf Landon's 1936 admonition to "stop the folly of uncontrolled spending [and] balance the budget—not by increasing taxes but by cutting expenditures, drastically and immediately."[45] Gingrich thought the best way to accomplish this was to slash $270 billion in projected Medicare costs. The effects of such an action, he hoped, would allow the Democrats' beloved Medicare entitlement to "wither on the vine."[46] Democrats, who had once taken Medicare and Social Security for granted, showed a renewed appreciation of these programs—even though, as taxpayers, they did not want the federal government to grow much more. Clinton reinforced their support by running a series of television advertisements denouncing the "Dolegingrich" cuts. The ads paid off: by 57 percent to 33 percent, Americans said the Democrats were better able to deal with the problems posed by the Medicare trust fund's shortfall.[47] Gingrich's assault on the New Deal gave Democrats a sword they would use with relish:

Republicans wanted to eliminate the guarantee of health care for the poor, the elderly, and the disabled. They were wrong and we stopped them. Republicans wanted to destroy the food stamp and school lunch programs that provide basic nutrition to millions of working-class families and poor children. They were wrong, and we stopped them. Republicans wanted to cut off young unwed mothers—because they actually thought their children would be better off living in an orphanage. They were dead wrong, and we stopped them. The bill Republicans passed last year was values-backward—it was soft on work and tough on children, and we applaud the president for stopping it.[48]

Like the Roosevelt Democrats of the 1930s, Clinton Democrats told voters that a Republican restoration would result in a Robin Hood–like reversal, as Republicans would give "a massive tax break to the wealthiest Americans, and pay for it by raising taxes on ordinary Americans and slashing health care for the elderly."[49] Dole repeatedly pledged never to touch Social Security, recalling how his late mother would admonish him, "All I've got is my Social Security; don't touch it."[50] But Dole was trapped by a post–cold war Republican establishment determined make government its new enemy. In 1994, Grover G. Norquist, a conservative antitax Republican activist, wrote that the sine qua non of Dole's presidential candidacy "will be Dole's ability to block any government-run health care system."[51] Dole's success in doing just that boosted his chances among Republicans, but ran afoul of the general electorate. Of the 15 percent who named Medicare as the most important factor in their voting decision, 67 percent backed Clinton. Moreover, 42 percent named the Republicans as "more

likely" to cut Medicare—just 17 percent thought Democrats would attack this holy grail of American politics. Finally, of the 9 percent who said that compassion was an important factor in determining their presidential vote, 72 percent chose Clinton.[52]

Besides Medicare, Clinton rested his case on another Democratic legacy: education. Ever since Jimmy Carter told the National Education Association that he would establish a Department of Education—a promise fulfilled in 1979—Democrats have made education a priority. They received an unexpected boost in 1983, when a Reagan-appointed National Commission on Excellence in Education issued a report titled *A Nation at Risk*. Using the language of the cold war, the commission sounded an alarm about declining U.S. educational standards: "If an unfriendly foreign power had attempted to impose on America the mediocre educational performance that exists today, we might well have viewed it as an act of war. As it stands, we have allowed this to happen to ourselves. We have even squandered the gains in student achievement made in the wake of the Sputnik challenge. Moreover, we have dismantled essential support systems which helped make those gains possible. We have, in effect, been committing an act of unthinking, unilateral educational disarmament."[53] A Gallup poll conducted in October 1996 gave the Democrats a 29-point advantage as the party best able to deal with the education issue.[54] The Republican Congress compounded their party's problem by advocating elimination of the Department of Education, slashing slated increases in federally sponsored school lunch programs, and jettisoning the Corporation for Public Broadcasting, which funded such popular children's television programs as *Sesame Street*. To Democrats, such stances were by-products of a Republican Party more motivated by the values of Scrooge than of opportunity for all: "The Republican budget tried to take Big Bird away from 5-year-olds, school lunches away from 10-year-olds, summer jobs away from 15-year-olds, and college loans away from 20-year-olds."[55]

But Clinton's vision of being a modern-day Roosevelt was mired in widespread public distrust of government. Unlike the halcyon days of the New Deal, 52 percent of those leaving the polls in 1996 believed the federal government should do less; just 41 percent said there

137

was more for government to do.[56] Voters rendered a judgment: they wanted a president who would preserve the best of the New Deal, Fair Deal, and Great Society while not enlarging the federal establishment very much. Clinton's shrewd political instincts anticipated such a result. The Democratic platform penned by his

Voters wanted a president who would preserve the best of the New Deal, Fair Deal, and Great Society while not enlarging the federal establishment.

underlings advised parents to "help their children with their homework, to read to them, to know their teachers, and above all, to teach their children right from wrong, set the best example, and teach children how to make responsible decisions."[57] The document also printed a toll-free 800 number for battered spouses who needed to find shelter and report their abusive partners to the authorities. Promising a "reinvented government" that would adhere to the values of opportunity, community, and responsibility, Clinton's New Democratic Party described its mission for the next century:

> Today's Democratic Party knows that the era of big government is over. Big bureaucracies and Washington solutions are not the real answers to today's challenges. We need a smaller government . . . and we must have a larger national spirit. Government's job should be to give people the tools they need to make the most of their own lives. Americans must take the responsibility to use them, to build good lives for themselves and their families. Personal responsibility is the most powerful force we have to meet our challenges and shape the future we want for ourselves, for our children, and for America.[58]

But Clinton's forward-looking rhetoric contained much that was mired in the New Deal past. While touting V-chips that would control children's access to television; promoting

Table 14.1

Two-Party Presidential Vote Compared, 1992 and 1996 (in percentages)

Demographic Category	Clinton '96 minus Clinton '92	Dole minus Bush
Nationwide	+6	+3
Sex		
Men	+2	+6
Women	+9	+1
Race		
Whites	+4	+6
Blacks	+1	+2
Hispanics	+11	−4
Age		
18–29 years old	+10	0
30–44 years old	+7	+3
45–59 years old	+7	+1
60 and older	−2	+6
Income		
Under $15,000	+1	+5
$15,000–$29,999	+8	+1
$30,000–$49,999	+7	+2
$50,000–$74,999	+5	+4
$75,000 and over	+5	+3
Education		
Less than high school	+5	0
High school graduate	+8	−1
Some college	+7	+3
College graduate	+5	+5
Postgraduate	+2	+4
Region		
East	+8	−1
Midwest	+6	+4
South	+5	+3
West	+5	+6
Religion		
White Protestant	+3	+6
Catholic	+9	+2
Jewish	−2	+5
Party		
Democrats	+7	0
Republicans	+3	+7
Independents	+5	+3
Philosophy		
Liberal	+10	−3
Moderate	+10	+2
Conservative	+2	+7

Sources: Voter Research and Surveys, exit poll, November 3, 1992, and Voter News and Surveys, exit poll, November 5, 1996.

Table 14.2

Issue Concerns and Candidate Preferences, 1996 (in percentages)

Issue Concern	Clinton Voters	Dole Voters	All Voters
Taxes	19	73	11
Medicare	67	26	15
Foreign Policy	35	56	4
Federal Deficit	27	52	12
Economy/Jobs	61	27	12
Education	78	16	12
Crime/Drugs	40	50	7

Source: Voter News and Surveys, exit poll, November 5, 1996.

school uniforms and family leave; launching a war on teenage smoking; continuing the ban against assault weapons; teaching every 8-year-old to read, every 12-year-old to use the Internet, and extending some college education to every 18-year-old were noble goals, they did not constitute a vision upon which future Democratic presidents could build. Clinton's dilemma was to find a way to move his administration and his party away from Franklin Roosevelt's and Lyndon Johnson's domestic victories, and empower Democrats with a purpose that would energize them in the years to come. Clinton played it safe by giving voters a "lite" version of the New Deal.

REPUBLICAN DISARRAY

But it is the defeat of the Republican Party's last grand warrior that may prove emblematic for what happens in the post–cold war era. Throughout the cold war, presidential contests were fought over the corpse of the Democratic Party. Now the same thing seems to be happening to the Republicans. In an age when voters want more than self-congratulatory kudos for beating communism, Republicans may find that success poses the greatest danger a political party can face. Former New Hampshire Republican governor Steve Merrill has perceptively observed: "It is time for reflection in our party. The losses we've suffered at the presidential level should cause us to reflect that we really have not explained our vision of the future as well as we should have."[59]

It is these losses that should give the Republicans pause. By any measure, the 38 percent and 41 percent of the votes received by George Bush and Bob Dole respectively are devastating performances. Not since the Carter-Mondale twin defeats in 1980 and 1984 has a presidential pair performed so poorly. As Table 14.1 shows, the 1992 and 1996 Republican vote resembled the plains of Bob Dole's native Kansas—in virtually every demographic category, a flat line could be drawn from one election to the next.

Thus, the next Republican ticket faces a daunting task: to win in 2000, it must outperform Dole-Kemp by *nine* percentage points. Recent history shows this to be nearly impossible. Only Dwight Eisenhower in 1952 following the Korean stalemate and Jimmy Carter in 1976 after the Watergate disaster improved on their party's previous nominees by nine points. The Republican dilemma is also compounded by the fact that there is no obvious heir apparent to the presidential nomination. The last time the GOP faced a leadership crisis was in 1964, when the Goldwater forces engineered a takeover. Today's Republican Party has at least four factions that would like to run it: the moderates (social liberals and economic conservatives led by New Jersey governor Christine Todd Whitman and Massachusetts governor William Weld), old-fashioned, balance-the-budget conservatives (once led by Bob Dole), supply-siders (whose leading spokespersons are Jack Kemp and Steve Forbes), and the religious right (led by Pat Robertson and Ralph Reed). Of these, the born-again Republicans have the most potential to wrest control away from the other groups. Already, the Christian Right controls the party machinery in such key states as Texas and Pennsylvania. Like the Democrats of the 1920s who squabbled over prohibition and did not win the presidency until they came to grips with the issue, Republicans must achieve a settlement over the question of abortion. Until that happens, whoever wins the Republican presidential nomination in 2000 must be acceptable to all four factions—a near-heroic feat if it can be accomplished. Barring a grand settlement, the prospective nominee faces what former Minnesota Republican senator David Durenberger aptly describes as the "Mondale problem":

> We are suffering currently from what is [known as] "leadership" in the Republican Party. What is it? Is it going to be known by what you're against or what you're for? It's so much easier to say you're *against* employer mandates and you're *against* large government and you're *against* taxes. Then what are you *for*? . . . Dole is *for* whatever the people are at the moment. Dole's problem is basically the Mondale problem. You can't get to be president unless you go through that damn convention, and if you go through that damn convention you probably won't be president.[60]

Thus, the obstacles that beset the Republican Party in post–cold war presidential contests seem especially large. As Table 14.2 indicates, Dole did quite well among the small number of voters still trapped in the cold war rubric—especially the 4 percent of those who said foreign policy mattered most. But it was Clinton's agenda that most voters responded to, and it seems likely to remain important four years hence. For Clinton backers, education, Medicare, and the economy were all-important, whereas Dole won the largest vote share from those who said taxes, foreign policy, and deficit reduction mattered most. Of these, deficit reduction and taxes are likely to remain important considerations. But the difficulties that Clinton and the 105th Congress face on entitlement issues also mean that the old Democratic standbys of Medicare and Social Security are likely to remain high on the voters' list of priorities. Add education and the environment to the post–cold war issues mix, and Democrats are well poised to walk across Bill Clinton's bridge to the twenty-first century. The altered set of issues, dubbed by White House strategists as "M2E2" (shorthand for Medicare, Medicaid,

education, and the environment), carry particular weight among female voters—especially single mothers dependent on the social safety nets cast by government. Republican representative Marge Roukema observed that unless Republicans consciously address these issues they will be "a long time coming back."[61]

THE VITAL CENTER

Republicans did heave a sigh of relief, however, when the final election count showed continuance of their congressional majority—the first back-to-back GOP Congresses in 68 years. A relieved Newt Gingrich told reporters: "It's pretty amazing, a truly historic moment."[62] Indeed it was. The power of incumbency certainly helped the GOP keep its hold on power—just as it did during the long years of Democratic domination. To confirm this point, 95 percent of House members from both parties who sought reelection won—including 83 percent of the Republican class of 1994. Likewise, the Republican "incumbent party" prevailed in the Senate, where 93-year-old Strom Thurmond (SC) won an eighth term, and the much-despised Jesse Helms (NC) was reelected to his fifth. Only South Dakota's hapless Larry Pressler bowed before a Democratic challenger.

But just as presidential contests have been altered since the end of the cold war, Congress has also been transformed. Most House members, for example, have won their seats since the Berlin Wall fell in 1989. In the new post–cold war Congress, successful Democratic and Republican candidates must make their respective pitches to self-described independents who hold the balance of power. And most of them like the new division they have created with a Democratic president and a Republican Congress. By a margin of 49 percent to 44 percent, voters leaving the polls expressed a preference for a Republican Congress if Clinton were to win again.[63] Aware of this, Republican strategists cobbled together an election night television commercial for viewing on the West Coast that all but threw Dole overboard: "Remember the last time Democrats ran everything? The largest tax increase in history. Government-run health care. More wasteful spending. Who wants that again? Don't let Oregon down. Don't let the media stop you from voting. And don't hand Bill Clinton a blank check. The polls close at eight."[64] Some credit the advertisement with helping Oregon Republican Gordon Smith win a close Senate race over Democrat Tom Bruggere.

Independents are renowned for their cognitive dissonance when it comes to the role of government. In 1967, social scientists Lloyd Free and Hadley Cantril observed a dichotomy between the public's preference for "ideological conservatism" and its penchant for "programmatic liberalism."[65] Voters wanted the federal government in the abstract to be kept to a minimum, but when asked about specific programs,

---

Most citizens do not trust either party, preferring to divide their ballots and demand that the parties find a consensus.

---

they voiced strong support for a more involved bureaucracy. Today, the contradictions maintain their conventional partisan overtones, with Republicans cast in the role of the "ideological conservatives" and Democrats acting as the "programmatic liberals." Delivering his 1996 State of the Union address, Bill Clinton tried to reconcile the two: "We know big government does not have all the answers. There is not a program for every problem. We know we need a smaller, less bureaucratic government in Washington—one that lives within its means."[66] But the elevation of such issues as tax cuts, entitlements, deficit reduction, education, and the environment has created a divided government decidedly different from its predecessors, and one that appeals to American sensibilities. Voters have never bought the concept of unified party government as either desirable or necessary to make government work. Back in 1944, pollster Elmo Roper found only 37 percent of respondents saying that split-party control of the presidency and Congress would be "bad because it has made it impossible to work on solutions to the important problems facing the country."[67] Today, most citizens say they do not trust either party, preferring the extra-constitu-

tional check that their divided ballots have created and demanding that the parties find a consensus. Questioning the candidates at their second debate, schoolteacher Sharon MacAfee spoke for many when she quoted the sentiments of a sixth-grader:

> If I were president, I would think about Abraham Lincoln and George Washington and what they did to make our country great. We should unite the white and black people and people of all cultures. Democrats and Republicans should unite also. We should all come together and think of the best ways to solve the economic problems of our country. I believe that when we are able to come together and stop fighting amongst ourselves, we will get along a lot better.[68]

After the election, both parties got the message. Speaking to an enthusiastic crowd of supporters, Bill Clinton disavowed partisanship: "The challenges we face, they're not Democratic or Republican challenges. They're American challenges. What we know from the budget battles of the last two years and from the remarkable success of the last few weeks of the Congress is the lesson we have learned for the last 220 years—what we have achieved as Americans of lasting good, we have achieved by working together. So let me say to the leaders of my Democratic Party and the leaders of the Republican Party, it is time to put country ahead of party."[69] Newt Gingrich agreed: "Our goal is to find common ground [with Clinton]. . . . We don't have to live in a world of confrontation. We ought to work with him and give him a chance to lead in the direction he campaigned on."[70]

The American desire for a fusion of the two parties is a dominant characteristic of the post–cold war era. As Daniel Bell prematurely postulated in 1960, Americans may be witnessing the "end of ideology."[71] If that is true 37 years later, it also means an end to the politics of passion, for passion is what gives ideology its force. That seems to suit the electorate just fine. In 1996, Americans settled down from the dizzying changes that characterized elections immediately following the end of the cold war. A grand settlement was reached: voters gave a resounding "NO!" to any big new agendas from either party, preferring that government give tax cuts that would empower them to do more for themselves, protect middle-class entitlements

141

such as Social Security and Medicare, and provide an enhanced federal role in such vital twenty-first-century concerns as education and the environment. Bill Clinton perceived the emerging consensus and placed himself squarely in favor of it: "The ground has shifted beneath our feet, but we have clearly created a new center, not the lukewarm midpoint between overheated liberalism and chilly conservatism, but instead, a place where throughout our history, people of goodwill have tried to forge new approaches to new challenges."[72]

Back in the summer of 1965, Bill Clinton wrote of his future in a letter to a friend, "Maybe I am beginning to realize that I am almost grown, and will soon have to choose that one final motive in life which I hope will put a little asterisk by my name in the billion pages of the book of life."[73] Clinton's two-term tenure in the White House assures him of an asterisk. But his place in American political history remains to be written. The last four years have witnessed the collapse of an old political order shaped by the cold war and dominated by the Republicans. During his first term in office, Clinton was unable to put his political imprint on the post–cold war era. He now faces the dilemma of those presidents, many of them relatively insignificant, who have no war or other major crises that allow them great power to shape their times. Washington, Lincoln, and Franklin Roosevelt, whose claims to greatness are universally accepted by historians, had the opportunity to use crises to make their names synonymous with a political era that they defined. Clinton seems to recognize this. Confiding to his staff late one evening in January 1995, he lamented that there was no longer the crackle of electricity surrounding the presidency: "I would have much preferred being president during World War II. I am a person out of my time."[74]

In many ways, Clinton's challenge is akin to Theodore Roosevelt's. Lacking a war or a severe economic crisis, Roosevelt lent his voice to the growing Progressive chorus. By the sheer force of his personality, he helped to enlarge what Herbert Croly called in 1909 "the promise of American life,"[75] and became one of the few presidents without a serious economic or military calamity to have his visage placed on Mount Rushmore. Whether Bill Clinton can emulate Theodore Roosevelt, even modestly, re-

mains to be seen. Thus far, Clinton has shown the Democrats how to win the presidency. Now he needs to give his party a continued rationale for keeping it.

ENDNOTES

1. Quoted in John F. Kennedy, "The Presidency and Foreign Policy," speech to California Democratic Clubs Convention, February 12, 1960.

2. See Bill Clinton, "Speech to the Democratic Leadership Council," Washington, DC, December 11, 1996, and John F. Harris, "Clinton Vows Wider NATO in Three Years," *Washington Post*, October 23, 1996, p. A1.

3. *Los Angeles Times*, survey, April 4–13, 1996. Text of question: "Which comes closer to your view? Whoever wins the presidential election in November, the result will have a major impact on my life. OR, Whoever wins the presidential election in November, the result will have no major impact on my life." Major impact, 39 percent; no major impact, 54 percent; don't know, 7 percent.

4. Quoted in Emmet John Hughes, *The Living Presidency* (New York: Coward, McCann and Geoghegan, 1973), p. 40.

5. Text of Kennedy's Speech: "If We Stand Our Ground, We Can Prevail," *New York Times*, August 30, 1996, p. A13.

6. John F. Kennedy, "Remarks to Delegates to the Eighteenth Annual American Legion Boys Nation," July 24, 1963, in *Public Papers of the Presidents of the United States: John F. Kennedy* (Washington, DC: U.S. Government Printing Office, 1964), p. 598.

7. Bill Clinton, *Between Hope and History: Meeting America's Challenges for the 21st Century* (New York: Times Books, 1996), p. 142.

8. The Republican Party's gains among southern whites have been well documented. See, for example, Thomas Byrne Edsall with Mary D. Edsall, *Chain Reaction: The Impact of Race, Rights and Taxes on American Politics* (New York: W. W. Norton, 1992). For a longer interpretation of the cold war's influence on American politics, see John Kenneth White, *Still Seeing Red: How the Old Cold War Shapes the New American Politics* (Boulder, CO: Westview Press, 1997).

9. George Ball, "The Rationalist in Power," *New York Review of Books*, April 22, 1993, p. 34.

10. Quoted in Alan Brinkley, *The End of Reform: New Deal Liberalism and the War* (New York: Knopf, 1995), p. 16.

11. Quoted in "Editorial Comment of Representative Newspapers on Vote Outcome," *New York Times*, November 5, 1936, p. 4.

12. Gallup poll, 1936.

13. Quoted in Kirk H. Porter and Donald Bruce Johnson, *National Party Platforms: 1840–1968*

(Urbana: University of Illinois Press, 1970), pp. 365–366.

14. Franklin D. Roosevelt, "Address at the Democratic State Convention," Syracuse, NY, September 29, 1936.

15. Quoted in Theodore H. White, *The Making of the President, 1964* (New York: New American Library, 1965), p. 130.

16. Ronald Reagan, "Remarks at the Annual Convention of the National Association of Evangelicals," Orlando, FL, March 8, 1983.

17. Quoted in Francis X. Clines, "Civics 101: Cultivating Grass Roots the Old Way," *New York Times*, November 4, 1992, p. B1.

18. George Bush, Acceptance Speech, Republican National Convention, Houston, Texas, August 20, 1992.

19. Quoted in Garry Wills, "The Born-Again Republicans," *New York Review of Books*, September 24, 1992, p. 10.

20. Dan Quayle, *Standing Firm* (New York: HarperCollins, 1994), p. 355.

21. Quoted in Ann Devroy, "Domestic Perils Sink President Bush," *Washington Post*, November 4, 1992, p. A21.

22. Robert J. Dole, Acceptance Speech, Republican National Convention, San Diego, California, August 15, 1996.

23. Quoted in "Dole Won't Confirm Reports He Will Urge Drug Tests for All on Welfare," *Boston Globe*, May 21, 1996.

24. Dole, Acceptance Speech.

25. Ibid.

26. "Transcript of the Second Presidential Debate," *Washington Post*, October 17, 1996, p. A12.

27. *The Republican Platform, 1996: Restoring the American Dream* (Washington, DC: Republican National Committee, 1996), p. 78.

28. Ibid., p. 4.

29. *The 1996 Democratic National Platform* (Washington, DC: Democratic National Committee, 1996), p. 32.

30. *Republican Platform, 1996*, p. 78.

31. Jack Kemp, Acceptance Speech, Republican National Convention, San Diego, California, August 15, 1996.

32. Quoted in Evan Thomas, "The Small Deal," *Newsweek*, November 18, 1996, p. 127.

33. William Safire, *Before the Fall: An Inside View of the Pre-Watergate White House* (New York: Ballantine Books, 1977), pp. 416–417.

34. "Shrill Emergency Broadcast Test Soon to Be a Cold War Relic," *New York Times*, November 17, 1996, p. 29.

35. Samuel Lubell, *The Future of American Politics* (New York: Harper & Row, 1965), p. 13.

36. "Text of Democratic Platform," reprinted in *New York Times*, June 26, 1936, p. 1.

37. Lyndon Baines Johnson, *The Vantage Point: Perspectives of the Presidency, 1963–1969* (New York: Holt, Rinehart & Winston, 1971), p. 213.

38. Clinton quoting Dole, "Transcript of the Second Presidential Debate," p. A12.

39. Quoted in Stefan Lorant, *The Presidency: A Pictorial History of Presidential Elections from Washington to Truman* (New York: Macmillan, 1951), p. 591.

40. Ted Morgan, *FDR* (New York: Simon & Schuster, 1985), p. 40.

41. Quoted in Theodore H. White, *The Making of the President, 1968* (New York: Atheneum Publishers, 1969), p. 359.

42. Gallup poll, August 3–8, 1951. Text of question: "Suppose a young person, just turned 21, asked you what the Republican Party/Democratic Party stands for today—what would you tell them?" The number-one Republican response, 16 percent, was "for the privileged few, moneyed interests." The number-one Democratic response, 19 percent, was "for the working man, for the public benefit, for the common man."

43. Gallup poll, October 26–29, 1996.

44. Clinton, *Between Hope and History*, p. 90.

45. Ibid., p. 369.

46. Quoted in *1996 Democratic Platform*, p. 11.

47. Gallup poll, October 26–29, 1996.

48. *1996 Democratic National Platform*, p. 21.

49. Ibid., p. 6.

50. "Transcript of the Second Presidential Debate," p. A15.

51. Quoted in Haynes Johnson and David S. Broder, *The System: The American Way of Politics at the Breaking Point* (Boston: Little, Brown, 1996), p. 384.

52. Voter News and Surveys, exit poll, November 5, 1996.

53. National Commission on Excellence in Education, *A Nation at Risk* (Washington, DC: U.S. Government Printing Office, 1983), p. 5.

54. Gallup poll, October 26–29, 1996.

55. *1996 Democratic National Platform*, p. 6.

56. Voter News and Surveys, exit poll, November 5, 1996.

57. *1996 Democratic National Platform*, p. 40.

58. Ibid., p. 17.

59. David S. Broder, "Factions, Competing Ideologies Challenge Coalition Builders," *Washington Post*, November 7, 1996.

60. Quoted in Johnson and Broder, *The System*, p. 445.

61. Broder, "Factions, Competing Ideologies Challenge Coalition Builders, p. A23.

62. Richard L. Berke, "Clinton Preparing for Second Term with Shuffle of Top Officials," *New York Times*, November 7, 1996, p. A1.

63. Voter News and Surveys, exit poll, November 5, 1996.

64. Warren P. Strobel, "President Improves on His 1992 Showing," *Washington Times*, November 6, 1996, p. A1.

65. Lloyd Free and Hadley Cantril, *The Political Beliefs of Americans* (New Brunswick, NJ: Rutgers University Press, 1967).

66. William J. Clinton, State of the Union Address, Washington, DC, January 23, 1996.

67. Cited in Everett Carll Ladd, "Public Opinion and the 'Congress Problem,'" *Public Interest*, Summer 1990, p. 66.

68. "Transcript of the Second Presidential Debate," p. A12.

69. Bill Clinton, Victory Speech, Little Rock, Arkansas, November 5, 1996.

70. Quoted in Adam Clymer, "Top Republicans Say They Seek Common Ground with Clinton," *New York Times*, November 7, 1996, p. A1.

71. Daniel Bell, *The End of Ideology* (Glencoe, IL: Free Press, 1960).

72. Clinton, "Speech to the Democratic Leadership Council," December 11, 1996.

73. Quoted in David Marinas, *First in His Class: A Biography of Bill Clinton* (New York: Simon & Schuster, 1995), p. 67.

74. Quoted in Bob Woodward, *The Choice* (New York: Simon & Schuster, 1996), p. 65.

75. Herbert Croly, *The Promise of American Life* (New York: Macmillan, 1909).

Appendix I

Winners in 1996 Races for the U.S. Senate

D   Democrat
R   Republican
*   Incumbent
☐   Winner
■   Winner and change
    in party control

ALABAMA
  Roger Bedford, D
■ Jeff Sessions, R
ALASKA
  Theresa Nangle Obermeyer, D
☐ Ted Stevens, R*
ARKANSAS
  Winston Bryant, D
■ Tim Hutchinson, R
COLORADO
  Tom Strickland, D
☐ Wayne Allard, R
DELAWARE
☐ Joseph R. Bidden Jr., D*
  Raymond J. Clatworthy, R
GEORGIA
☐ Max Cleland, D
  Guy Millner, R
IDAHO
  Walt Minnick, D
☐ Larry E. Craig, R*
ILLINOIS
☐ Richard J. Durbin, D
  Al Salvi, R
IOWA
☐ Tom Harkin, D*
  Jim Lightfoot, R
KANSAS
  Sally Thompson, D
☐ Pat Roberts, R

  Jill Docking, D
☐ Sam Brownback, R
KENTUCKY
  Steven L. Beshear, D
☐ Mitch McConnell
LOUISIANA
☐ Mary L. Landrieu, D
  Woody Jenkins, R
MAINE
  Joseph Brennan, D
☐ Susan E. Collins, R
MASSACHUSETTS
☐ John Kerry, D*
  William F. Weld, R
MICHIGAN
☐ Carl Levin, D*
  Ronna Romney, R
MINNESOTA
☐ Paul Wellstone, D*
  Rudy Boschwitz, R
MISSISSIPPI
  James W. Hunt, D
☐ Thad Cochran, R*
MONTANA
☐ Max Baucus, D*
  Dennis Rehberg, R
NEBRASKA
  Ben Nelson
■ Chuck Hagel, R
NEW HAMPSHIRE
  Dick Swett, D
☐ Robert C. Smith, R*
NEW JERSEY
☐ Robert G. Torricelli, D
  Richard A. Zimmer, R

NEW MEXICO
  Art Trujillo, D
☐ Pete V. Domenici, R*
NORTH CAROLINA
  Harvey B. Gantt, D
☐ Jesse Helms, R*
OKLAHOMA
  Jim Boren, D
☐ James M. Inhofe, R*
OREGON
  Tom Bruggere, D
☐ Gordon Smith, R
RHODE ISLAND
☐ Jack Reed, D
  Nancy J. Mayer, R
SOUTH CAROLINA
  Elliott Close, D
☐ Strom Thurmond, R*
SOUTH DAKOTA
■ Tim Johnson, D
  Larry Pressler, R*
TENNESSEE
  Houston Gordon, D
☐ Fred Thompson, R*
TEXAS
  Victor M. Morales, D
☐ Phil Gramm, R*
VIRGINIA
  Mark Warner, D
☐ John W. Warner, R*
WEST VIRGINIA
☐ John D. Rockefeller 4th, D
  Betty A. Burks, R
WYOMING
  Kathy Karpan, D
☐ Mike Enzi, R

Appendix II

Winners in 1996 Races for the U.S. House of Representatives

D Democrat
R Republican
O Other
* Incumbent
☐ Winner
■ Winner and change
in party control

ALABAMA
DISTRICT 1
Don Womack, D
☐ Sonny Callahan, R*
DISTRICT 2
Bob E. Gaines, D
☐ Terry Everett, R*
DISTRICT 3
Ted Little, D
■ Bob Riley, R
DISTRICT 4
Robert Wilson, D
■ Robert Aderholt, R
DISTRICT 5
☐ Robert E. Cramer, D*
Wayne Parker, R
DISTRICT 6
Mary Lynn Bates, D
☐ Spencer Bachus, R*
DISTRICT 7
☐ Earl F. Hilliard, D*
Joe Powell, R

ALASKA AT-LARGE
Georgianna Lincoln, D
☐ Don Young, R*

ARIZONA
DISTRICT 1
John Cox, D
☐ Matt Salmon, R*
DISTRICT 2
☐ Ed Pastor, D*
Jim Buster, R
DISTRICT 3
Alexander Schneider, D
☐ Bob Stump, R*
DISTRICT 4
Maria Elena Milton, D
☐ John Shadegg, R*
DISTRICT 5
Mort Nelson, D
☐ Jim Kolbe, R*
DISTRICT 6
Steve Owens, D

☐ J.D. Hayworth, R*
Robert Anderson, O

ARKANSAS
DISTRICT 1
☐ Marion Berry, D
Warren Dupwe, R
DISTRICT 2
☐ Vic Snyder, D
Bud Cummins, R
DISTRICT 3
Ann Henry, D
☐ Asa Hutchinson, R
DISTRICT 4
Vincent Tolliver, D
☐ Jay Dickey, R*

CALIFORNIA
DISTRICT 1
Michela Alioto, D
☐ Frank Riggs, R*
Emil Rossi, O
DISTRICT 2
Roberts A. Braden, D
☐ Wally Herger, R*
DISTRICT 3
☐ Vic Fazio, D*
Tim Lefever, R
DISTRICT 4
Katie Hirning, D
☐ John Doolittle, R*
DISTRICT 5
☐ Robert T. Matsui, D*
Robert S. Dinsmore, R
DISTRICT 6
☐ Lynn Woosley, D*
Duane C. Hughes, R
DISTRICT 7
☐ George Miller, D*
Norman H. Reece, R
DISTRICT 8
☐ Nancy Pelosi, D*
Justin Raimondo, R
DISTRICT 9
☐ Ronald V. Dellums, D*
Deborah Wright, R
DISTRICT 10
■ Ellen O. Tauscher, D
Bill Baker, R*
DISTRICT 11
Jason Silva, D
☐ Richard Pombo, R*
DISTRICT 12
☐ Tom Lantos, D*
Storm Jenkins, R

DISTRICT 13
☐ Pete Stark, D*
James S. Fay, R
DISTRICT 14
☐ Anna G. Eshoo, D*
Ben Brink, R
DISTRICT 15
Dick Lane, D
☐ Tom Campbell, R*
DISTRICT 15
☐ Zoe Lofgren, D*
Chuck Wojslaw, R
DISTRICT 17
☐ Sam Farr, D*
Jess Brown, R
DISTRICT 18
☐ Gary A. Condit, D*
Bill Conrad, R
DISTRICT 19
Paul Barile, D
☐ George Radanovich, R*
DISTRICT 20
☐ Cal Dooley, D*
Trice Harvey, R
DISTRICT 21
Deborah A. Vollmer, D
☐ Bill Thomas, R*
DISTRICT 22
■ Walter Holden Capps, D
Andrea Seastrand, R*
DISTRICT 23
Robert R. Unruhe, D
☐ Elton Gallegly, R*
DISTRICT 24
☐ Brad Sherman, D
Rich Sybert, R
DISTRICT 25
Diane Trautman, D
☐ Howard P. McKeon, R*
DISTRICT 26
☐ Howard L. Berman, D*
Bill Glass, R
DISTRICT 27
Doug Kahn, D
☐ James E. Rogan, R
DISTRICT 28
David Levering, D
☐ David Dreier, R*
DISTRICT 29
☐ Henry A. Waxman, D*
Paul Stepanek, R
DISTRICT 30
☐ Xavier Becerra, D*
Patricia Jean Parker, R

DISTRICT 31
☐ Matthew G. Martinez, D*
John V. Flores, R
DISTRICT 32
☐ Julian C. Dixon, D*
Larry Ardito, R
DISTRICT 33
☐ Lucille Roybal-Allard, D*
John P. Leonard, R
DISTRICT 34
☐ Esteban E. Torres, D*
David G. Nunez, R
DISTRICT 35
☐ Maxine Waters, D*
Eric Carlson, R
DISTRICT 36
☐ Jane Harman, D*
Susan Brooks, R
DISTRICT 37
☐ J. Millender-McDonald, D*
Michael E. Voetee, R
DISTRICT 38
Rick Zbur, D
☐ Steve Horn, R*
DISTRICT 39
Bob Davis, D
☐ Ed Royce, R*
DISTRICT 40
Robert Conaway, D
☐ Jerry Lewis, R*
DISTRICT 41
Richard L. Waldron, D
☐ Jay C. Kim, R*
DISTRICT 42
☐ George E. Brown, D*
Linda M. Wilde, R
DISTRICT 43
Guy C. Kimbrough, D
☐ Ken Calvert, R*
DISTRICT 44
Anita Rufus, D
☐ Sonny Bono, R*
DISTRICT 45
Sally J. Alexander, D
☐ Dana Rohrabacher, R*
DISTRICT 46
■ Loretta Sanchez, D
Robert K. Dornan, R*
DISTRICT 47
Tina Louise Laine, D
☐ Christopher Cox, R*
DISTRICT 48
Dan Farrell, D
☐ Ron Packard, R*

DISTRICT 49
Peter Navarro, D
☐ Brian P. Bilbray, R*
DISTRICT 50
☐ Bob Filner, D*
Jim Baize, R
DISTRICT 51
Rita Tamerius, D
☐ Randy Cunningham, R*
DISTRICT 52
Darity Wesley, D
☐ Duncan Hunter, R*

COLORADO
DISTRICT 1
☐ Diana DeGette, D
Joe Rogers, R
DISTRICT 2
☐ David E. Skaggs, D*
Pat Miller, R
DISTRICT 3
Al Gurule, D
☐ Scott McInnis, R*
DISTRICT 4
Guy Kelley, D
☐ Bob Schaffer, R
DISTRICT 5
Mike Robinson, D
☐ Joel Hefley, R*
DISTRICT 6
Joan Fitz-Gerald, D
☐ Dan Schaefer, R*

CONNECTICUT
DISTRICT 1
☐ Barbara B. Kennelly, D*
Kent Sleath, R
DISTRICT 2
☐ Sam Gejdenson, D*
Edward W. Munster, R
DISTRICT 3
☐ Rosa DeLauro, D*
John Coppola, R
DISTRICT 4
Bill Finch, D
☐ Christopher Shays, R*
DISTRICT 5
■ James H. Maloney, D
Gary A. Franks, R*
DISTRICT 6
Charlotte Koskoff, D
☐ Nancy L. Johnson, R*

DELAWARE AT-LARGE
Dennis E. Williams, D
☐ Michael N. Castle, R*

FLORIDA
DISTRICT 1
Kevin Beck, D
☐ Joe Scarborough, R*
DISTRICT 2
☐ Allen Boyd, D
Bill Sutton, R
DISTRICT 3
☐ Corrine Brown, D*
Preston James Fields, R
DISTRICT 4
☐ Tillie Fowler, R*
DISTRICT 5
☐ Karen L. Thurman, D*
Dave Gentry, R
DISTRICT 6
Newell O'Brien, D
☐ Cliff Stearns, R*
DISTRICT 7
George Stuart, D
☐ John L. Mica, R*
DISTRICT 8
Al Krulick, D

☐ Bill McCollum, R*
DISTRICT 9
Jerry Provenzano, D
☐ Michael Bilirakis, R*
DISTRICT 10
Henry Green, D
☐ C. W. Bill Young, R*
DISTRICT 11
☐ Jim Davis, D
Mark Sharpe, R
DISTRICT 12
Mike Canady, D
☐ Charles T. Canady, R*
DISTRICT 13
Sanford Gordon, D
☐ Dan Miller, R*
DISTRICT 14
Jim Nolan, D
☐ Porter J. Goss, R*
DISTRICT 15
John L. Byron, D
☐ Dave Weldon, R*
David Golding, Ind
DISTRICT 16
Jim Stuber, D
☐ Mark Foley, R*
DISTRICT 17
☐ Carie P. Meek, D*
Wellington Rolle, R
DISTRICT 18
☐ Ileana Ros-Lehtinen, R*
DISTRICT 19
☐ Robert Wexler, D
Beverly Kennedy, R
DISTRICT 20
☐ Peter Deutsch, D*
Jim Jacobs, R
DISTRICT 21
☐ Lincoln Diaz-Balart, R*
DISTRICT 22
Kenneth D. Cooper, D
☐ Clay Shaw Jr., R*
DISTRICT 23
☐ Alcee L. Hastings, D*
Robert Paul Brown, R

GEORGIA
DISTRICT 1
Rosemary D. Kaszans, D
☐ Jack Kingston, R*
DISTRICT 2
☐ Sanford D. Bishop Jr., D*
Darrel Ealum, R
DISTRICT 3
Jim Chafin, D
☐ Mac Collins, R*
DISTRICT 4
☐ Cynthia A. McKinney, D*
John Mitnick, R
DISTRICT 5
☐ John Lewis, D*
DISTRICT 6
Michael Coles, D
☐ Newt Gingrich, R*
DISTRICT 7
Charlie Watts, D
☐ Bob Barr, R*
DISTRICT 8
Jim Wiggins, D
☐ Saxby Chambliss, R*
DISTRICT 9
Ken Poston, D
☐ Nathan Deal, R*
DISTRICT 10
David Bell, D
☐ Charles Norwood, R*
DISTRICT 11
Tommy Stephenson, D

☐ John Linder, R*
HAWAII
DISTRICT 1
☐ Neil Abercrombie, D*
Orson Swindle, R
DISTRICT 2
☐ Patsy T. Mink, D*
Tom Pico, R
Amanda Toulon, O

IDAHO
DISTRICT 1
Dan Williams, D
☐ Helen Chenoweth, R*
DISTRICT 2
John D. Seidl, D
☐ Michael D. Crapo, R*

ILLINOIS
DISTRICT 1
☐ Bobby L. Rush, D*
Noel Naughton, R
DISTRICT 2
☐ Jesse Jackson Jr., D*
Frank H. Stratman, O
DISTRICT 3
☐ William O. Lipinski, D*
Jim Nalepa, R
DISTRICT 4
☐ Luis V. Gutierrez, D*
William Passmore, O
DISTRICT 5
■ Rod R. Blagojevich, D
Michael P. Flanagan, R*
DISTRICT 6
Stephen De La Rosa, D
☐ Henry J. Hyde, R*
DISTRICT 7
Danny Davis, D
Randy Borow, R
DISTRICT 8
Elizabeth Ann Hull, D
☐ Philip M. Crane, R*
DISTRICT 9
☐ Sidney R. Yates, D*
Joseph Walsh, R
DISTRICT 10
Philip R. Torf, D
☐ John Edward Porter, R*
DISTRICT 11
Clem Balanoff, D
☐ Jerry Weller, R*
DISTRICT 12
☐ Jerry F. Costello, D*
Shapley R. Hunter, R
DISTRICT 13
Susan W. Hynes, D
☐ Harris W. Fawell, R*
DISTRICT 14
Doug Mains, D
☐ Dennis Hastert, R*
DISTRICT 15
Laurel Lunt Prussing, D
☐ Thomas W. Ewing, R*
DISTRICT 16
Catherine M. Lee, D
☐ Donald Manzullo, R*
DISTRICT 17
☐ Lane Evans, D*
Mark Baker, R
DISTRICT 18
Mike Curran, D
☐ Ray LaHood, R*
DISTRICT 19
☐ Glenn Poshard, D*
Brent Winters, R
DISTRICT 20
Jay C. Hoffman, D

■ John M. Shimkus, R
INDIANA
DISTRICT 1
☐ Peter J. Visclosky, D*
Michael Edward Petyo, R
DISTRICT 2
Marc Carmichael, D
☐ David M. McIntosh, R*
DISTRICT 3
☐ Tim Roemer, D*
Joe Zakas, R
DISTRICT 4
Gerald L. Houseman, D
☐ Mark Souder, R*
DISTRICT 5
Douglas L. Clark, D
☐ Steve Buyer, R*
DISTRICT 6
Carrie Dillard-Tramell, D
☐ Dan Burton, R*
DISTRICT 7
Robert F. Hellmann, D
☐ Edward A. Pease, R
DISTRICT 8
Jonathan Weinzapfel, D
☐ John Hostettler, R*
DISTRICT 9
☐ Lee H. Hamilton, D*
Jean Leising, R
DISTRICT 10
☐ Julia M. Carson, D
Virginia Blankenbaker, R

IOWA
DISTRICT 1
Bob Rush, D
☐ Jim Leach, R*
DISTRICT 2
Donna Smith, D
☐ Jim Nussle, R*
DISTRICT 3
■ Leonard Boswell, D
Mike Mahaffey, R
DISTRICT 4
Connie McBurney, D
☐ Greg Ganske, R*
DISTRICT 5
MacDonald Smith, D
☐ Thomas Latham, R*

KANSAS
DISTRICT 1
John Divine, D
☐ Jerry Moran, R
DISTRICT 2
John Frieden, D
☐ Jim Ryun, R
DISTRICT 3
Judy Hancock, D
☐ Vince Snowbarger, R
DISTRICT 4
Randy Rathbun, D
☐ Todd Tiahrt, R*

KENTUCKY
DISTRICT 1
Dennis Null, D
☐ Edward Whitfield, R*
DISTRICT 2
Joe Wright, D
☐ Ron Lewis, R*
DISTRICT 3
Mike Ward, D*
■ Anne Northup, R
DISTRICT 4
Denny Bowman, D
☐ Jim Bunning, R*
DISTRICT 5
☐ Harold Rogers, R*

DISTRICT 6
☐ Scotty Baesler, D*
Ernest Fletcher, R

LOUISIANA
DISTRICT 1
☐ Robert Livingston, R*
DISTRICT 2
☐ William Jefferson, D*
DISTRICT 3
☐ Billy Tauzin, R*
DISTRICT 4
☐ Jim McCrery, R*
DISTRICT 5
Francis Thompson, D
■ John Cooksey, R
DISTRICT 6
☐ Richard Baker, R*
DISTRICT 7
■ Chris John, D
Hunter Lundy, D

MAINE
DISTRICT 1
■ Thomas Allen, D
James Longley, R*
DISTRICT 2
☐ John Baldacci, D*
Paul Young, R

MARYLAND
DISTRICT 1
Steven Eastaugh, D
☐ Wayne Gilchrest, R*
DISTRICT 2
Connie DeJuliis, D
☐ Robert Ehrlich, R*
DISTRICT 3
☐ Benjamin Cardin, D*
Patrick McDonough, R
DISTRICT 4
☐ Albert Wynn, D*
John Kimble, R
DISTRICT 5
☐ Steny Hoyer, D*
John Morgan, R
DISTRICT 6
Stephen Crawford, D
☐ Roscoe Bartlett, R*
DISTRICT 7
☐ Elijah Cummings, D*
Kenneth Kondner, R
DISTRICT 8
Donald Mooers, D
☐ Constance Morella, R*

MASSACHUSETTS
DISTRICT 1
☐ John Oliver, D*
Jane Swift, R
DISTRICT 2
☐ Richard Neal, D*
Mark Steele, R
DISTRICT 3
■ James McGovern, D
Peter Blute, R*
DISTRICT 4
☐ Barney Frank, D*
Jonathan Raymond, R
DISTRICT 5
☐ Martin Meehan, D*
DISTRICT 6
■ John Tierney, D
Peter Torkildsen, R*
DISTRICT 7
☐ Edward Markey, D*
Patricia Long, R
DISTRICT 8
☐ Joseph Kennedy, D*
Philip Hyde, R

DISTRICT 9
☐ Joe Moakley, D*
Paul Gryska, R
DISTRICT 10
☐ William Delahunt, D
Edward Teague, R

MICHIGAN
DISTRICT 1
☐ Bart Stupak, D*
Bob Carr, R
DISTRICT 2
Dan Kruszynski, D
☐ Peter Hoekstra, R*
DISTRICT 3
Betsy Flory, D
☐ Vernon Ehlers, R*
DISTRICT 4
Lisa Donaldson, D
☐ Dave Camp, R*
DISTRICT 5
☐ James Barcia, D*
Lawrence Sims, R
DISTRICT 6
Clarence Annen, D
☐ Fred Upton, R*
DISTRICT 7
Kim Tunnicliff, D
☐ Nick Smith, R*
DISTRICT 8
■ Debbie Stabenow, D
Dick Chrysler, R*
DISTRICT 9
☐ Dale Kildee, D*
Patrick Nowak, R
DISTRICT 10
☐ David Bonior, D*
Susy Heintz, R
DISTRICT 11
Morris Frumin, D
☐ Joseph Knollenberg, R*
DISTRICT 12
☐ Sander Levin, D*
Jhn Pappageorge, R
DISTRICT 13
☐ Lynn Rivers, D*
Joe Fitzsimmons, R
DISTRICT 14
☐ John Conyers, D*
William Ashe, R
DISTRICT 15
☐ Carolyn Kilpatrick, D
Stephen Hume, R
DISTRICT 16
☐ John Dingell, D*
James DeSana, R

MINNESOTA
DISTRICT 1
Mary Rieder, D
☐ Gil Gutknecht, R*
DISTRICT 2
☐ David Minge, D*
Gary Revier, R
DISTRICT 3
Stanley Leino, D
☐ Jim Ramstad, R*
DISTRICT 4
☐ Bruce Vento, D*
Dennis Newinski, R
DISTRICT 5
☐ Martin Sabo, D*
Jack Uldrich, R
DISTRICT 6
☐ William Luther, D*
Tad Jude, R
DISTRICT 7
☐ Collin Peterson, D*

Darrell McKigney, R
DISTRICT 8
☐ James Oberstar, D*
Andy Larson, R

MISSISSIPPI
DISTRICT 1
Henry Boyd, D
☐ Roger Wicker, R*
DISTRICT 2
☐ Bennie Thompson, D*
Danny Covington, R
DISTRICT 3
John Eaves, D
■ Charles Pickering, R
DISTRICT 4
Kevin Antoine, D
☐ Mike Parker, R*
DISTRICT 5
☐ Gene Taylor, D*
Dennis Dollar, R

MISSOURI
DISTRICT 1
☐ William Clay, D*
Daniel O'Sullivan, R
DISTRICT 2
Joan Horn, D
☐ James Talent, R*
DISTRICT 3
☐ Richard Gephardt, D*
Deborah Wheelehan, R
Michael Crist, D
DISTRICT 4
☐ Ike Skelton, D*
Bill Phelps, R
DISTRICT 5
☐ Karen McCarthy, D*
Penny Bennett, R
DISTRICT 6
☐ Patsy Danner, D*
Jeff Bailey, R
DISTRICT 7
Ruth Bamberger, D
☐ Roy Blunt, R
DISTRICT 8
Emily Firebaugh, D
Richard Kline, R
☐ Jo Ann Emerson, O
DISTRICT 9
Harold Volkmer, D*
■ Kenny Hulshof, R

MONTANA AT-LARGE
Bill Yellowtail, D
■ Rick Hill, R

NEBRASKA
DISTRICT 1
Patrick Combs, D
☐ Doug Bereuter, R*
DISTRICT 2
James Davis, D
☐ Jon Christensen, R*
DISTRICT 3
John Webster, D
☐ William Barrett, R*

NEVADA
DISTRICT 1
Bob Coffin, D
☐ John Ensign, R*
DISTRICT 2
Thomas Wilson, D
☐ Jim Gibbons, R

NEW HAMPSHIRE
DISTRICT 1
Joe Keefe, D
☐ John E. Sununu, R

DISTRICT 2
Deborah Arnesen, D
☐ Charles Bass, R*
Carole Lamirande, O

NEW JERSEY
DISTRICT 1
☐ Robert Andrews, D*
Mel Suplee, R
DISTRICT 2
Ruth Katz, D
☐ Frank LoBiondo, R*
DISTRICT 3
John Leonardi, D
☐ Jim Saxton, R*
DISTRICT 4
Kevin Meara, D
■ Christopher Smith, R*
DISTRICT 5
Bill Auer, D
☐ Marge Roukema, R*
DISTRICT 6
☐ Frank Pallone, D*
Steven Corodemus, R
DISTRICT 7
Larry Lerner, D
☐ Bob Franks, R*
DISTRICT 8
■ William Pascrell, D
Bill Martini, R*
DISTRICT 9
☐ Steve Rothman, D
Kathleen Donovan, R
DISTRICT 10
☐ Donald Payne, D*
Vanessa Williams, R
DISTRICT 11
Chris Evangel, D
☐ R. Frelinghuysen, R*
DISTRICT 12
David Del Vecchio, D
☐ Mike Pappas, R
DISTRICT 13
☐ Robert Menendez, D*
Carlos Munoz, R

NEW MEXICO
DISTRICT 1
John Wertheim, D
☐ Steven Schiff, R*
DISTRICT 2
Shirley Baca, D
☐ Joe Skeen, R*
DISTRICT 3
☐ Bill Richardson, D*
William Redmond, R

NEW YORK
DISTRICT 1
Nora Bredes, D
☐ Michael Forbes, R*
DISTRICT 2
Kenneth Herman, D
☐ Rick Lazio, R*
DISTRICT 3
Dal Lamagna, D
☐ Peter King, R*
DISTRICT 4
■ Carolyn McCarthy, D
Daniel Frisa, R*
DISTRICT 5
☐ Gary Ackerman, D*
Grant Lally, R
DISTRICT 6
☐ Floyd Flake, D*
Jorawar Misir, R
DISTRICT 7
☐ Thomas Manton, D*
Rose Birtley, R

DISTRICT 8
☐ Jerrold Nadler, D*
Michael Benjamin, R
DISTRICT 9
☐ Charles Schumer, D*
Robert Verga, R
DISTRICT 10
☐ Edolphus Towns, D*
Amelia Smith-Parker, R
DISTRICT 11
☐ Major Owens, D*
Claudette Hayle, R
DISTRICT 12
☐ Nydia Velazquez, D*
Miguel Prado, R
DISTRICT 13
Tyrone Butler, D
☐ Susan Molinari, R*
DISTRICT 14
☐ Carolyn Maloney, D*
Jeffrey Livingston, R
DISTRICT 15
☐ Charles Rangel, D*
Edward Adams, R
Jose Suero, O
Ruben Vargas, 0
DISTRICT 16
☐ Jose Serrano, D*
Rodney Torres, R
Owen Camp, O
DISTRICT 17
☐ Eliot Engel, D*
Denis McCarthy, R
DISTRICT 18
☐ Nita Lowey, D*
Kerry Katsorhis, R
DISTRICT 19
Richard Klein, D
☐ Sue Kelly, R*
Joseph Dio Guardi, O
DISTRICT 20
Yash Aggarwalt, O
☐ Benjamin Gilman, R*
DISTRICT 21
☐ Michael McNulty, D*
Nancy Norman, R
Lee Wasserman, O
DISTRICT 22
Steve James, D
☐ Gerald Solomon, R*
DISTRICT 23
Bruce Hapanowicz, D
☐ Sherwood Boehlert, R*
DISTRICT 24
Donald Ravenscroft, D
☐ John McHugh, R*
DISTRICT 25
Marty Mack, D
☐ James Walsh, R*
DISTRICT 26
☐ Maurice Hinchey, D*
Sue Wittig, R
DISTRICT 27
Thomas Fricano, D
☐ Bill Paxon, R*
DISTRICT 28
☐ Louise Slaughter, D*
Goeffrey Rosenberger, R
DISTRICT 29
☐ John LaFalce, D*
David Callard, R
DISTRICT 30
Francis Pordum, D
☐ Jack Quinn, R*
DISTRICT 31
Bruce Mac Bain, D
☐ Arno Houghton, R*

NORTH CAROLINA
DISTRICT 1
☐ Eva Clayton, D*
Ted Tyler, R
DISTRICT 2
■ Bob Etheridge, D
David Funderburk, R*
DISTRICT 3
George Parrott, D
☐ Walter Jones, R*
DISTRICT 4
■ David Price, D
Frederick Heineman, R*
DISTRICT 5
Neil Cashion, D
☐ Richard Burr, R*
DISTRICT 6
Mark Costley, D
☐ Howard Coble, R*
DISTRICT 7
☐ Mike McIntyre, D
Bill Caster, R
DISTRICT 8
☐ William Hefner, D*
Curtis Blackwood, R
DISTRICT 9
Michel Daisley, D
☐ Sue Myrick, R*
DISTRICT 10
Ben Neill, D
☐ Cass Ballenger, R*
DISTRICT 11
James Ferguson, D
☐ Charles Taylor, R*
DISTRICT 12
☐ Melvin Watt, D*
Joseph Martino, R

NORTH DAKOTA
AT-LARGE
☐ Earl Pomeroy, D*
Kevin Cramer, R

OHIO
DISTRICT 1
Mark Longabaugh, D
☐ Steve Chabot, R*
DISTRICT 2
Thomas Chandler, D
☐ Rob Portman, R*
DISTRICT 3
☐ Tony Hall, D*
David Westbrock, R
DISTRICT 4
Paul McLain, D
☐ Michael Oxley, R*
DISTRICT 5
Annie Saunders, D
☐ Paul Gillmor, R*
DISTRICT 6
■ Ted Strickland, D
Frank Cremeans, R*
DISTRICT 7
Richard Blain, D
☐ Dave Hobson, R*
DISTRICT 8
Jeffrey Kitchen, D
☐ John Beohner, R*
DISTRICT 9
☐ Marcy Kaptur, D*
Randy Whitman, R
DISTRICT 10
■ Dennis Kucinich, D
Martin Hoke, R*
DISTRICT 11
☐ Louis Stokes, D*
James Sykora, R

DISTRICT 12
Cynthia Ruccia, D
☐ John Kasich, R*
DISTRICT 13
☐ Sherrod Brown, D*
Kenneth Blair, R
DISTRICT 14
☐ Thomas Sawyer, D*
Joyce George, R
DISTRICT 15
Clifford Arnebeck, D
☐ Deborah Pryce, R*
DISTRICT 16
Thomas Burkhart, D
☐ Ralph Regula, R*
DISTRICT 17
☐ James Traficant, D*
James Cahaney, O
DISTRICT 18
Robert Burch, D
☐ Robert Ney, R*
DISTRICT 19
Thomas Coyne, D
☐ Steven LaTourette, R*
Thomas Martin, O

OKLAHOMA
DISTRICT 1
Randolph Amen, D
☐ Steve Largent, R*
DISTRICT 2
Glen Johnson, D
☐ Tom Coburn, R*
DISTRICT 3
Darryl Roberts, D
■ Wes Watkins, R
DISTRICT 4
Ed Crocker, D
☐ J. C. Watts, R*
DISTRICT 5
James Forsythe, D
☐ Ernest Istook, R*
DISTRICT 6
Paul Barby, D
☐ Frank Lucas, R*

OREGON
DISTRICT 1
☐ Elizabeth Furse, D*
Bill Witt, R
DISTRICT 2
Mike Dugan, D
☐ Robert Smith, R
DISTRICT 3
☐ Earl Blumenauer, D*
Scott Bruun, R
DISTRICT 4
☐ Peter DeFazio, D*
John Newkirk, R
DISTRICT 5
Darlene Hooley, D
☐ Jim Bunn, R*

PENNSYLVANIA
DISTRICT 1
☐ Thomas Foglietta, D*
James Cella, R
DISTRICT 2
☐ Chaka Fattah, D*
Larry Murphy, R
DISTRICT 3
☐ Robert Borski, D*
Joseph McColgan, R
DISTRICT 4
☐ Ron Klink, D*
Paul Adametz, R
DISTRICT 5
Ruth Rudy, D
☐ John Peterson, R

DISTRICT 6
☐ Tim Holden, D*
Christian Leinbach, R
DISTRICT 7
John Innelli, D
☐ Curt Weldon, R*
DISTRICT 8
John Murray, D
☐ Jim Greenwood, R*
DISTRICT 9
Monte Kemmler, D
☐ Bud Shuster, R*
DISTRICT 10
Joe Cullen, D
☐ Joseph McDade, R*
DISTRICT 11
☐ Paul Kanjorski, D*
Stephen Urban, R
DISTRICT 12
☐ John Murtha, D*
Bill Choby, R
DISTRICT 13
Joseph Hoeffel, D
☐ Jon Fox, R*
Thomas Burke, O
DISTRICT 14
☐ William Coyne, D*
Bill Ravotti, R
DISTRICT 15
☐ Paul McHale, D*
Bob Kilbanks, R
DISTRICT 16
James Blaine, D
☐ Joseph Pitts, R
DISTRICT 17
Paul Kettl, D
☐ George Gekas, R*
DISTRICT 18
☐ Michael Doyle, D*
David Fawcett, R
DISTRICT 19
Scott Chronister, D
☐ William Gooding, R*
DISTRICT 20
☐ Frank Mascara, D*
Mike McCormick, R
DISTRICT 21
Ron DiNicola, D
☐ Philip English, R*

RHODE ISLAND
DISTRICT 1
☐ Patrick Kennedy, D*
Giovanni Cicione, R
DISTRICT 2
☐ Robert Weygand, D
Richard Wild, R

SOUTH CAROLINA
DISTRICT 1
☐ Mark Sanford, R*
Joseph Innella, O
DISTRICT 2
☐ Floyd Spence, R*
Maurice Raiford, O
DISTRICT 3
Debbie Dorn, D
☐ Lindsey Graham, R*
DISTRICT 4
Darrell Curry, D
☐ Bob Inglis, R*
DISTRICT 5
☐ John Spratt, D*
Larry Bigham, R
DISTRICT 6
☐ James Clyburn, D*
Gary McLeod, R

SOUTH DAKOTA AT-LARGE
Rick Weiland, D
■ John Thune, R

TENNESSEE
DISTRICT 1
Kay Smith, D
☐ William Jenkins, R
DISTRICT 2
Stephen Smith, D
☐ John Duncan, R*
DISTRICT 3
Charles Jolly, D
☐ Zach Wamp, R*
DISTRICT 4
Mark Stewart, D
☐ Van Hilleary, R*
DISTRICT 5
☐ Bob Clement, D*
Steven Edmondson, R
DISTRICT 6
☐ Bart Gordon, D*
Steve Gill, R
DISTRICT 7
Don Trotter, D
☐ Ed Bryant, R*
DISTRICT 8
☐ John Tanner, D*
Tom Watson, R
DISTRICT 9
☐ Harold Ford Jr., D
Rod DeBerry, R

TEXAS
DISTRICT 1
☐ Max Sandlin, D
Ed Merritt, R
DISTRICT 2
☐ Jim Turner, D
Brian Babin, R
DISTRICT 3
Lee Cole, D
☐ Sam Johnson, R*
DISTRICT 4
☐ Ralph Hall, D*
Jerry Hall, R
DISTRICT 5
John Pouland, D
■ Pete Sessions, R
DISTRICT 6
☐ Joe Barton, R*
Catherine Anderson, O
Janet Richardson, O
Doug Williams, UST
DISTRICT 7
Al Siegmund, D
☐ Bill Archer, R*
DISTRICT 8
Cynthia Newman, D
Kevin Brady, R
Robert Musemeche, D
Gene Fontenot, R
DISTRICT 9
Nick Lampson, D
Stephen Stockman, R*

Geraldine Sam, D
DISTRICT 10
☐ Lloyd Doggett, D*
Teresa Doggett, R
DISTRICT 11
☐ Chet Edwards, D*
Jay Mathis, R
DISTRICT 12
High Parmer, D
■ Kay Granger, R
DISTRICT 13
Samuel Silverman, D
☐ William Thornberry, R*
DISTRICT 14
Charles Morris, D
☐ Ron Paul, R
DISTRICT 15
☐ Ruben Hinojosa, D
Tom Haughey, R
DISTRICT 16
☐ Silvestre Reyes, D
Rick Ledesma, R
DISTRICT 17
☐ Charles Stenholm, D*
Rudy Izzard, R
DISTRICT 18
☐ Sheila Jackson-Lee, D*
Larry White, R
Jerry Burley, R
George Young, R
DISTRICT 19
John Sawyer, D
☐ Larry Combest, R*
DISTRICT 20
☐ Henry Gonzalez, D*
James Walker, R
DISTRICT 21
Gordon Wharton, D
☐ Lamar Smith, R*
DISTRICT 22
Scott Cunningham, D
☐ Tom DeLay, R*
DISTRICT 23
Charles Jones, D
☐ Henry Bonilla, R*
DISTRICT 24
☐ Martin Frost, D*
Ed Harrison, R
DISTRICT 25
Ken Bentsen, D*
Brent Perry, R
Dolly McKenna, R
Beverley Clark, D
John Devine, R
John Sanchez, R
DISTRICT 26
Jerry Frankel, D
☐ Dick Armey, R*
DISTRICT 27
☐ Solomon Ortiz, D*
Joe Gardner, R
DISTRICT 28
☐ Frank Tejeda, D*
Mark Cude, R

DISTRICT 29
☐ Gene Green, D*
Jack Rodriguez, R
DISTRICT 30
☐ Eddie Bernice Johnson, D*
John Hendry, R
Marvin Crenshaw, D
James Sweatt, D
Lisa Kitterman, R
Lisa Hembry, Ind

UTAH
DISTRICT 1
Gregory Sanders, D
☐ James Hansen, R*
DISTRICT 2
Ross Anderson, D
☐ Merrill Cook, R
DISTRICT 3
Bill Orton, D*
■ Christopher Cannon, R

VERMONT AT-LARGE
Jack Long, D
Susan Sweetser, R
☐ Bernard Sanders, O*

VIRGINIA
DISTRICT 1
☐ Herbert Bateman, R*
DISTRICT 2
☐ Owen Pickett, D*
John Tate, R
DISTRICT 3
☐ Robert Scott, D*
Elsie Holland, R
DISTRICT 4
☐ Norman Sisisky, D*
Anthony Zevgolis, R
DISTRICT 5
☐ Virgil Goode, D
George Landrith, R
DISTRICT 6
Jeffrey Grey, D
☐ Robert Goodlatte, R*
DISTRICT 7
Roderic Slayton, D
☐ Thomas Bliley, R*
DISTRICT 8
☐ James Moran, D*
John Otey, R
DISTRICT 9
☐ Frederick Boucher, D*
Patrick Muldoon, R
DISTRICT 10
Robert Weinberg, D
☐ Frank Wolf, R*
DISTRICT 11
Thomas Horton, D
☐ Thomas Davis, R*

WASHINGTON
DISTRICT 1
Jeff Coopersmith, D
☐ Rick White, R*
DISTRICT 2
Kevin Quigley, D
Jack Metcalf, R*

DISTRICT 3
■ Brian Baird, D
Linda Smith, R*
DISTRICT 4
Rick Locke, D
☐ Richard Hastings, R*
DISTRICT 5
Judy Olson, D
☐ George Nethercutt, R*
DISTRICT 6
☐ Norm Dicks, D*
Bill Tinsley, R
DISTRICT 7
☐ Jim McDermott, D*
Frank Kleschen, R
DISTRICT 8
Dave Little, D
☐ Jennifer Dunn, R*
DISTRICT 9
■ Adam Smith, D.
Randy Tate, R*

WEST VIRGINIA
DISTRICT 1
☐ Alan Mollohan, D*
DISTRICT 2
☐ Robert Wise, D*
Greg Morris, R
DISTRICT 3
☐ Nick Rahall, D*

WISCONSIN
DISTRICT 1
Lydia Spottswood, D
☐ Mark Neumann, R*
DISTRICT 2
Paul Soglin, D
☐ Scott L. Klug, R*
DISTRICT 3
■ Ron Kind, D
James Harsdorf, R
DISTRICT 4
☐ Gerald D. Kleczka, D*
Tom Reynolds, R
DISTRICT 5
☐ Thomas M. Barrett, D*
Paul D. Melotik, R
DISTRICT 6
Al Lindskoog, D
☐ Tom Petri, R*
DISTRICT 7
☐ David R. Obey, D*
Scott West, R
DISTRICT 8
■ Jay Johnson, D
David Prosser, R
DISTRICT 9
Floyd Brenholt, D
☐ F. J. Sensenbrenner, R*

WYOMING AT-LARGE
Pete Maxfield, D
☐ Barbara Cubin, R*

Contributors

Janet K. Boles is an associate professor of political science at Marquette University. She is coauthor of *The Historical Dictionary of Feminism* and editor of *American Feminism.* She specializes in studying women in politics, the women's movement, and feminist public policy. Boles is a past president of the Women and Politics Research Section of the American Political Science Association.

William Crotty is the Thomas P. O'Neill Chair in Public Life and professor of political science at Northeastern University. He has written a number of books on political parties and elections, including *The Party Game, Party Reform,* and *Decision for the Democrats*; he is an editor of several other works, including the four-volume *Political Science: Looking to the Future.* Crotty has served as president of the Midwest Political Science Association, the Policy Studies Organization, and the Political Organizations and Parties Section of the American Political Science Association, from which he received the Samuel J. Eldersveld Lifetime Achievement Award.

Debra L. Dodson is a senior research associate at the Center for the American Woman and Politics, a unit of the Eagleton Institute of Politics at Rutgers University. Dodson has written extensively about the impact of women in public office and abortion politics. She is currently writing a book about women's impact on policy making in the U.S. Congress and conducting research that explores the dynamics of cultural issues in contemporary electoral politics. She holds a Ph.D. in political science from the University of Michigan.

Frank B. Feigert is Regents Professor of Political Science at the University of North Texas. He has authored or coauthored three books on American political parties and has published articles on parties and voting behavior in such journals as the *American Political Science Review, Western Political Quarterly, Electoral Studies, Legislative Studies Quarterly, Public Opinion Quarterly, Publius,* and *American Politics Quarterly,* as well as in several anthologies.

Kenneth M. Goldstein is a professor of political science at Arizona State University. He received his Ph.D. at the University of Michigan and has served as polling consultant for national networks and newspapers. He has written a number of articles and professional papers and specializes in American voting behavior, political attitudes, the media, and survey research.

John S. Jackson III is the Provost of Southern Illinois University at Carbondale. His teaching and research specialties are political parties, party leadership, presidential elections, and Congress. He is coauthor with William Crotty of *Presidential Primaries and Elections* and coauthor of *The Politics of Presidential Selection.* His work has appeared in the *Journal of Politics, American Politics Quarterly, Polity, Midwest Journal of Political Science, Western Political Quarterly,* and *Legislative Studies Quarterly.*

John A. Kromkowski is assistant dean of the College of Arts and Sciences at The Catholic University of America and president of the National Center for Urban Ethnic Affairs

151

Contributors

in Washington, D.C. He has written extensively on ethnic concerns and urban politics. In addition, he coordinates seminars and internship programs in four countries and is conducting research on domestic institutions and political representation in the United States and the development of pluralism in Eastern Europe.

Jarol B. Manheim earned his Ph.D. from Northwestern University and is a professor of political communication and director of the National Center for Communication Studies at George Washington University. His research appears in the leading journals of political science, journalism, and communication. His books include *All of the People, All the Time*, which examines the techniques of strategic political communication used in campaigns, lobbying, and public relations, whether for candidates, corporations, special interests, or foreign governments.

Jerome M. Mileur is a professor of political science at the University of Massachusetts at Amherst. He is coauthor with George T. Sulzner of *Campaigning for the Massachusetts Senate*, editor of *The Liberal Tradition in Crisis*, and coeditor with John K. White of *Challenges to Party Government*. He has been editor of *Polity*, executive director of the Committee for Party Renewal, and a member of the Massachusetts Democratic State Committee. Mileur is now a director of the Center for Party Development.

Candice J. Nelson is an associate professor of government and director of the Campaign Management Institute at American University. She is the coauthor of *The Money Chase: Congressional Campaign Finance Reform* and *The Myth of the Independent Voter* and coeditor of *Campaigns and Elections American Style*. Prior to coming to American University she was a Visiting Fellow at the Brookings Institution, and she has also been an American Political Science Association Congressional Fellow.

Dean E. Robinson earned his B.A. from Stanford University and his Ph.D. from Yale University. Currently an assistant professor at the University of Massachusetts at Amherst, he teaches in the areas of race and ethnic politics, American government, and American political thought. He is the author of many articles and professional papers, and his book, *Black Nationalism in the United States*, is forthcoming

John S. Shockley is a professor of political science at Western Illinois University. He received his Ph.D. from the University of Wisconsin and has published in the areas of minority politics, American government, public law, and campaign finance reform. He is the author of *Chicano Revolt in a Texas Town*, as well as numerous articles, professional papers, and chapters in texts.

John T. Tierney is a member of the political science faculty at Boston College. With widely varying interests in American national politics, he has written several books, including *Organized Interests and American Democracy*, coauthored with Kay Lehman Schlozman. He has contributed articles to many scholarly journals and edited volumes on topics including the politics of government corporations, health care policy making, American foreign policy, and the ties that bind lobbyists and legislators. He is currently at work on a book about the intensifying political conflict surrounding federal land management policy in the western states.

John Kenneth White is an associate professor of politics at The Catholic University of America. He is author of *The Fractured Electorate, The New Politics of Old Values, Seeing Red*, coeditor with Peter W. Colby of *New York State Today*, and coeditor with Jerome M. Mileur of *Challenges to Party Government*. He is a former executive director of the Committee for Party Renewal and currently vice president of the Center for Party Development.